C000228643

ELEMENTARY

Language LEADER

TEACHER'S BOOK
and Test Master CD-ROM

John Waterman

CONTENTS

CONTENTS

List of photocopiable worksheets

1 A	Mega cities	Group work	*to be, there is, there are*
1 B	Old town, new town	Pair work	Saying where places are
2 A	What's my job	Group work	Present simple questions and short answers
2 B	Off to university	Pair work	Present simple questions
3 A	Questions, questions	Group work	Questions with question words
3 B	Festival fun	Group work	Question formation and making suggestions
4 A	A dream hotel	Pair work	Articles, asking for information
4 B	Bingo	Whole class	Numbers
5 A	Good, better, the best – a quiz	Pair/group work	Comparative and superlative adjectives
5 B	What's the best car?	Group/pair work	Comparative and superlative adjectives
6 A	Food, drink or dish	Pair/group work	*some, any, much, many, a lot of*
6 B	What am I bid?	Pairs and whole class	Countable and uncountable nouns with *some, any, much, many, a lot of*
7 A	Find the differences	Pair work	Present continuous
7 B	Say 'Yes', say 'No'	Group work	Giving advantages and disadvantages
8 A	When you were a child	Individual and whole class	Ability and possibility in the past (*could*)
8 B	Could you …?	Group work	Polite requests and responses
9 A	Match!	Pair/group work	Pronunciation of past simple tense and irregular verb forms
9 B	TV or car?	Pair/group work	Giving advantages and disadvantages and reason
10 A	Money	Individual	Words and phrases connected with money
10 B	Help me, please!	Group work	*should, shouldn't*
11 A	A safe future	Pair/group work	*will, won't*
11 B	Design your flat	Pair/group work	*going to*, making and responding to suggestions
12 A	Have you ever … ?	Group work	Present perfect and past simple
12 B	A holiday postcard	Individual	Present perfect, past simple, *going to*

INTRODUCTION

To the teacher: introduction by the authors

We are pleased to welcome you to this new course: *Language Leader*. In this introduction we outline some of our ideas about the course. We have done our very best to write a series of books that teachers (and students!) will enjoy using, and we very much hope that, although we may be physically far apart, we share with you – as teachers – a common set of beliefs and practices, and a common sense of purpose.

Approach

Language Leader is an international course with a global focus, and is aimed at citizens of the 21st century world – people who cross (and communicate across) national borders. We believe that students are curious about the modern world, and that this course engages with it. *Language Leader* enables students to be better informed and helps them understand and express their ideas and feelings about the world.

We believe it is important to offer students stimulating topics that engage their interest and increase their motivation for learning. We have made use of our diverse backgrounds, personalities and interests as authors, in the hope of providing students with a rich variety of different topics. Each unit contains an 'umbrella topic' with a different subtopic in each lesson, allowing us to explore a range of issues within a single topic and also to recycle vocabulary. We think that the approach to the topics in the course will challenge students and allow them to develop their powers of expression and analysis and their critical thinking skills. *Language Leader* reflects our belief that language learning is not merely a form of training, but should be situated in a broader educational context. We hope that students who use the series will not only learn English, but – through English – will also learn interesting things about the world and about themselves. Perhaps, sometimes, they may not even be aware that they are actually learning English!

Language Leader is not based on one particular teaching 'philosophy' or methodology, but is informed by sound pedagogical principles, plus an intuitive sense – the result of many years' experience – of what works in the classroom. Having said this, we use a broadly communicative methodology and a text and task-based approach. Pair and group work is an important part of the learning process. The Common European Framework has informed many of the speaking activities.

Language development

Throughout the units, there is careful development and logical staging of new language, as well as substantial recycling of previous language, enabling students to move forward rapidly. The Review, Language Reference and Extra Practice sections consolidate and extend students' learning.

The texts in *Language Leader* not only provide context for grammar and vocabulary but systematically develop students' reading and listening skills. The reading texts are authentic or semi-authentic, or at lower levels based on real sources, and are taken from a variety of genres (for example, newspapers, magazines, literature and publicity materials). Listening skills are also developed throughout the course. Each unit has a number of listening activities and there is a wide variety of different listening texts (for example, radio programmes, conversations, interviews, talks and lectures), as well as a varied range of activity types.

There is considerable variety in the length of these reading and listening texts: some are relatively short, but *Language Leader* also offers students an opportunity to deal – in a supported way – with some longer texts. Students who suddenly find themselves in an English-speaking environment – whether in their home country or abroad – often have difficulty with the large quantities of spoken and written English that they are exposed to. This course helps them to build up their confidence in handling extended amounts of English. In addition, many of the reading and listening exercises are based on exam-type questions.

There are constant opportunities throughout the course for students to improve their speaking skills, with speaking exercises in every unit. Students can comment on the topics and discuss the issues that arise, as well as talk about more personal experiences and knowledge, through a variety of exercises, such as information gaps, personalised question and answer activities, role plays and debates.

The Scenario lessons are, we believe, an important communicative feature of *Language Leader*. Every unit includes a Scenario lesson, devoted to extended speaking practice in a real-life situation. Information has to be processed – and decisions made – leading to a specific outcome. Students are given language support to carry out the task.

The course covers all the key grammar points. These points are all contextualised and students are generally encouraged to analyse and understand grammar through an inductive approach with reference to examples in the texts. The grammar is practised in motivating and interesting activities. The Language reference and Extra practice section at the back of the book extends students' knowledge of grammar and provides essential further practice. It can be used in the class or for independent study at home.

Lack of vocabulary is one of the main problems many students face. Consequently, students struggle to make sense of texts and express themselves. They need more words. To address this, *Language Leader* has a wide range of vocabulary, and students are able to acquire and use this vocabulary through contextualisation and recycling.

Writing skills and study skills

Writing in English has become increasingly important, but is often students' weakest skill and something that they don't really enjoy. Even with very able students, it often drags down their scores in examinations in which they would otherwise do well. We consider, however, that writing is also a skill in which – with a little help – students can make significant progress. *Language*

Leader has a page in every unit that is devoted to the development of writing skills, and there are also further writing activities throughout the course. Because of the systematic approach to the development of writing skills in the course, students should be able to make real progress in their writing, and derive great satisfaction from this. Again, there is wide variety in the length and type of tasks. We place considerable emphasis, even at the lower levels, on discourse features of written English, with frequent analysis of text models and plenty of writing practice at both paragraph and text level. In addition, we have included activities designed to encourage students to be rigorous in checking their own writing.

Each unit also includes a Study skills page, which aims to encourage students to be independent learners with a high level of self-awareness. The skills that we cover in this section are not just for students who are on educational courses in schools, colleges and universities; they are also transferable skills which will be useful to students in many different contexts, including their careers and personal lives.

Flexibility

Of course, we hope that you will use every page in the book! But the *Language Leader* format deliberately lends itself to different teaching situations and can be adapted easily depending on the length and type of course you are teaching.

To conclude, we trust that you and your students will find *Language Leader* interesting, motivating and enjoyable. We also hope that it will meet your students' needs as well as providing something new. We welcome your comments on the course and hope to have the pleasure of meeting you in the future!

Gareth Rees, Ian Lebeau (Elementary and Pre-intermediate)
David Cotton, David Falvey, Simon Kent (Intermediate and Upper Intermediate)

Language Leader: course description

Language Leader is a general English series for adults and young adults. The course has a topic-based multi-strand syllabus which includes comprehensive work on grammar, vocabulary, pronunciation and integrated skills, where strong emphasis is placed on reading, writing and study skills as well as speaking and listening. With its purposeful approach *Language Leader* is particularly suitable for general English students working towards exams, and those learners who may go on to, or are already in, further education.

Language Leader has four levels and takes learners from Elementary to Upper Intermediate; each level offers 90 – 120 hours of work.

Coursebook

The twelve Coursebook units are divided into double-page lessons, each with a clear aim, which are designed to make the course flexible and easy-to-use.

- **Input lessons:** in *Language Leader Elementary* there are two input lessons in each unit. Here, new language is presented through informative texts with a balanced mix of grammar, vocabulary, pronunciation and skills work.
- **Scenario:** in the third lesson, learners integrate and practise the language presented in the previous lessons through a communicative task. This major speaking activity is carefully staged; the Key language section gives extra support by developing functional exponents and the Other useful phrases boxes provide helpful fixed phrases.
- **Study and Writing Skills:** the fourth lesson consists of a Study skills section, followed by Writing skills, which helps students to write a particular text type.

Language Leader Coursebook also features the following:

- **Review:** the Review spreads occur after every three units; these provide mixed practice for ongoing revision. The Language check section is a quick self-edit exercise and Look back encourages reflection on the previous units.
- **Language reference/ Extra practice:** this section consists of one cross-referenced spread for each unit. The left-hand page includes a grammar summary for the unit, plus reference lists for Key language and Vocabulary. The right-hand page provides extra practice for consolidation.

CD-ROM

- This component is attached to the back of the Coursebook.
- It provides extra practice and self-assessment for the learners with a variety of exercises, including listening. With the help of the Language Reference and the Dictionary, the CD-ROM helps learners develop their learning skills. The unique Writing section includes models for different writing tasks from everyday notes to academic essays.

Class CDs

- These provide all the recorded material from the Coursebook.

Workbook

- This contains further practice of areas covered in the corresponding units of the Coursebook and introduces Extra vocabulary to build lexis in the topic area.
- To help the development of language skills, useful strategies are introduced through Read better and Listen better boxes.
- In each unit there is a Translation exercise for students to compare English with their L1, and Dictation exercises provide more listening and writing.

Workbook CD

- Attached to the back of the Workbook, the CD contains all the recorded material for extra practice.

INTRODUCTION

Teacher's Book

- This provides all the support teachers need from detailed teaching notes to extra photocopiable activities.
- There are **warning points** to alert teachers about possible problem areas as well as **teaching tips** to help them. Taking into account teachers' busy schedules, the Teacher's Book notes are designed as lesson plans, with ideas for **extension** and **adjustment,** which are especially useful for mixed ability groups.

(!) warning points   (N) extension

(※) teaching tips   (🔧) adjustment

Test Master CD-ROM

- Attached to the back of the Teacher's Book, the Test Master CD-ROM is an invaluable resource to accompany *Language Leader*. The tests are based strictly on the content of the Coursebooks, providing a fair measure of students' progress.
- The audio files for the listening tests are conveniently located on the same CD-ROM.
- The tests can be printed out and used as they are, or can be adapted using Microsoft® Word to edit them to suit different teaching situations.
- The Test Master CD-ROM contains the following:
  - Placement Test (to identify levels)
  - Unit Tests (one 'A' and one 'B' test for each unit)
  - Progress Tests (one 'A' and one 'B' test for every three units plus additional optional speaking and writing tests)
  - Final Test (one 'A' and one 'B' version)

Syllabus areas

- **Topics:** to motivate learners the units are based on up-to-date topics of international interest or new angles on familiar subjects. Themes have been carefully chosen to engage the learners and to provide a springboard for their own ideas and communicative needs.
- **Grammar:** *Language Leader* follows an established syllabus progression and learners are actively involved in developing their knowledge of grammar. The Grammar sections in the input lessons focus on the main language points presented through the texts and learners are encouraged to work out the rules for themselves. They are supported by the Grammar tip boxes and cross-referred to the corresponding Language reference and Extra practice pages at the back of the book for reinforcement.
- **Vocabulary:** vocabulary input is derived from the unit topics and texts, allowing the teacher to build on words and phrases the students already know to create lexical sets. Additional attention is paid to word building and lexical patterns. The vocabulary is recycled through the speaking activities in each unit, revised in the Review lesson and Extra practice and practised further in the Workbook.

- **Pronunciation:** regular pronunciation sections are integrated with the presentation of new language or included on the Scenario spread as part of the communicative task. The pronunciation syllabus covers word and sentence stress, difficult sounds, contractions and intonation.
- **Reading:** there is a wide range of reading material in *Language Leader* and a variety of exercise types developing the reading skills. The informative texts have been chosen for their interest and to provide a context for the grammar and vocabulary items being studied. The texts are based on real-life sources (magazines, websites, etc) and related activities include comprehension, vocabulary and reading sub-skills work.
- **Listening:** students are given many opportunities to develop a wide range of listening skills in *Language Leader,* both in terms of text types and activity types (e.g. checking predictions, table and note-completion). There is more listening practice in the Workbooks and CD-ROMs to further build the learners' confidence.
- **Speaking:** opportunities for oral practice of language and freer discussion appear regularly in every lesson. There is at least one explicit speaking activity per lesson and a major communicative task in the Scenario lesson.
- **Writing:** the writing syllabus introduces students to different genres and develops students' writing through analysis of models and practice in producing different text styles.
- **Study skills:** a systematic approach to developing study skills fosters independent dictionary use, encourages students to take notes effectively and gives them help in approaching exams and learning outside the classroom.

External organisations and link to examinations

- **Common European Framework of Reference:** the ethos of the CEFR is reflected throughout *Language Leader* in a variety of ways. For example, the outcomes of the Scenario lessons reflect the 'Can do' descriptors and help students use the language they have learnt effectively. Also, great emphasis is placed on the development of independent learning across the course including the extensive work on study skills, good study habits and self-assessment. For more information on *Language Leader* and the CEFR see the website www.pearsonlongman.com/languageleader.
- **Bologna Process:** as part of this initiative to harmonise tertiary education, many institutions now offer credit-bearing English language programmes. *Language Leader* reflects the values of the Bologna Process with its emphasis on individual responsibility for learning.
- **Link to examinations:** ELT examination exercise-types occur regularly throughout *Language Leader* to help prepare students for a range of common exams (IELTS in particular). The website provides grids correlating *Language Leader* to international ELT exams.

INTRODUCTION

How a unit works (Elementary)

Input lesson (1)

The contents of each unit are clearly labelled at the top of the opening page.

Stimulating topic-related quotation to engage learners.

Reading exercises aid comprehension of the text and develop skills.

The informative reading text provides a context for the language and vocabulary being studied.

Speaking exercises personalise the language and encourage communication.

Writing exercises practice short contextualised text construction.

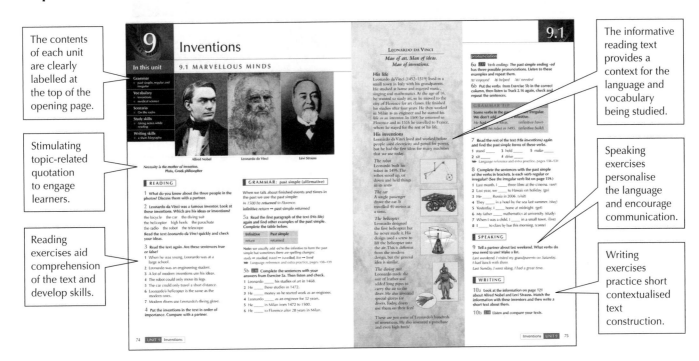

Input lesson (2)

Listening exercises guide students through audio texts and encourage different styles of listening.

Vocabulary exercises present and practise topic-specific lexis.

Clear presentation of grammar followed by useful practice.

Concept-check questions encourage students to work out the grammar rules themselves.

The regular Grammar tip boxes focus on key points.

Cross reference directs students to the Language reference and Extra practice spread at the back of the book.

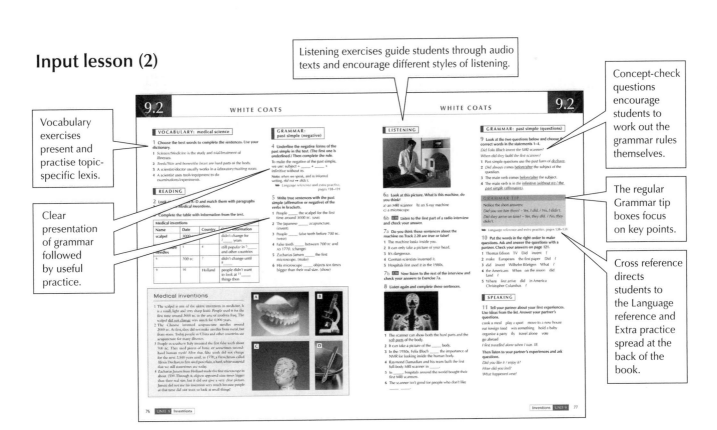

INTRODUCTION

Scenario

Scenario lessons practise Key language from the unit through a meaningful final task.

Students are given preparation for the task through different activities.

The Key language of the lesson is presented and practised.

Students are given practice in correct pronunciation of the Key language.

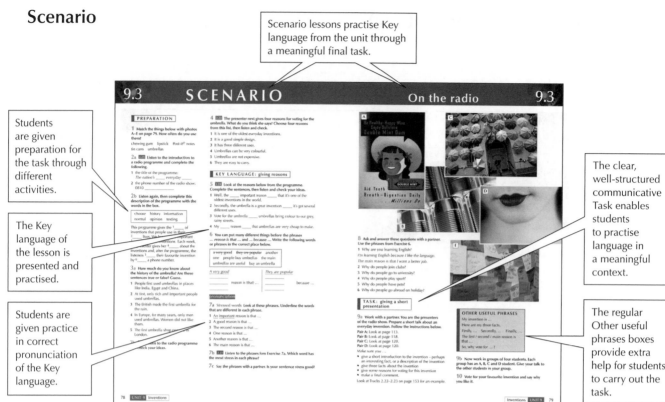

The clear, well-structured communicative Task enables students to practise language in a meaningful context.

The regular Other useful phrases boxes provide extra help for students to carry out the task.

Study and writing skills

Writing Skills focus on a different genre of writing in each unit.

The Study skills section develops students' ability to work on their own and in the classroom environment.

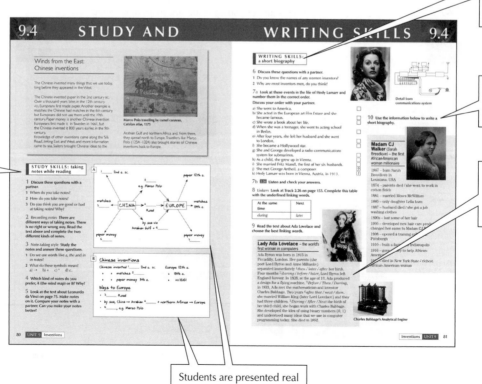

Students are given a guided writing task

Students are given model texts to follow and analyse.

Students are presented real life tasks with alternatives.

INTRODUCTION

Other sections
Review

Review lessons occur after every three units; they revise and consolidate the Grammar, Vocabulary and Key language from the previous units.

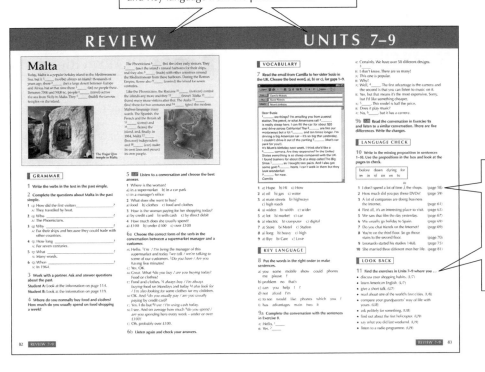

Students are encouraged to check and comment on their own learning, and reflect on what they have learned.

Language reference / Extra practice

There is one Language reference and Extra practice spread for each unit at the back of the book.

Grammar is cross-referenced to separate grammar points in each unit.

Extra practice exercises for the Grammar, Key language and Vocabulary studied in the unit.

The students are given a summary of the Key language and Vocabulary they have studied in the unit.

Cities

1.1 CITY FACTS

Lesson topic and staging

The lesson looks at famous cities around the world. Students do vocabulary work on adjectives to describe a city, for example *big ≠ small*, *noisy ≠ quiet*. This language is then contextualised in a reading, Ten facts about São Paulo. The lesson then moves on to grammar and the verb *to be*. Students use the reading to complete a grammar table on the verb and then do some controlled grammar practice. Students then listen to two conversations: one about Kraków in Poland and the other about Istanbul in Turkey. The lesson finishes with a role-play based on the listening in which students talk about their city/town.

Objectives

By the end of the lesson students should have:

- expanded their range of adjectives for describing places
- revised the meaning and form of the present simple form of the verb *to be*
- learned (more) about a number of major cities: São Paulo, Kraków and Istanbul
- been able to describe their city/town in basic terms

Timings

If short of time, leave exercises 6 and 7 until the beginning of the next lesson where they can be used as a quick revision activity.

A possible lesson break would be after the reading on page 6 and before the Grammar work on page 7.

WARM-UP

This warm-up is a quiz on the capital cities of the world.

- Write the following six countries and six capitals on the board jumbled as follows and ask students to match them:

1	Mexico	a) Paris
2	Russia	b) New Delhi
3	France	c) Madrid
4	Canada	d) Mexico City
5	India	e) Moscow
6	Spain	f) Ottawa

- Check students' answers (1d; 2e; 3a; 4f; 5b; 6c).

VOCABULARY: cities and adjectives

1 Ask students to look at exercise 1 and match the photos on pages 6 and 7 with the cities from the box.

> **A** London; **B** São Paulo; **C** Istanbul; **D** Kraków

i Photo A shows a night-time view of London, looking down the River Thames towards the financial district called the City of London. The two tall buildings are Tower 42 on the left, and the Swiss Re building, more commonly known as 'the Gherkin' after its unusual shape.

Photo B shows a major road through São Paulo.

Photo C shows the Yeni mosque in the Eminönü district of Istanbul.

Photo D shows Wawel Cathedral in Kraków. It is a very famous and important building in Poland.

2 Students do activity as per Coursebook.

- When you check students' answers correct any pronunciation problems they have, e.g.
wet /vet/ ✗ /wet/ ✓
cheap /tʃep/ ✗ /tʃiːp/ ✓

> 2d; 3h; 4a; 5b; 6c; 7f; 8e

- Ask students to give you adjectives to describe London in photo A and write their answers on the board (e.g. *London is big, beautiful, noisy and expensive*).

- Get students to discuss the other three photos and then ask for a few answers from the whole class.

🔧 If you have a strong class, encourage them to use linking words (e.g. *London is big and beautiful but it is also noisy and expensive*).

READING

3 Ask students to look at the photo of São Paulo on page 7 and see if any of them can tell the class something about the city.

- Tell students to read the statements in 3a and 3b first, before reading the text.

i São Paulo is one of the biggest cities in the world. Its population of over 18 million makes it the biggest city in Brazil. It is also the richest! But it is very noisy and dirty – it has one of the worst traffic problems in the world.

> **3a: 1** big and noisy
> **3b: 2** false (fact 2); **3** false (fact 3); **4** true (fact 1);
> **5** false (fact 5); **6** false (fact 8).

GRAMMAR: *to be*

4   Check that students understand the way the table is organised and the technical language used to describe different forms, such as *Affirmative* and *Negative*, if you think they aren't familiar with them.

- Tell students to study the table and use the text to complete spaces 1–4.

- Check their answers and point out the use of contractions. If you feel they need extra practice at this moment, get them to do the exercises on page 123.

💡 You might want to point out the difference in usage between the contracted forms (e.g. *I'm, he's,* etc.) and the uncontracted forms (e.g. *I am, he is,* etc.): this is covered on page 122 in the Language Reference.

> **2** they're; **3** isn't; **4** aren't

5a Students do activity as per Coursebook.

> **1** London is the capital of the UK. *It's* an old city; **2** Istanbul *isn't* the capital of Turkey; **3** São Paulo and Brasilia *are* in Brazil; **4** Kraków and London *aren't* hot in winter.

5b Students do activity as per Coursebook. Encourage them to extend their answers by referring them back to exercise 2, e.g. *London is big and beautiful but it is also noisy and expensive.*

GRAMMAR TIP

It's worth spending a little time going over the short answers with students as they will use them in later exercises.

6   Students do activity as per Coursebook.

> Answers will vary depending on students' opinions.

📝 To extend this activity, write the following questions on the board. Elicit the answers for 1 and 2 and ask students to answer the rest in pairs.

1   Are you from Mexico?
2   Are you an English student?
3   Is Ronaldinho Brazilian?
4   Is Madonna American?
5   Is your city/town small?
6   Is your town/city expensive?
7   Are you a noisy class?
8   Are you intelligent students?
9   Are India and China in Europe?
10 Are Poland and England in Europe?

7   Get students to work on this exercise in pairs.

> **2** Are the buses expensive in your city? **3** Is New York in Europe? **4** Is Tokyo a big city? **5** Are you happy in your city? **6** Are you famous in your city?

LISTENING

1.2

8a Ask students to read the questions before they listen.

> 1c; 2b

8b Ask students to read the task before they listen. You could also ask students which city they would prefer to visit and why.

> **Kraków: 2** south; **3** cold
> **Istanbul: 4** noisy; **5** wet; **6** famous

SPEAKING

9   Students do activity as per Coursebook. You may want to let them read the two conversations on page 146 first.

🔧 If you think your students will find this task difficult, write the prompts below on the board. Choose a student to be the teacher and model the conversation with him/her.

teacher: Good morning. What's your name?
student: …
teacher: And where are you from?
student: …
teacher: That's interesting. Tell me something about it.
student: It's …
teacher: Really. And what about the weather?
student: …
teacher: Are the restaurants good?
student: …
teacher: That's interesting. Thank you.

💡 It is better for weaker students to play the role of the teacher in the first round. Then get students to swap roles so that the teacher becomes the student and vice versa.

> **Track 1.2**
> **1**
> *Teacher, Pavel*
> T: Good morning. Come in. What's your name?
> P: Pavel.
> T: OK, Pavel. Have a seat. Where are you from?
> P: From Kraków, in Poland.
> T: Oh, OK. Tell me something about Kraków.
> P: Well, it's a beautiful city. It's very old. It's in the south of Poland. It isn't the capital of Poland – that's Warsaw.
> T: Is it a big city?
> P: No, it isn't. It's quite small.
> T: Anything else?
> P: It's cold in winter. And er … for you, it's very cheap!
> T: OK, good, Pavel. We're on page …
> *continued…*

2

Teacher, Ayla

T: Hello! Come in. Are you Ayla?

A: Yes, that's right.

T: OK. Where are you from, Ayla?

A: Istanbul, in Turkey.

T: OK, what's Istanbul like?

A: Sorry?

T: Tell me something about Istanbul.

A: Oh, OK. It's a big city, very beautiful, but very noisy! The mosques are very famous.

T: I see. What about the weather?

A: It's hot in summer and it's wet in winter, but spring and autumn are nice.

T: Are the restaurants good?

A: Yes, they are, very good!

HOMEWORK OPTIONS

Students do the exercises on pages 6–7 of the Workbook.

Students do/finish the extra practice activities 1, 2, 3, 9 and 10 on page 123 in the Language Reference.

Students write a similar conversation to the ones in exercise 9b of the Coursebook.

1.2 PLACES IN A CITY

IN THIS LESSON

Lesson topic and staging

The lesson continues the focus on cities around the world with a special focus on places within a city. Students begin the lesson by expanding their vocabulary of places in a city such as canals, churches, harbours and mountains. This language is contextualised in a reading on famous cities: Sydney, Mumbai and Venice. The lesson then turns to grammar with a focus on *there is, there are*. Students work with this structure before applying it in an information-gap speaking activity about other famous cities. The lesson then moves on to a listening in which people talk about the city they are from before finishing on a pronunciation exercise on contractions.

Objectives

By the end of the lesson students should have:

- expanded their range of vocabulary for places in a city
- revised the meaning and form of *there is, there are* for saying what a place has
- learned (more) about a number of major cities around the world
- improved their awareness and pronunciation of contracted forms

Timings

If short of time, you could drop exercise 6 on page 9 and give it for homework.

A good lesson break would be after exercise 3 on page 8 and before the grammar on page 9.

WARM-UP

- Tell students to open their books and look at photo A on page 8. Ask them what they can see in the photo. When they have finished, tell them they have a couple of minutes to look at photos B–J and see what they know about them.

- When students are ready, get a few of them to tell the rest of the group about the photos. Encourage other students to correct any wrong information or to complete any 'missing' information, for example:

  student a: I think photo F is of China.

  student b: No, it isn't. It's Mumbai, a big city in India.

VOCABULARY: places in a city

1a Students do activity as per Coursebook.

- Check students' answers and their pronunciation.

> **A** a beach; **B** a theatre; **C** an airport; **D** a park,
> a fountain; **E** a bridge; **F** a cinema; **G** a canal,
> a church; **H** a temple; **I** a harbour, a mountain;
> **J** a museum

i Photo A shows Bondi Beach in Sydney. This is one of the busiest beaches in Sydney.

Photo B is the Stockholm Royal Opera House.

Photo E shows Harbour Bridge and the Opera House in Sydney.

Photo G shows the Grand Canal in Venice. This is the most important waterway in the city. In the distance you can see the Basilica di Santa Maria della Salute.

Photo H shows the west gate of the Pure Water Temple in Kyoto. The temple was built in the late 16th century.

Photo I shows the waterfront of Cape Town, South Africa. In the background you can see Table Mountain.

Photo J shows the Field Museum of Natural History in Chicago, USA.

1b You could do this with the whole class or in small groups. If done in small groups, students will probably 'teach' each other the 'new' words. You could also encourage students to think of examples from their own towns/cities.

READING

2 Students do activity as per Coursebook. Ask students which city they would like to visit and why.

Give students a pre-reading task. You could write up the cities in the text on the board and ask students what they know about the places. This should throw up some information about them.

> **2** beaches; **3** films; **4** water

3 Ask students to answer the questions from memory.

- Tell them to check their answers by looking at the text.
- Check their answers.

> **2b; 3b; 4b; 5c; 6a**

GRAMMAR: *there is, there are*

4a Students do activity as per Coursebook. You might like to give some more examples of the grammar using objects in the classroom, e.g. *There's a window in the classroom. There are 12 chairs in the classroom.*

(!) Students may have trouble with number 4, because they need to use *any*. This is covered in exercise 4b below.

> **2** there are; **3** there isn't; **4** there aren't any

4b Ask the whole class to think about this question.

We use *any* in negative sentences to talk about plural nouns (e.g. *There aren't any canals in my city*).

(!) We can also use *any* in questions. This is explained in the table in exercise 5, and in the Language Reference.

5 Students do activity as per Coursebook.

> **2** not; **3** Is; **4** isn't; **5** are; **6** any; **7** are

For a full explanation and further practice activities, go to pages 122–123 in the Language Reference.

6 Students do activity as per Coursebook.

> **2** are; **3** aren't; **4** isn't a; **5** Are; **6** are

GRAMMAR TIP

Draw students' attention to the grammar tip and check that they understand it.

SPEAKING

7 This is an information-gap activity where two students have to exchange information to complete a table about various cities. Explain the activity and divide students into As and Bs.

- Give students time to read the table and think about the questions they are going to ask. It would help to get a pair of students to demonstrate a question and answer.

- Quickly check students' answers. You could write the answers on the board to help weaker students.

Remember to monitor students and make notes while they are doing this activity.

It is normal for many students to use their own language when working unobserved in pairs or small groups. Do your best to encourage them to speak English as much as possible in class. A lot of valuable practice takes place in pair and group work and it is worth explaining that to your students.

LISTENING

1.3

8a Give students time to read the task before you play the recording.

2b; 3d; 4a

Track 1.3

1
Hello! I'm Yukako and I'm from Kyoto. Kyoto's in the west of Japan. My city's old and there are a lot of old buildings. There are a lot of temples. They're very quiet. I love the old buildings.

2
Hi there! I'm Pablo. I'm from Lima, in Peru. In my city there are hundreds of cafés. They're great. I love them.

3
Hi. I'm Stefan and I'm from Chicago, in the United States. In the city there are a lot of museums. I love the museums in Chicago.

4
Hello. I'm Peter and I'm from Cape Town in South Africa. In Cape Town there's a beautiful mountain and there are a lot of beaches. The beaches are fantastic. I love them.

8b Students do activity as per Coursebook. Give them time to read the task before you play the recording.

2b; 3b; 4b

pronunciation

1.4

9a Explain that this activity focuses on contractions. You might want to drill the following: *I am – I'm*; *You are – You're*; *He is – He's*, etc.

- Tell students that contractions are normal in spoken and written English. Full forms normally only occur in formal written English these days.

- Give students time to read the six sentences before you play the recording.

- If the students say it was difficult to hear the difference, you could play the sentences again before checking their answers.

☼ A helpful way to drill a sentence is to break it up and drill each part. Start at the end of the sentence and put the sentence back together by getting students to repeat after you. For example:

teacher: ... Chicago.	students: ... Chicago.
teacher: ... from Chicago.	students: ... from Chicago.
teacher: I'm from Chicago.	students: I'm from Chicago.

Audioscript and answers:
Track 1.4
1 I'm from Chicago.
2 They're very quiet.
3 There's a beautiful mountain.

9b Students do activity as per Coursebook.

WRITING

10 This writing activity consolidates the work of the lesson. Think of a town or city that all the students will know and use it to write a model text with the whole group on the board.

- Ask students to write about their town or city. If all the students come from the same town, ask them to write about other cities or towns they know well. Tell them not to mention the name of the place when they write because they will read out their descriptions and get the other students to guess the place.

- Monitor the activity and help students if necessary.

- When most of the students are ready ask two or three to read their descriptions to the group. Tell the other students not to call out the names of the place.

- When each student has finished reading get a few of the other students to guess the place but do NOT confirm the answer until they have all spoken.

HOMEWORK OPTIONS

Students do the exercises on pages 8–9 of the Workbook.

Students do/finish the extra practice activities 4, 5 and 11 on page 123 in the Language Reference.

1.3 SCENARIO: ON THE STREET

IN THIS LESSON

Lesson topic and staging

Students do preparatory work on place names such as *bookshop* and *swimming pool*. This is practised before students go into a reading about the English city, Cambridge. This leads into a listening about places of interest in Cambridge. In the next stage of the lesson students focus on the Key Language of prepositions of place. A number of further activities prepare them for the main focus of the lesson – the task. In this task students have to use their language resources to locate places on a map.

Objectives

By the end of the lesson students should have:

- expanded their range of language for naming places in a city/town
- learned language used to locate places: *between X and Y*, *next to X …*, *opposite Y*, *in Z*
- learned (more) about the English town, Cambridge
- talked about locations in their city/town in basic terms

Common European Framework

Students can use a map to ask and answer questions about the location of places within a town/city.

Timings

If short of time, you could drop exercise 4. Students could do this for homework.

A possible lesson break would be after exercise 7b and before the Key Language on page 11.

Make sure you leave sufficient time at the end of the lesson to prepare for, complete and discuss the task in exercise 10.

PREPARATION

1

(!) In Romance languages *library* is a false friend and may be confused in English with *bookshop*.

- Students do activity as per Coursebook. Check students' pronunciation at the same time as you check their answers.

> **2** post office; **3** bus station; **4** college; **5** public toilets; **6** market; **7** tourist information centre; **8** car park; **9** shopping centre; **10** zoo; **11** swimming pool; **12** gardens; **13** railway station; **14** library; **15** building site

`1.5`

2a Students do activity as per Coursebook.

> **2** zoo; **3** car park; **4** swimming pool; **5** building site; **6** bus station

---

Track 1.5
1 (railway station)
2 (zoo)
3 (car park)
4 (swimming pool)
5 (building site)
6 (bus station)

2b Ask students what they think about the various noises. The answers are subjective so be prepared for different opinions.

> **Possible answers: 'nice':** 2, 4; **'nasty':** 1, 3, 5, 6

3a Ask small groups of students to make a list of five noisy places and five quiet places in their town/city. You could get students to write up their lists on the board and compare them.

3b Start the activity by asking students a few questions about the area near your institution to model the activity. Check students understand *I'm not sure*. It may help students if you say the sentence and get students to repeat it after you.

4 Get students to look at the photos of Cambridge and ask them to tell you anything they know about the city.

- Quickly check students know all the words in the box and get them to complete the task.
- Ask students if they would like to visit Cambridge and what they would like to do there.

> **2** population; **3** gardens; **4** famous; **5** students; **6** language

(i) The top picture on page 10 shows King's College, part of Cambridge University. Underneath you can see King's Parade, a busy shopping street.

`1.6`

5 Tell students that they are going to listen to a talk about Cambridge. Play the recording once.

> At an English language school.

6 Get students to study the map on page 10 before they do the task. Students do activity as per Coursebook.

> **Students should tick:** bookshop, post office, market, shopping centre, bus station, park, railway station, library, zoo

7a Students do activity as per Coursebook. This is a difficult listening so make sure students read the sentences before you play the recording.

- You could let students check their answers in pairs as this will prepare them for listening again.

- Play the recording again so students can confirm or change their answers.

7b Get students to look at the map and check their answers. If you think they won't know the meaning of the prepositions of place, look first at the Language Reference on page 122. Students can refer to this when checking their answers.

1b; 2c; 3a; 4b

Track 1.6

School administrator, 2 students

SA: Good morning everyone. Welcome to Cambridge and to the Cam English School. Right, now, please look at your maps. There are a lot of interesting places in the city centre. First of all, please find Trinity Street and King's Parade – they're on the left of your map. There are a lot of beautiful colleges on these streets. Opposite Trinity College there's a good bookshop and a small post office.

In the middle of the map, between Trinity College and the main post office, there's the main shopping area, with the market and the shopping centre. The market's nice, with food and clothes and a lot of other things. And it's cheap! The shopping centre's … well … to tell you the truth, it's ugly, but there are a lot of shops. On the right of the map, there's the bus station, next to the park. It's quite busy in the mornings and evenings. Take the bus from there to the railway station, or to London. Any questions so far?

S1: Yes. Is there a library?

SA: Yes, there is. It's in the shopping centre. On your map, there's a person with a book.

S1: Oh, yes. Thank you.

S2: Excuse me, is there a zoo?

SA: No, I'm afraid there isn't, not in the city. OK then, that's all for now. Don't forget – tomorrow at three o'clock, there's a guided tour of the city. Have a good time and learn a lot of English!

KEY LANGUAGE: saying where places are

8 Students do activity as per Coursebook.

The small post office is opposite Trinity College.
The theatre is between King's College and the tourist information centre.
The Zoology Museum is next to the Whipple Museum.

---

pronunciation

1.7

9a

(!) The /ə/ or schwa is the most common sound in the English language. It's the only phoneme or sound that has its own name! It only occurs in unstressed syllables. It helps if students can locate the main stress in a word because the schwa is often found in one or more of the other syllables.

- Explain to students that they are going to practise the most important sound in English but first they need to understand the idea of stress in words.

- Write these words on the board and ask students how many syllables they have (each word has two syllables).

garden   market   bookshop

- Say the words to the students and ask them which syllable is 'louder' or 'bigger' and mark their answers on the words as follows:

    •   •   •
garden   market   bookshop

- Explain that the 'big' or 'loud' syllable is the stressed syllable; now ask students to mark the stress on the words in exercise 9a.

    •   •   •   •
station opposite famous England

- Now ask students to listen to the recording. Ask them if they hear the sound in the underlined parts. Pronounce the /ə/ and get them to repeat it after you.

- Now pronounce the words or play the recording and get students to repeat the words.

Audioscript and answers:
Track 1.7
station, opposite, famous, England

1.8

9b Get students to do the same with the stressed and unstressed syllables in the words. Can they find the schwas? The word cinema has two. You could write the words on the board and get students to come out and mark the main stress and underline the schwas.

Audioscript and answers:
Track 1.8
canal; fountain; library; cinema; quiet; million

TASK: describing where places are

Task summary: Students will work in pairs, A and B. They both have the same map of a town but some of the places on their maps are not named (six places in each). Student A has the answers that Student B needs and vice versa. The students' task is to complete the map. A successful task outcome is when students have completed the six spaces on each map, i.e. a total of 12 spaces.

10 Explain the basic situation, task and task outcome. Tell students that they should not look at the other person's map, and should only communicate with English.

- Look together at the *Other useful phrases* at the bottom of page 11 in the Coursebook. The purpose of the box is to provide useful language for students to help them successfully complete the task.

- Use the map of Cambridge centre on page 10 to explain and practise the phrases.

- Get a student A to ask the first question and get a student B to reply. This will model the conversation.

- Monitor students while they are doing the task and write down concrete examples of correct and incorrect English. It's better not to intervene unless individual pairs have a breakdown in communication.

- Once students have finished, ask how many students completed all their spaces. What did they find easy? Did they have any problems? What kind of problems did they have? If they have generally achieved the task, congratulate them.

- Finally, use your notes to give feedback on the language areas needed to complete the map.

HOMEWORK OPTIONS

Students do the exercises on page 10 of the Workbook.

DICTIONARY REMINDER

Ask your students to make a note to bring their dictionaries to class for the next lesson.

1.4 STUDY AND WRITING SKILLS

IN THIS LESSON

Lesson topic and staging

In the first part of the lesson students look at the pronunciation of the letters of the alphabet, and then different uses of a monolingual English dictionary before practising the uses themselves. In the second part of Lesson 1.4 students analyse a basic text about a city (Toronto, Canada). They look at how information is organised by topic and paragraph before examining the type of language used and how it is linked by the conjunction *and*. Students then combine what they have worked on in the lesson to write a simple factfile on a city they know.

Objectives

By the end of the lesson students should have:

- learned some of the main uses of a monolingual English dictionary
- practised the skills necessary to use a monolingual dictionary
- learned (more) about the city of Toronto, Canada
- analysed the structure of a factfile
- planned and written a short, simple factfile about a city they know

Common European Framework

Students can write a short, simple text about a city they know.

Timings

If short of time, you could drop exercise 13. Students could do this activity for homework.

A possible lesson break would be after exercise 9 on page 12, before the Writing Skills section on page 13.

WARM-UP

- Tell students that the first part of the lesson will be about how to use a dictionary.

- Write up these questions for students to discuss in pairs or small groups.

Preteach: *monolingual dictionary* (a dictionary in only one language), *bilingual dictionary* (a dictionary that has translations of words into another language)

   1 Do you have a dictionary?

   2 Is it a monolingual or a bilingual dictionary?

   3 When do you use the dictionary?

STUDY SKILLS: using your dictionary (1)

1.9

1

(!) This exercise may prove to be very difficult depending on the students' language and the script they use, for example Arabic, Cyrillic, Greek and so on. Of course, your students will have used the Roman script before but the English alphabet may still cause them problems even if they use Roman script in their own language!

- Make the distinction clear between sounds and letters: there are 26 letters in the alphabet but there are many more sounds in the language, and it is not always possible to predict the pronunciation of a word in English from its spelling. Students listen to and then repeat the alphabet.

(☼) You may want to write it on the board in upper and lower case (*A*, *a*), to help students when they listen and repeat.

> **Audioscript and answers:**
> **Track 1.9**
> A B C D E F G H I J K L M N O P Q R S T U V W
> X Y Z

(✎) To extend this activity, give students a ball. The first student says a letter of the alphabet and throws it to another student who says the next letter of the alphabet and so on. If a student makes a mistake, start from the beginning of the alphabet again.

1.10

2 This exercise uses phonemes (sounds) to help students with the pronunciation of the alphabet. Start by writing an example word for each phoneme (1–7) in the Coursebook on the board (e.g. /eɪ/ *make*, /iː/ *see*, /e/ *bed*, /aɪ/ *sky*, /uː/ *blue*, /əʊ/ *boat*, /ɑː/ *car*).

- Get students to repeat the words after you, then repeat the words one by one followed by the sound, e.g.

  teacher: Make.   students: Make.
  teacher: /eɪ/.   students: /eɪ/.

- Test students by pointing at random at different sounds and getting them to say them.
- Tell students to complete groups 1–7 with the letters in the box.
- Check students' answers and write them on the board next to the seven sounds.

> **Audioscript and answers:**
> **Track 1.10**
> 1 /eɪ/ A H J K
> 2 /iː/ B C D E G P T V
> 3 /e/ F L M N S X Z
> 4 /aɪ/ I Y
> 5 /uː/ Q U W
> 6 /əʊ/ O
> 7 /ɑː/ R

- If students need more practice, drill the words on the board group by group.

3 In pairs, students do activity as per Coursebook.

> 2 G; 3 H; 4 J; 5 Q; 6 U; 7 Y; 8 Z

4a Spell the words/phrases below slowly to students. You may want to write the following useful phrase on the board for students: *Can you say that again, please?*

> 1 ugly; 2 cheap; 3 fountain; 4 harbour;
> 5 swimming pool; 6 tourist information centre

4b Students do activity as per Coursebook.

5 This activity practises alphabetical ordering, which is a very important skill when looking words up in a dictionary. Explain the purpose of the activity and give students 30 seconds to complete the task.

- Time them and when the 30 seconds are over, stop students and check their answers.

(🔧) If your students are not very strong, particularly if their L1 uses a completely different script from English, they will need longer to complete the task.

> 2 chair; 3 city; 4 cold; 5 famous; 6 harbour; 7 is;
> 8 market; 9 mountain; 10 museum; 11 music;
> 12 no; 13 park; 14 yes

6a Students do activity as per Coursebook. If students do not have a dictionary, skip this activity or tell students to do it for homework.

> Answers will depend on the dictionary the students use. In Wordwise, the answers are *underage, grasshopper, marathon, headache, seabed, food chain, radioactive, think, engrave.*

6b In pairs, students compare their answers. They may not be the same if their dictionaries are different.

7 Read the words/phrases below to the students. When you have finished allow them time to check their spelling if they have dictionaries. If you have brought a class set of dictionaries, students can check their spellings in small groups of three or four.

> **Suggested words for dictation: 1** expensive;
> 2 cities; 3 canals; 4 theatre; 5 railway station;
> 6 next to; 7 alphabet; 8 dictionary

8 To prepare students for this activity, ask them what information a dictionary can give you (e.g. it can teach you about grammar, pronunciation, etc.).

• Tell students to put the labels in the correct places. Tell students not to try to understand every word. The object is to understand the different parts of a dictionary entry.

> **a** pronunciation; **b** definition; **c** grammar;
> **d** different meanings of the words; **f** example

9 Introduce the concept of a part of speech by looking at sentences 1–4 with your students.

• Students do the activity as per Coursebook.

> **2** n; **3** adj; **4** adj; **5** adj; **6** n; **7** adj; **8** n; **9** adj; **10** n;
> **11** n; **12** n

WRITING SKILLS: a description of a city

10 Explain to students that the aim of this part of the lesson is to study a factfile about a famous city and then to write a similar one about a city that they know well.

Preteach: *location* (a place), *tourist attractions* (things that tourists like to see or do), *points of the compass* (north / northeast / northwest, south / southeast / southwest, etc.)

• Students do activity as per Coursebook.

☼ It is often a good idea to tell students the aim of a lesson so that they are focused and know why they are doing something and what the end result will be.

> **1** Location; **2** Climate; **3** Size; **5** Tourist attractions

11a Students do activity as per Coursebook.

☼ This activity repeats the work of exercise 9 but it is important that students work at making their texts more attractive, however basic, by using adjectives.

> **2** adj; **3** adj or n (the language); **4** adj; **5** n; **6** n; **7** n;
> **8** adj; **9** adj

11b Students do activity as per Coursebook.

> **2** modern; **3** busy; **4** beautiful; **5** wonderful

12 Start by introducing the link-word *and* on the board. Write up the following sentences and ask students for a word to join/link the parts of the sentence.

London is big ___ noisy.
Toronto has a lot of museums ___ theatres.

• Students could do the exercise in pairs.

> **1** London is a big and expensive city. / London is big and expensive.
> **2** There are museums and theatres in the city.
> **3** Venice is a small and beautiful city. / Venice is small and beautiful.
> **4** There are canals and a lot of churches in the city.
> **5** Sydney is a large and noisy city. / Sydney is large and noisy.
> **6** There is an opera house and a beautiful harbour.

13 This task is the culmination of all the work students have done so far in this lesson. Get students in pairs to decide on a city they know well. It is important that they know enough about the city to cover the sections listed in exercise 10.

• Tell students the aim of this part of the lesson, i.e. to write a factfile for the city they choose.

• Students make notes on the city. Tell them to look at the text on Toronto for ideas.

• Get students to divide the notes into general description, location, etc.

• Write the following on the board and get students to fill in the spaces:

> _____ is in the _____ of _____. It's on/near _____.

• Tell students to use the text about Toronto to help them write the sections of their factfile.

• Tell the students to ask you if they need help. Alternatively, walk around the classroom while students are working so that you can help anybody who needs you.

• If time, get a couple of students to read their factfile to the class. Can other students add any information about the city?

🔧 If you feel students need more support, you could first write another factfile with the whole class on the board following the steps suggested.

HOMEWORK OPTIONS

Students complete the written task. If they have already finished, they could write about another city they know well.

Students do the exercises on page 11 of the Workbook.

2 Work and study

2.1 WORKING LIFE

Lesson topic and staging

The lesson focuses on the world of work. Students begin by looking at the vocabulary of jobs and places of work. A short reading explores the working lives of a Korean businesswoman and two Dutch airline pilots. The texts provide a context for the grammar focus on the present simple tense that follows. The grammar deals with affirmative and negative forms. Students have to work out the meaning and form of the tense and go on to practise it. In the final activity of the lesson students make simple notes about themselves and then, working in pairs, use each other's notes to tell the class about their partner.

Objectives

By the end of the lesson students should have:

- learned more words and phrases for jobs and workplaces
- revised the meaning and form of the present simple
- improved their scanning and inference skills
- learned more about their classmates

Timings

If short of time, you could drop exercises 4 and 9. Students could do these exercises for homework.

A possible lesson break would be after exercise 4 and before the Grammar focus on page 15.

WARM-UP

This is a quick revision activity.

- Put students in small groups and give them three minutes to write down as many place names from the previous unit as they can.
- Get students to tell you the words on their lists and write them on the board to ensure they have the correct spelling.

VOCABULARY: jobs and places of work

1a Students do activity as per Coursebook.

- Check their pronunciation as you check the answers.

> **B** a lawyer; **C** a lecturer; **D** a doctor;
> **E** an accountant; **F** a businesswoman; **G** a pilot

1b See if students can tell you where the people from exercise 1a work. Give them an example, *A teacher works in a school.*

- Ask students to match the pictures with the workplaces. Students will probably not know the word *court* but it will become clear by a process of elimination.

With stronger students you could ask them to write full sentences, e.g. *An accountant works in an office.*

> **Suggested answers:**
> **B** in a court; **C** in a university; **D** in a hospital;
> **E** in an office; **F** in an office; **G** on a plane

2 Students discuss the questions in pairs or groups.

READING

3 Get students to look at the photos F and G and tell you what they think the texts are about. Tell them not to read the text yet.

- Tell students to read the sentences in exercise 3 before they read the texts.

> **2** false (she works for a big clothes shop);
> **3** true (she buys clothes); **4** false (see 3); **5** true;
> **6** false (Jos says, 'We speak a lot of English …')

4 You could ask students to do this from memory and check their answers by reading the texts.

> **2** Marco; **3** Youna; **4** Marco; **5** Marco

GRAMMAR: present simple

Students often find the use of the auxiliary *do/does* very difficult, and may have problems with third person singular forms. They may make mistakes like these:

I do go to a lot of countries. She like her job.

She don't live in Europe. They doesn't work in a school.

5 This activity examines basic concepts of the tense. Ask students to work in pairs to complete the exercise. Make sure students are clear about what a) and b) mean.

Students may be confused by 3 and match it with a) or b). *Live* is viewed in English as a state unless it is described as temporary. If temporary, we use the progressive form: *They're living in a flat until they can find the right house.*

> **1b; 2a; 3a; 4b**

6 Tell students to read the sentences before they look for the appropriate verbs from the text.

> **2** buy; **3** doesn't meet; **4** live; **5** don't fly; **6** see

7 Students do activity as per Coursebook.

> **2** meet; **3** don't meet; **4** doesn't meet; **5** don't meet

For a full explanation and further practice activities, go to page 124 in the Language Reference.

GRAMMAR TIP

Read through the grammar tip and make sure students understand the rules for spellings.

For a full explanation and further practice activities, go to page 124 in the Language Reference.

8 Students do activity as per Coursebook.

> **2** fly; **3** doesn't; **4** don't; **5** uses; **6** don't

9 Make sure students understand that the sentences should be true for themselves. Do the first item as an example.

SPEAKING

10a This activity pulls together all the work students have done in the lesson. Complete the sentences for yourself on the board as a model for students. Show them that they can write anything about themselves they want to in the last sentence.

- Point out use of the negative auxiliary in *I don't like …*
- Get students to write sentences about themselves.
- When students are writing their sentences, look out for typical mistakes with the tense and correct them.

10b In this activity students have to transform their partner's sentences from first to third person.

- Use the list of sentences about yourself on the board to show students how to turn sentences from first into third person.

  My name is Janet Davis.→ Her name is Janet Davis.

- Ask students to swap sentences with their partners and give them some time to think about the changes they will need to make, but without writing them.

- When students are ready ask a few people to tell the class about their partner.

HOMEWORK OPTIONS

Students do/finish the extra practice activities 1, 2, 3 and 6 on page 125 in the Language Reference.

Students do the exercises on pages 12–13 of the Workbook.

Students write sentences like those in exercise 10b about someone else, for example a friend or family member.

2.2 STUDENT LIFE

IN THIS LESSON

Lesson topic and staging

The lesson focuses on the world of study. Students begin by looking at a website for a university in New Zealand. This provides the context for the grammar: present simple question forms. Students have to work out the rules of the question form which they then apply in a number of exercises based on the topic of study. The lesson then moves to a listening based in a language school in the UK. A student is asked a number of questions about her life and study habits. Students use the basis of the listening to interview other students about their everyday life and study habits. The lesson finishes with a simple writing activity where students write sentences about the different classmates they interviewed.

Objectives

By the end of the lesson students should have:

- learned more words and phrases on the topic of study and university
- learned (more) about applying for a place in an English-speaking university
- improved their scanning and inference skills
- revised the meaning and form of present simple question forms with *do* and *does*
- become more confident about asking and answering questions using the present simple

Timings

If short of time, drop exercises 1b and 10. Students could do exercise 10 for homework.

A possible lesson break would be after exercise 4b and before additional practice of the grammar in exercises 5, 6 and 7 on page 17.

WARM-UP

This warm-up activity gets students to think about the idea of studying abroad. Many students may not have this opportunity but it is something that will interest them in principle.

- Write these questions on the board and ask students to discuss them in small groups or pairs.

  1 Do you want to study abroad? Why (not)?

  2 Which country do you want to study in?

  3 What do you want to study?

- When most of the students are ready discuss the questions with the whole group. Note: the focus here is on their answers so it is better not to correct their answers unless it is clear the group does not understand them.

⚪ The IELTS (the International English Language Testing System) and TOEFL (Test of English as a Foreign Language) are tests of English language proficiency to see if non-native speakers' English is good enough to enter an English-speaking university.

Different universities ask for different scores for entry; a score of 6.0 in IELTS or 550 in TOEFL is normally a minimum requirement for university entrance.

READING

1a

Preteach: *lecturer* (a university teacher)

- Students do activity as per Coursebook. Give students a time limit of 15 seconds to answer the question. This forces them to scan rather than read the text in detail.

> It is for foreign students.

1b

Preteach: *staff* (the people who work for an organisation), *hall of residence* (a college or university building where students live)

- Point out the different parts of the web page. Then ask students to find the links (a connection between one page on the Internet and another).

> 2 Clubs and societies; 3 Staff; 4 Accommodation

2

Preteach: *foundation course* (a course of study that prepares you to start a university course), *IELTS* and *TOEFL* (exams foreign students take to get into an English-speaking university), *qualifications* (official exams you pass that show what level of education or training you have), *part-time job* (a job that you do for less than the usual number of hours)

- Ask students to read the questions before they match them.

> 2b; 3a; 4f; 5e; 6d; 7h; 8g

3

Ask students to read the sentences before they read the text again.

> 2 true (*We give you an official letter to help you.*); 3 false (*... we don't have one-year foundation courses*); 4 true (*... available for all foreign students.*); 5 true (*The exams are in June every year.*); 6 true (*Students live in the halls of residence on campus and in private flats off campus.*); 7 false (*The kitchens have everything you need.*); 8 false (*Students work in cafés, bars and shops.*)

GRAMMAR: present simple questions

⚪ Students often find present simple question forms difficult because of the use of the auxiliary verb *do/does*. You might want to use translation to demonstrate the difference between students' language and English. Although they may be able to complete the grammar rules they may find using the grammar much more difficult. It will probably take them some time to master the use of the auxiliaries. Gentle and continual correction will help.

4a

Check that students understand the grammatical terms, especially *infinitive* (the basic form of the verb, e.g. *go, play*, etc.) and *short answers* (the answer to a *yes/no* question, e.g. *Do you like sport? – Yes, I do / No, I don't.*).

- Tell students to use the text to help them write the rules.

> 1 does; 2 without; 3 don't; 4 don't use

4b

Students do activity as per Coursebook.

> 1 teach; 2 Does, teach; 3 do, teach; 4 does, teach

For a full explanation and further practice activities, go to pages 124–125 in the Language Reference.

5

Check students understand that there are two parts to the exercise. Remind them to look at the table in exercise 4b if they need help.

⚪ Questions 1–5 are *yes/no* questions. Question 6 is an 'information' question and some students may be confused by the form.

> 2 Does; 3 Does; 4 Do; 5 Do; 6 do
> Students will provide answers relevant to their own situation in the second part of this exercise.

6a

This activity focuses on word order. Explain the exercise by doing number 2 with the whole class.

⚪ If some of your students work, questions 5–8 may not seem relevant to them. Remind them that they are 'students' of English.

Students may be confused by question **3** where *do* is used twice: as an auxiliary and as the main verb.

> 2 Do you work for a small company? 3 What do you do in a normal day? 4 Do you like your job? 5 Do you go to school, college or university? 6 What subjects do you study? 7 Do you like your course? 8 Do you live in a hall of residence?

6b Put students in pairs to ask and answer questions.

If your students need help with pronunciation, you could write the questions up on the board once they've put them in order, and drill them, building up from *Do you* to form the whole questions, i.e.:

Do you …

Do you work for a …

Do you work for a small company?

Do you …

Do you like …

Do you like your job?

Do you …

Do you go …

Do you go to school?

LISTENING

1.11

7

Preteach: *free time* (time when you are not busy)

- Tell students the listening is an interview with a student.
- Get students to read the questions before they listen and try and complete them.
- Remind students that they should only focus on the questions at the moment.

> 3 have; 4 use; 5 have; 6 travel; 7 live; 8 meet;
> 9 play; 10 do

Track 1.11

Teacher, Gina

T: Gina, do you have time for me to ask a few questions?

G: Of course. What are they about?

T: Well, it's a survey about student life – your studies, your home life and your free time.

G: OK, fine.

T: Right, well, first of all, about your studies. Do you study English at the weekend?

G: Yes, I do. On Sundays, I study for about an hour.

T: Do you bring a dictionary to class?

G: No, I only have a big old dictionary at home.

T: Do you have a computer?

G: Yes. It's our family computer.

T: And at the school, do you use the library and study centre?

G: No, I don't. I don't have time in the week.

T: OK. Now some questions about work, travel and home. You study, but do you also have a job?

G: A job – no, I don't. But I have children! That's a job really.

T: Yes, true. Do you travel to school by train, bus or car?

G: By bus. It's cheap.

T: Do you live alone, with family or with friends?

continued…

G: You know that answer! With my family.

T: Indeed, sorry. One or two questions now about your free time. Do you meet your classmates outside school?

G: Yes, I do. We go to a café after class every day, for a quick coffee and a chat.

T: Do you play sports?

G: No, I don't! I don't like sports!

T: OK, and finally, what other things do you do in your free time?

G: I don't have a lot of free time – I'm a mother, you know! In the little time I have, I read books.

T: OK. Thank you for your time, Gina.

8 Explain the exercise and play the recording.

If your students are not very strong, divide the questions up amongst them, e.g. group A listens for the answers to *Study habits* or questions 1, 4, 7 and 10. Group B listens for *Work, travel and home life* or questions 2, 5 and 8. Group C listens for *Free time* or questions 3, 6 and 9.

> **2** no (big old dictionary at home); **3** yes (family computer); **4** no (no time in the week); **5** no, but she's a mother; **6** by bus (it's cheap); **7** family; **8** yes (coffee after class); **9** no (doesn't like sports); **10** reads (she doesn't have a lot of time – she's a mother)

SPEAKING

9 Explain the task and tell students it is very important that they write down the answers their classmates give them.

- Get students to ask questions to no more than two or three other students and check that they are all taking notes.
- Remember to monitor and write down examples of correct and incorrect English.

If your students are not very strong, get them to ask you questions 1–10 first.

WRITING

10 Use the information for yourself or another student and ask students to help you write up a model text on the board.

- Students do the same for another one or two students.

HOMEWORK OPTIONS

Students do/finish the extra practice activities 4 and 7 on page 125 in the Language Reference.

Students do the exercises on pages 14–15 of the Workbook.

Students write about another student the way they did in exercise 10.

2.3 SCENARIO: IN AN OFFICE

SCENARIO: IN AN OFFICE

IN THIS LESSON

Lesson topic and staging

The lesson focuses on the world of work: office jobs and enquiring about jobs. Students learn about office jobs in English and language to do with looking for jobs. Students then use the language to make questions used when asking about jobs. This extends the topic of work and the grammar of question formation with the present simple. This work is then contextualised in a listening task about a woman looking for work in an employment agency. Students do more work on forming questions in preparation for the main task: making enquiries about different jobs in an employment agency. Students use all the language from the unit and the lesson to role-play the situation. In the last stage students have to discuss which of three jobs available they find most attractive.

Objectives

By the end of the lesson students should have:

- learned more words and phrases on the topic of work
- developed their awareness of word stress
- revised present simple question forms with *do* and *does*
- learned about making basic enquiries about a job in English

Common European Framework

Students can ask and answer basic questions about an office job and what it involves.

Timings

If short of time, you could drop exercises 1 and 2. Students could do these exercises for homework.

A possible lesson break would be after the listening in exercise 5 and before working on Key Language for the role-play on page 19.

Make sure you leave sufficient time at the end of the lesson to prepare for, complete and discuss the task in exercises 9 and 10.

WARM-UP

This warm-up activity revises jobs and places of work from Lesson 2.1.

- Write these sentences on the board and get students to complete them from memory.
  1 A web designer works in an _____.
  2 A _____ works in a court.
  3 A _____ works in a university.
  4 A doctor works in a _____.
  5 A businessman/businesswoman works in an _____.

6 A pilot works on a _____.
7 An _____ works in an office.

- When students are ready check their answers or ask them to check their answers on page 14 of the Coursebook.

  1 office; 2 lawyer; 3 lecturer; 4 hospital; 5 office; 6 plane; 7 accountant
  Note students may give other answers for 7, for example 'secretary', but point out that the indefinite article is *an* and not *a*.

PREPARATION

1 Students do activity as per Coursebook.

  1 send; 2 answer; 3 use; 4 organise; 5 do; 6 go to/organise

2 Get students in pairs to discuss the questions. Encourage them to talk as much as they can instead of just saying *Yes* or *No*.

3a
Preteach: *working hours* (the times you begin and finish a job), *salary* (the money you get every month for your job)

- Students do activity as per Coursebook.

  2c; 3b; 4c; 5e; 6d; 7e; 8a; 9d; 10b

3b Get students to complete the questions in pairs; check the answers and then get them to ask and answer the questions with their partner.

  2 communication; 3 salary; 4 qualifications; 5 hours

- Ask students to talk about the questions with their partners.
- Ask a couple of students what their partner said to them.

1.12

4
Preteach: *work duties* (the jobs you are responsible for at work, e.g. doing the photocopying, etc.)

- Explain the situation to students and ask them to read the list.
- Play the recording and then get students to check answers in pairs.
- Check answers with the whole class.

  Students should tick: working hours; salary; work duties
  She doesn't want the job (because the salary is very low – only £1,000 a month).

<table>
<tr><td>

Track 1.12

Agent, Petra

A: Hello. How can I help you?

P: Hello. Can you tell me about the office *assistant* job, please?

A: Certainly. Let me find the information. Let me see … Right. The office assistant job … with DP Computer Export?

P: Yes, that's right.

A: OK. What information do you want?

P: Well, first of all, where is it? Is it in the city centre?

A: Yes, it is. It's a *modern* office and there's good *transport*.

P: Fine. What are the working hours and salary?

A: Well, you work from Monday to Friday, from nine o'clock to half past five. And the salary is … let me see … yes … it's 1,000 pounds a month.

P: OK, but what does an office assistant do? What are the work duties?

A: Well, in this job you *answer* the phone, you do the *filing* and you do the *photocopying*. You also write and send *emails* and *letters*. OK?

P: Yes, thank you. What qualifications do I need?

A: Well, you need a school *certificate* and basic English. I'm sure you have those.

P: Yes, I do. And what skills do I need?

A: Erm … you need good *computer* skills and good *communication* skills. OK?

P: Yes, that's fine. Thank you.

A: So, are you interested in the job?

P: Erm, well, … the salary isn't very good … Do you have any other jobs?

</td></tr>
</table>

5 Explain the exercise and get students to read Petra's notes before they listen. They may be able to complete some of the answers before they listen again.

• Play the recording and check students' answers.

🔧 If your students are not very strong, you can put up the answers on the board in the wrong order and get students to match them and then listen to check their answers.

> **2** 9; **3** Friday; **4** £1,000; **5** answer; **6** emails; **7** letters; **8** filing; **9** certificate; **10** English

> **KEY LANGUAGE:**
> **asking for information (1)**

`1.13`

6 Get students to work in pairs to complete as many questions as possible.

• Play the recording and students check their answers and complete the questions they couldn't do.

• Check students' answers.

💡 You might want to get students to repeat the questions in preparation for the task in exercise 9.

<table>
<tr><td>

Audioscript and answers:
Track 1.13

1 What information do you want?

2 Where is <u>it</u>?

3 Is it in the <u>city</u> centre?

4 What are the working hours and <u>salary</u>?

5 What does an <u>office</u> assistant do?

6 What are the work <u>duties</u>?

7 What <u>qualifications</u> do I need?

8 What <u>skills</u> do I need?

</td></tr>
</table>

pronunciation

`1.14`

7a Remind students of the work on word stress from Lesson 1.3, exercises 9a and 9b on page 11.

• Get students to write the number of syllables in each word.

• Play the recording so students can check their answers.

• Go over the words slowly to double-check students have the correct answer. You may want to play the recording again.

> **1** 2 syllables (du-ties); **3** 4 syllables (in-for-ma-tion);
> **4** 2 syllables (of-fice); **5** 3 syllables (sa-la-ry);
> **6** 5 syllables (qua-li-fi-ca-tion)

<table>
<tr><td colspan="3">

Track 1.14

</td></tr>
<tr><td>

1 duties
2 Internet

</td><td>

3 information
4 office

</td><td>

5 salary
6 qualification

</td></tr>
</table>

💡 Two-syllable words normally carry the main stress on the first syllable. If a word ends in *-sion* or *-tion* the main stress falls on the syllable before the last one.

`1.15`

7b Students do activity as per Coursebook.

<table>
<tr><td>

Audioscript and answer:
Track 1.15

● internet

</td></tr>
</table>

7c Students do activity as per Coursebook.

> ● ● ● ● ●
> duties information office salary qualification

8a Get students to look at the audioscript on page 146 and mark the stress. You could play the recording again to check their answers.

> assistant; modern; transport; answer; filing;
>
> photocopying; emails; letters; certificate;
>
> computer; communication

8b Students do activity as per Coursebook.

TASK: asking and answering questions

Task summary: In the task students play the parts of someone who works in an employment agency and someone looking for a job. Student A, as the agent, provides information about a job, and Student B, as the jobseeker, asks for information. Students then swap roles and repeat the role-play with different information. A successful task outcome is when both students have managed to ask for and give the necessary information.

9   Explain the basic situation, task and task outcome. Give students their roles and check they understand what they have to do.

*   Give Student As time to prepare for the role-play by looking at the information on page 110.

*   Give Student Bs sufficient time to prepare by reading the notes and making sure they can form the right questions.

It is a good idea to create the right atmosphere for a role-play by moving furniture if appropriate and possible. Here ask students to move the furniture so that there is a desk between the jobseeker and the agent.

*   Tell students they should be polite and friendly in the role-play. Then ask them to start.

*   Monitor the role-plays but do not interrupt students unless there is a breakdown in communication. Write down examples of correct and incorrect uses of the key language (the main language points students are working on).

*   Ask students what they found easy, and what problems they had if any. If they have generally achieved the task, congratulate them.

*   Finally, use your notes to give feedback on the language areas needed to complete the role-play.

10   This closing activity gives students a chance to express their personal opinions about the three jobs from the lesson. Students can talk about the jobs in pairs.

*   Bring the whole class back together and ask a few students their opinions.

HOMEWORK OPTION

Students could research a job that interests them, and then tell the other students about the job at the beginning of next class.

Students do the exercises on page 16 of the Workbook.

DICTIONARY REMINDER

Ask your students to make a note to bring their dictionaries to class for the next lesson.

2.4 STUDY AND WRITING SKILLS

IN THIS LESSON

Lesson topic and staging

In the first part of the lesson students look at word stress and parts of speech. They do various activities to see how these two aspects of language are shown in a monolingual English dictionary, and then apply what they have learned by completing sentences with the correct part of speech. In the second part of the lesson students analyse a basic curriculum vitae (CV). Firstly, students look at how information is organised within a CV. They then go on to look at capitalisation before writing their own CV.

Objectives

By the end of the lesson students should have:

*   identified how a monolingual English dictionary shows word stress and parts of speech

*   practised marking stress and showing parts of speech

*   learned when to use capital letters

*   learned (more) about how a simple CV is structured

*   planned and written a short, simple CV

Common European Framework

Students can write a short, simple CV.

Timings

If short of time, you could drop exercises 10 and 11. Students could do these exercises for homework.

A possible lesson break would be after exercise 5b, before the Writing Skills section on page 20.

WARM-UP

*   Remind students of the lesson on dictionaries in Unit 1. See what different things you can find in a dictionary entry, for example definitions, pronunciation, parts of speech, etc.

STUDY SKILLS: using your dictionary (2)

1.16

1   Remind students of word stress and let them read the four words in the exercise.

*   Play the recording.

> •   •   •   •
> 1 employment 2 lecture 3 organise 4 photocopy

Track 1.16

1 employment	3 organise
2 lecture	4 photocopy

2 Ask students to find out how the dictionary shows the stressed syllable.

The (primary) stress is shown by a ' before the stressed syllable in the phonetic spelling.

3a Students do activity as per Coursebook.

☀ There are several ways to show stress. *Language Leader* uses small black blobs to show stress, for example:

●
employment

This system can also be used to show how many syllables a word has and where the main stress is. This 'picture' helps students to remember and then later pronounce a word, for example:

● ● ●
employment

Encourage students to mark the main stress on any words they want to learn for 'active' use, i.e. words students can recognize and produce.

`1.17`

3b Students do activity as per Coursebook.

Audioscript and answers:
Track 1.17
A email, pilot, visit
B complete, design
C company, organise
D accountant, designer, location

4 Students do activity as per Coursebook.

The numbers indicate different definitions for that word: in this case the words can also be different parts of speech – both nouns and verbs.

5a Students do activity as per Coursebook.

Verb	Noun	Verb and noun
complete	accountant	design
organise	company	email
	designer	pilot
	location	visit

Complete can also be an adjective.

5b Students do activity as per Coursebook. If students have dictionaries, this is a good moment to show them how to find different parts of speech in an entry.

2 emails; 3 location; 4 visits; 5 designs;
6 company; 7 pilot; 8 complete; 9 organises;
10 designer

WRITING SKILLS: a CV

6

Preteach: *accounts* (a record of the money that a business or a person receives and spends in a particular period of time), *BA Hons* (a Bachelor of Arts Honours degree is the qualification you get when you successfully complete three years of study at a university), *first-class degree* (the best degree that you can get from a university), *A level* (an examination in a particular subject which students in England and Wales take when they are 18. Students must pass at least two A levels in order to go to a university, and usually need to pass three.)

• Set the scene by pointing to the CV on page 21 and asking students what it is (normally it's a list of the education and previous jobs that you have had that you show companies when you're trying to get a new job). Tell students that they are going to look at a CV and then write their own CV.

• Then ask them to read the CV and see if Nina Cassidy would be good for the job. Tell them they have to find reasons from her CV for their answer.

Nina is a good person for the job. She has a university education and studied computing at university. She has worked in design before (Cambridge Book Design and Euro Business Design). She also has experience in managing people and projects (Project assistant and Team manager). Her computing skills are also good. She also speaks 'advanced' French, which she will need if she lives in Paris and leads a French-speaking team.

7 Students do activity as per Coursebook.

2 Date of birth; 3 Address; 4 Telephone; 5 Email;
6 Education/Training; 7 Employment; 8 Other
Skills; 9 Interests

8 Students do activity as per Coursebook.

2 false (*First-class degree*); 3 true (*BA (Hons)
Maths and Computing; Maths (A)*); 4 true (*Heffer's
Booksellers*); 5 false (*French (advanced)*); 6 false
(*Sport: tennis and horse-riding; Travel: Europe and
Japan; Cinema and theatre*)

9a Check that students understand the term 'capital letters'.

• Do the first two examples with the whole class so they understand the activity. Then get students to work individually or in pairs.

> **people's names:** Nina Cassidy (exception is in an email address where names are often in lower case); **cities:** London, Cambridge, Canterbury (Chelsea is a part of London rather than a city); **languages:** English, French, Japanese; **companies:** Euro Business Design, Cambridge Book Design, Heffer's Booksellers; **countries:** Japan (Europe is a continent rather than a country); **streets:** Ivy Road; **school and university names:** Cambridge University, Canterbury School for Girls; **nationalities:** British

9b Students do activity as per Coursebook.

> Martin Jeffers; Canadian; 22 Rose Street, London; London Metropolitan University; MA (Business and Computing); World Computer Company; Russian (elementary); Music: guitar and piano

10 Students do activity as per Coursebook.

> Martin Jeffers – Name; Canadian – Nationality; 22 Rose Street, London – Address; London Metropolitan University, MA (Business and Computing) – Education/Training; World Computer Company – Employment; Russian (elementary) – Other Skills; football – Interests; Music: guitar and piano – Interests

11 This task is the culmination of all the work students have done so far in this lesson.

- Get students to look at the list in exercise 7 and to provide information in note form for their CV.

- When they are ready ask them to look at the layout in the CV and to use it as a model for their CV.

- Ask students to write their CVs. If there is not enough time, they can complete them for homework.

- If translation is allowed, you could help them in their mother tongue, especially when translating qualifications into English. Write phrases like these on the board and practise them:

  How do you say 'Matura' in English? (Poland)

  Can I say 'OSS' in English? (Turkey)

- If there is time, you could get students to swap their CVs with a classmate. The classmates should be encouraged to help by reading their partner's CV and offering advice and encouragement where necessary. It is beneficial to develop the 'editor' in all students, as research suggests that students who can perform this role become more critical language learners.

HOMEWORK OPTIONS

If students have finished their CVs and they have access to computers, ask them to word process their CVs in English for next lesson.

Students do the exercises on page 17 of the Workbook.

DICTIONARY REMINDER

Ask your students to make a note to bring their dictionaries to class for the next lesson.

Water

3.1 WET AND DRY

IN THIS LESSON

Lesson topic and staging

The lesson focuses on the part water plays in our lives: from everyday use to its role in deserts. Students take a general knowledge quiz on water before working with a vocabulary activity based on verbs connected with water. Students then listen to a TV programme about deserts. The listening contextualises the grammar focus on question words: *what, when, where, why, who, how* and *which*. After some controlled practice using question words, students finish the lesson with a speaking activity based on personal questions they write using question words.

Objectives

By the end of the lesson students should have:

- learned more language (nouns and verbs) used to talk about water
- revised *Yes/No* questions, for example *Do you drink two litres of water every day?*
- revised and extended their knowledge and use of question words
- learned (more) about the part water plays in our lives

Timings

If short of time, you could drop exercise 2 on page 22. Students could do exercises 2a and 2b for homework and discuss exercise 2c in the next lesson.

A possible lesson break would be after exercise 2c and before the listening focus on page 23.

WARM-UP

- This activity revises the use of capital letters from Lesson 2.4, exercise 9. Write the following text on the board:

  my name is jo wright and I study marine biology at the university of wales. when i finish my degree i want to work for the dolphin research center in florida, usa.

- Get students in pairs to rewrite it using capital letters. The corrected text is:

  My name is Jo Wright and I study Marine Biology at the University of Wales. When I finish my degree I want to work for the Dolphin Research Center in Florida, USA.

READING

1 Students do activity as per Coursebook. There are a number of words that students may not know but most can be guessed from the context of the questions and the answers.

   1a; 2b; 3b; 4a; 5b; 6a; 7b; 8a

VOCABULARY: verbs connected with water

💡 If your students don't have dictionaries with them, put them in bigger groups. That way they will be able to teach each other.

2a Students do activity as per Coursebook.

   boil; cook; drink; freeze; swim; wash; waste

2b This exercise revises *Yes/No* questions. Get students to complete the questions; tell them that one verb is used more than once.

   2 boil; **3** swim; **4** cook; **5** wash; **6** drink

2c Quickly revise short answers by writing this question on the board: *Do you drink coffee?*

- Ask students what the positive and negative answers are and write them on the board, i.e. *Yes, I do. No, I don't.*

- Students do activity as per Coursebook.

💡 It's important that students use these speaking activities to 'stretch' their English. Some students are happy to answer *Yes* or *No*. They need to push themselves to say as much as they can – even if the English is not perfect! You can illustrate this by comparing a dialogue between three students. Which student, B or C, is best?

STUDENT A: Do you drink a lot of tea in the morning?
STUDENT B: No.
STUDENT A: And you?
STUDENT C: Yes, I do. I love tea. I drink four or five teas every day. Do you like it?

LISTENING

3a This activity introduces the topic of the listening – deserts – and key vocabulary students will need for it. Students do activity as per Coursebook.

   a desert
   A sand; **B** cactus; **C** camel; **D** plant; **E** rock

3b You could ask this question to the whole class.

i Some of the most famous deserts in the world are the Sahara in North Africa, the Kalahari in South West Africa, the Gobi desert in Mongolia and China, the Atamaca desert in Chile, the Sonora desert in Mexico and the Great Western desert, commonly known as the 'Outback', in Australia.

`1.18`

4a Let students read the list and see if they can predict the answers before they listen.

> rain; temperature; the sea; animals; food

Track 1.18
Presenter, Dr Simmonds
(Track 1.19)
P: Dr Simmonds, my idea of a desert is a very hot place with a lot of sand. Is this correct? I mean, what is a desert, exactly?
S: Well, there are different kinds of desert – hot deserts and cold deserts. And hot deserts aren't always hot; the temperature changes, for example, from 38 degrees to ten degrees …
P: Ten degrees! That's cold! When are deserts that cold?
S: At night. They're hot during the day but cold at night.
P: Mmm, interesting.
S: Also, only about 30 percent of the world's deserts are sand – a lot of deserts are just rocks and stones. But all deserts have one thing in common: they're very dry, with a maximum of 250 mm of rain a year.
P: Really? So, why are deserts dry?
S: Well, for a number of reasons. Sometimes they're a long way from the sea and rain doesn't reach them. Sometimes mountains stop the rain.
(Track 1.20)
P: OK, so there isn't any water – so how do animals and plants live in deserts?
S: Life in deserts isn't easy. A lot of desert animals sleep in the day and come out at night to look for food. The kangaroo rat gets all its water from its food. And desert plants have water in them. The Saguaro cactus in North America has five tonnes of water in its body and it sometimes lives for 200 years.
P: Wow! What about people? How do they live in the desert?
S: Desert people often live in groups, and move from place to place. They often live at the edges of deserts, not in the middle. The Aborigines of Australia eat desert plants and animals and live that way, but it's a hard life!

4b As in 4a let students read the sentences before they listen. They may be able to answer some of the ideas from memory or with common sense.

> 1✓; 2✓; 3✓; 4✗; 5✗; 6✓

`1.19`

4c Students do activity as per Coursebook. This exercise practises intensive listening and asks students to pick out specific numbers. You might want to quickly revise numbers in tens and hundreds before students listen again.

> **1** 38, 10; **2** 30; **3** 250

`1.20`

4d Students do activity as per Coursebook.

🔧 If your students are strong, do the exercise as in the book. However if you want to give your students more support, you could jumble up the answers on the board and students have to listen and fill the answers in.

> **2** come out; **3** has; **4** move; **5** eat; **6** animals

GRAMMAR: question words

5a Give students a couple of examples of questions words.
- Tell them to look at the quiz in exercise 1 on page 22 and the audioscript for Track 1.18 on page 147 and underline all the question words.
- Ask students to give you the question words and write them on the board. Check their pronunciation.

5b Ask students to do the first part of the activity individually and then check their answers.
- Get the students to complete the exercise in pairs before checking answers with the whole group.

> **2** Who; **3** Where; **4** When; **5** How; **6** Why; **7** Which

For a full explanation and further practice activities, go to pages 126–127 in the Language Reference.

GRAMMAR TIP

Read through the tip box. Point out that when *What* and *Which* are added to a noun at the beginning of a question they become determiners. Determiners are used to ask about or 'determine' the identity of someone or something, e.g. *Which school do you go to? What football team do you support?*

6 Students do activity as per Coursebook.

> **2** How; **3** Why; **4** Who; **5** Where; **6** Which; **7** What's; **8** When

SPEAKING

Task summary: The final activity of the lesson asks students to write a mini quiz about water on their own. They do this by rearranging a question that has been jumbled up. Students then work in pairs and ask and answer questions to complete the quiz.

7   Explain the activity to students by giving an example. Write the following on the board and ask students to rearrange it to make a question:

the oceans? – What percentage of – is in – the earth's water (answer: *What percentage of the world's water is in the oceans?*)

• Write these answers on the board and ask which is correct: *25%, 60%, 97%, 100%* (answer: *97%*).

• Tell students that they are going to write four questions each and then they are going to ask their partner the questions.

• Divide the students into As and Bs. Tell Student As to look at the information on page 110 and Student Bs to look on page 115.

• Give students time to read the information and form the questions. You could walk around the class and deal with any questions that individuals may have.

• Check students are all ready and then ask Student As to start.

> **Student A questions:**
> **1** What percentage of our bodies is water? (about 70 percent); **2** What percentage of the world is desert? (about 25 percent); **3** Why do we drink fresh water not sea water? (because sea water has a lot of salt); **4** How long do camels live without water? (two or three weeks)
> **Student B questions:**
> **1** What percentage of the world's people live in deserts? (about 5 percent); **2** What percentage of the world's water is in the seas and oceans? (about 95 percent); **3** How long do people live without water? (only a few days); **4** Where does water come from in your house? (a tap)

HOMEWORK OPTIONS

Students do/finish the extra practice activities 1 and 2 on page 127 in the Language Reference.

Students do the exercises on pages 18–19 of the Workbook.

Students write two or three questions about water and bring them to the next lesson where they could be used in the 'Warm-up' stage of the lesson.

3.2 BLUE PLANET

IN THIS LESSON

Lesson topic and staging

The lesson explores the world of whales and dolphins. Students begin by learning more vocabulary connected with water and then they read a leaflet about whale watching. The leaflet gives information about different whales and also provides the context for the grammar focus on language used to describe frequency. Students move on to examine adverbs of frequency like *always, sometimes*, etc. and expressions of frequency such as *twice a month, every day* and *once a year*. After working on this area the lesson finishes with a speaking activity. Students personalise the language of frequency by asking and answering questions about their routines and habits.

Objectives

By the end of the lesson students should have:

• learned more vocabulary about animals, places and actions (verbs) connected with water

• learned (more) about whales

• developed their ability to scan a text

• revised and extended their knowledge and use of adverbs and expressions of frequency

• learned (more) about each other's routines and habits

Timings

If short of time, you could drop exercise 1b on page 24. Students could do the exercise for homework and discuss the answers in the next lesson.

A possible lesson break would be after exercise 4 on page 24.

WARM-UP

• This activity revises the language of Lesson 3.1. Elicit a couple of facts about water and deserts that students can remember from last lesson. Write them on the board, for example: *Ninety percent of an iceberg is under water. Temperatures change from very hot during the day to very cold at night in a desert.*

• Ask students to work in groups and write down as many facts about water and deserts as they can remember from last lesson.

• Give them three minutes to make their lists.

• Stop students and see how many facts the group remembers.

• If students have written questions about water, collect them in, number them and ask the whole class the questions.

☼ As the focus is on facts and not grammar, don't worry if students' sentences are not perfect grammatically.

VOCABULARY: words connected with water

1a Ask students to work in pairs or small groups to do this activity.

- Check students' pronunciation when you check their answers.

i There are five oceans and several dozen seas. Seas are usually smaller than oceans and they are partially enclosed by land. But apart from that, they are exactly the same thing. A lake is a large, inland body of water, normally fresh.

> **Animals:** dolphin, penguin, seagull, shark, tuna, whale
> **Places:** ocean, sea
> **Actions (verbs):** dive, float, jump

🔧 If you think students won't know most of this vocabulary, draw the animals on the board and ask students: *What is this in English?*

To elicit places ask students to complete these names:
_____ *Baikal (Siberia) or Victoria (Africa) or Superior (America);*
the Pacific _____;
the Mediterranean _____.

You could elicit the actions by miming them.

1b Students do activity as per Coursebook.

> **2** jump; **3** Penguins/Whales; **4** Tuna; **5** Seagulls;
> **6** Sharks; **7** Sea

READING

☀ This activity practises scanning skills (the ability to pick out specific information from a text). It is important that students understand their task and read the leaflet quickly to find the information required. Many students will want to read the text intensively but that is not the aim of the task.

2 Give students time to read the three questions first. Then tell them to find the answers quickly in the text.

> **1** West Ireland; **2** daily trips, twice a day;
> **3** Humpback, killer, minke and fin whales. The question doesn't ask about dolphins.

3 Ask students what the biggest animal is. (Fin whale)

- Next ask them to put the animals in order of size, from biggest to smallest.

☀ This activity develops students' ability to scan the text for specific information.

> **2** humpback whale; **3** minke whale; **4** killer whale;
> **5** bottlenose dolphin

4 This exercise also develops students' scanning skills. Students do activity as per Coursebook.

> **2** fin whales; **3** minke whales; **4** killer whales;
> **5** bottlenose dolphins; **6** grey whales

GRAMMAR: adverbs of frequency

5a Exercise 5 elicits the adverbs *always* and *never*. Students do activity as per Coursebook.

> **1a; 2c**

5b Students do activity as per Coursebook.

> **1** always; **2** never

6 Students do activity as per Coursebook.

🔧 If your students are not very strong, you could provide the following scale for them: minke (80%); fin (70%); humpback (50%); killer (10%); grey (0%).

> minke whales: usually; humpback whales: sometimes; killer whales: occasionally

For a full explanation and further practice activities, go to pages 126–127 in the Language Reference.

7a Students do activity as per Coursebook.

> **1** often; **2** never; **3** never

7b Get students to look at the sentences in 7a and try to work out the rule for themselves.

> Adverbs of frequency come after the verb *to be*, e.g. *Blue whales* **are always** *the first to return to home in spring.*
> Adverbs of frequency come before other verbs, e.g. *Whales* **always move** *from one place to another.*

8 Explain what an *expression of frequency* is (two or more words that work like an adverb of frequency).

> **2** three times a week; **3** weekly (once a week);
> **4** twice a month; **5** once a year

9a This exercise focuses on the position of expressions of frequency in a sentence. Check students understand the grammatical term *subject*.

> a

9b Students do activity as per Coursebook. Ask students if any of the facts surprise them.

> **2** Dolphins usually live in large groups. **3** Baby fin whales drink 230 litres of milk every day. **4** Blue whales never jump out of the water. **5** Humpback whales occasionally dive for 45 minutes. **6** Killer whales sometimes eat fish. **7** Blue whales travel to the Arctic once a year. **8** Grey whales are often in the Pacific Ocean near America.

10 This activity asks students to relate the language practised to their own lives. Explain the activity to students and encourage them to use adverbs and expressions of frequency in their answers, for example:

I often swim in the sea.

I swim in the sea three or four times a week.

- Give students time to read the sentences and ask any questions they have.
- Monitor while students write their answers and help any students who need it.

SPEAKING

11a The last activity personalises all the work on the grammar of the lesson.

⊕ Encourage students to talk as much as possible about the sentences. Demonstrate the idea by getting a student to ask you a question and giving a very short answer. Then ask the same student to ask you the same question again. This time give a much longer answer and ask them the question too so that you have more of a conversation.

- Tell students that the aim of this activity is to speak as much as possible about the questions.
- Ask them to work in pairs and to ask and answer any of the questions that interest them.
- While students are talking monitor them and take notes discreetly. Make sure that you note down correct and incorrect examples of the target language (the language points that students have been studying). Note about six correct and six incorrect examples.
- When the students are finished ask some of them to tell the whole group one interesting thing about their partner, for example:

Sabahat uses the Internet every day. She spends two or three hours every night on the Internet.

- Read out the good examples of students' English that you noted down.
- Then write the incorrect examples of English on the board. Ask students to work in groups and correct the mistakes.
- Work with the whole group and correct the mistakes.

11b This activity helps students write/record what they've produced orally. Ask a few students to read out their sentences.

HOMEWORK OPTIONS

Students do/finish the extra practice activities 3, 4, 6 and 9 on page 127 in the Language Reference.

Students do the exercises on pages 20–21 of the Workbook.

3.3 SCENARIO: AT A FESTIVAL

IN THIS LESSON

Lesson topic and staging

The lesson looks at festivals around the world that celebrate water. Students read about four different festivals and takes notes on them. They then listen to the festival organisers of the Lowell Water Festival (a Southeast Asian Water festival celebrated every year in Lowell, USA) discussing the festival's programme. The functional language of making and responding to suggestions is drawn out of the listening, for example *What about having a music show on Friday?* Students go on to practise the meaning, form and pronunciation of this language, which prepares them for the main focus of the lesson – the task. In the task students decide which events they would like to see at the Lowell Festival and then decide in pairs or small groups what to do at the festival.

Objectives

By the end of the lesson students should have:

- learned about water festivals around the world
- developed their ability to take notes from a text
- learned some functional language for making and responding to suggestions
- used functional language for making and responding to simple suggestions on how to spend time

Common European Framework

Students can make and respond to simple suggestions.

Timings

If short of time, you could drop exercises 1 and 2 on page 26. Students could do these exercises for homework.

A possible lesson break would be after exercise 4c and before the focus on the Key Language of making suggestions.

Make sure you leave sufficient time at the end of the lesson to prepare for, complete and discuss the task in exercise 12.

WARM-UP

This activity revises adverbs and expressions of frequency from Lesson 3.2. It is a quick class survey to find out which member of the class spends most time sitting in front of a screen (TV, computer or handheld, e.g. Nintendo's *Game Boy*).

- Draw the following table on the board and ask students to copy it.

Name:				
How often do you …	every day	five times a week	two or three times a week	never
watch TV?				
go on the Internet?				
play computer or video games?				

- Ask students to work in pairs. They interview their partner and note down their answers. They should answer in full sentences, using adverbs of frequency.

- When students are finished find out who the most frequent 'user' is for each question, for example by asking *Does anyone watch TV every day?* and finding out how many hours per day.

PREPARATION

1 Ask students if they know any famous festivals, e.g. the Carnival in Rio de Janeiro, Brazil.

- Ask them if they know of any water festivals i.e. festivals that have water as their central theme.

Preteach: *temple* (a building where people in some religions go to pray, e.g. a Hindu temple), *race* (a competition in which people try to run or drive faster than each other), *parade* (an event in which people walk through the streets and play music to celebrate something), *drum* (a round musical instrument which you hit with your hand or a stick)

- Get students to look at pictures A–C and tell you what they see.

- Ask students to quickly read about the three water festivals and to match photos A–C with the festivals.

> **A** 2; **B** 1; **C** 3

2 This activity develops students' note-taking skills. Students do activity as per Coursebook. Tell them not to complete the information on the Lowell Water Festival. They don't need to write all the activities in the right-hand column, just some examples.

Festival	Month	Days	Example activities
Songkran	April	three days	clean their houses, visit temples, visit old relatives, throw water at people, dance shows and music concerts
Abu Dhabi F1	December	five days	a lot of races and competitions, a big parade, a large boat show, international food
Vilagarcia	August	one day	a parade, people throw water over each other, a drum dance, people jump in the sea

3 This activity also develops students' note-taking skills. Ask students to look at the picture of the Lowell Festival and tell you what they can see.

- Tell them to read the programme and complete the table on the festival.

Lowell	August	two days	a parade, dances, music, a talk, a boat tour, a fashion show, Thai boxing, a drum workshop, traditional boat races, children's activities, short films from Thailand, a barbecue and party

> 1.21

4a Students do activity as per Coursebook.

> Three people: two men (Andy and Li) and a woman (Cassie).

Track 1.21
Andy, Cassie, Li

A: Right then, does anyone have any ideas for the last few spaces? Cassie?

C: Well, what about having a music show on Friday evening? There aren't any other music shows in the festival. Is that OK, Li?

L: Yes, I think that's a good idea. Let's have traditional music and modern music. I know a Malaysian pop band – and that traditional Cambodian group wants to come again.

A: Excellent. And let's have the dance workshop on Saturday afternoon. What do you think?

L: Erm, … I'm not so sure, Andy.

C: Yeah, … I don't agree with you.

A: You don't? Why not?

C: Well, Andy, the traditional boat races are very popular, and the dance workshops need a lot of people. I'd like to have the dance workshop in the morning, and I'd like to have the international food market in the afternoon. People often go to the market during the races and before the barbecue.

A: OK. I agree. What about Saturday evening? What would you like to have then, Li?

L: Why don't we have a drum concert then? The Burmese drum circles are very exciting.

A: Great idea, Li. That way people either watch a film or watch the drum concert, if they don't come to the barbecue, of course.

L: Fantastic. Right, that's all then. Let's go and get something to eat.

A: Great. I'm starving. Let's go for a burger.

C: A burger? Huh, OK.

4b Make sure students understand the context and have read the festival programme and noted the times carefully before doing the activity.

🔧 If your students need more support, you could give them the missing events jumbled up and they listen and match them to the correct numbers.

> **1** music show; **2** dance workshop; **3** international food market; **4** drum concert

4c Explain that Andy (A) and Li (L) are men and Cassie (C) is a woman.

> **2** A; **3** C; **4** L; **5** L; **6** A

KEY LANGUAGE: making suggestions

5 Students do activity as per Coursebook.

🔧 If your students are not very strong, provide them with the words jumbled up on the board.

> **2** What; **3** What; **4** What; **5** Why

6 Make sure students understand the word *suggestion*.

> Asking for ideas: 1, 3, 4; Making suggestions: 2, 5

7 Make sure students are clear about the form of the different suggestions.

● Check students' answers and drill the four phrases.

> The two other ways to make suggestions are *Let's* … and *I'd like* …
> **2** Let's; **3** I'd like; **4** Why don't we
> The three different forms of the main verb are the infinitive without *to* (*Let's* … , *Why don't we* …), the infinitive with *to* (*I'd like* …) and the *-ing* form (*What about* …).

8 Students do activity as per Coursebook.

> **2** play; **3** going; **4** to go; **5** visiting; **6** to play

pronunciation

1.22

9a

👁 This exercise demonstrates how we use our voice through intonation, especially pitch and stress to show enthusiasm. You could demonstrate this idea before students listen. Firstly, imagine you are meeting a very old friend for the first time in years. Say *Oh, hello* with real surprise and happiness to the students.
Now imagine that you are meeting someone at a party who you aren't at all interested in, in fact you really don't like them. Say, *Oh, hello.* Can students tell the difference?

● Students read the questions and then listen.

● Check their answers and ask them how they know.

> **1** Yes; **2** Yes; **3** No

> **Track 1.22**
> C: I'd like to have the dance workshop in the morning, and I'd like to have the international food market in the afternoon. People often go to the market during the races and before the barbecue.
> A: OK. I agree.
> L: Fantastic. Right, that's all then. Let's go and get something to eat.
> A: Great. I'm starving. Let's go for a burger.
> C: A burger? Huh, OK.

1.23

9b Explain to students that *intonation* is the up and down of your voice – the music. Intonation shows how we feel: happy, sad, bored, tired and so on.

● Get students to listen to the start of the track and repeat *OK* in both ways.

● Let students listen to other examples of strong interest on the rest of the track. You could use your hand to show the high start and then fall of the word.

> **a** neutral; **b** strong interest

> **Track 1.23**
> a) Ok.   b) Ok.
> 1 Yes, …   4 Great idea, Li.
> 2 Excellent.   5 Fantastic.
> 3 OK. I agree.   6 Great.

1.24

10 Students listen and choose the correct intonation.

● Students then use the examples in exercise 10 to practise with their partners. Student A should say something and Student B says a) or b). It's important that students tell each other what type of intonation they used because they can have problems showing enough enthusiasm in their voices.

> **2** SI; **3** SI; **4** WI; **5** WI; **6** SI

> **Track 1.24**
> 1 Great idea.   4 OK.
> 2 Yes.   5 Fantastic.
> 3 Excellent.   6 Great.

11 This exercise is a rehearsal for the task that follows. Ask students to give you a list of things they normally do at the weekend and write their ideas on the board in note form. For example: go to the cinema, see friends, visit grandparents, go swimming, cook, etc.

● Ask students to make suggestions in three different ways using *go to the cinema*. Write them on the board: *Let's go to the cinema. What about going to the cinema? Why don't we go to the cinema?*

- Tell students to check how to say *Yes* and *No* by looking at the OTHER USEFUL PHRASES box on page 27.

- Now ask students for different ways to say *No*. Point out that it's important in English not to be too direct, i.e. to say *No!* is normally rude. We prefer to be less direct and say things like *Erm, … I'm not so sure*, or *Well, that's a good idea but how about …*

- Let students talk and decide what they want to do at the weekend. Monitor and take notes.

- If time, give students feedback on how they did.

TASK: making and responding to suggestions

Task summary: In the task students look at the completed programme for the Lowell Festival and choose events they'd like to go to or see. They then work in pairs or groups and try to decide what to see and do at the festival. A successful task outcome is when students have successfully discussed what they want to see, and have come to an agreement.

12a Let students read the Lowell programme again and decide what they want to do. Check they understand they can only choose one event for each time period.

12b Put students in pairs or small groups to do the task.

- Explain the basic situation, task and task outcome

- Remind them of the type of language they can use. Look together at the OTHER USEFUL PHRASES at the bottom of the page.

- As students do the task, monitor and take notes.

- When they are finished give feedback on task achievement by asking some of the pairs or groups what they decided to do. Ask the whole group if they had any problems or have any questions.

- Move on to language performance and use your notes to give feedback on examples of correct and incorrect use of the key language, making and responding to suggestions.

HOMEWORK OPTIONS

Students could write a short conversation about making and responding to suggestions.

Students do the exercises on page 22 of the Workbook.

DICTIONARY REMINDER

Ask your students to make a note to bring their dictionaries to class for the next lesson.

3.4 STUDY AND WRITING SKILLS

IN THIS LESSON

Lesson topic and staging

In the first part of the lesson students examine practical language to help them get more from their English lessons. Students learn a list of common classroom objects, then examine classroom instructions and questions they can use to find out more about words (e.g. *Where is the stress in 'glacier'?*). In the second part of the lesson students use an illustrated diagram, vocabulary, sequencers like *first of all* and *finally* and the pronouns *it* and *they* to build a paragraph describing the water cycle. Students then move on to write a paragraph describing the water cycle in the Antarctic.

Objectives

By the end of the lesson students should have:

- learned a range of useful vocabulary for common classroom objects

- revised and extended their knowledge and use of classroom language

- learned a set of questions for asking about words

- used visual information, sequencers and pronouns to build a paragraph describing a simple process

- learned (more) about water cycles

Common European Framework

Students can write a paragraph describing a simple process.

Timings

If short of time, you could drop exercises 1 and 2. Students could do these exercises for homework.

A possible lesson break would be after exercise 4 and before the Writing Skills section of the lesson on page 28.

WARM-UP

This is a quick activity to revise the language for making and responding to suggestions from Lesson 3.3.

- Tell students that it is Saturday and they have to decide with a classmate how they will spend the day. Remind students of the language they could use to do this. Give students a time limit to do this; three to five minutes is enough.

- Ask a couple of students what plans they have made.

- Ask the students if they have any questions.

STUDY SKILLS: classroom language

1 Get students to work in small groups to find the objects. Many of them should be somewhere in the class, so use the real objects to help explain any words they don't know.

• Check students' answers and pronunciation at the same time.

To extend this activity, if you feel that students need more practice with the list, tell them to close their books, work in small groups and try to write down all ten words and phrases from memory.

2a Get students to do this activity in pairs.

> **Suggested answers:**
> **1** T; **2** T; **3** T; **4** both; **5** T; **6** T; **7** both; **8** both; **9** both; **10** T

2b Students do activity as per Coursebook.

> **a** 4; **b** 9; **c** 1; **d** 7; **e** 2

3a Students do activity as per Coursebook.

• Drill the sentences as you check students' answers.

> **2** What; **3** How; **4** Where; **5** How; **6** How; **7** What

Students often speak their own language in the classroom when they are frustrated, don't understand or are tired. Students are much less likely to use their mother tongue if they have the English 'tools' to ask for help.

`1.25`

3b Students do activity as per Coursebook.

> **Audioscript and answers:**
> **Track 1.25**
> **1d**
> – What does 'glacier' mean?
> – A large river of ice that moves down a mountain.
> **2f**
> – What part of speech is 'glacier'?
> – It's a noun.
> **3a**
> – How do you spell 'glacier'?
> – G-L-A-C-I-E-R.
> **4b**
> – Where is the word stress in 'glacier'?
> – It's on the first syllable.
> **5g**
> – How do you pronounce it?
> – /ˈglæsɪə/
> **6e**
> – How do you say 'glacier' in Polish?
> – *Lodowiec*.
> **7c**
> – What is *lodowiec* n English?
> – In English, it's 'glacier'.

4 Explain that each student has some pictures of things they probably don't know the words for in English, and that they need to ask their partner for the word, spelling and word stress for each. They also have the information to give about their partner's pictures.

• Give them time to look at their page. Monitor the activity and help where necessary.

WRITING SKILLS: a description of a process

5a Tell students that the aim of this part of the lesson is to write a paragraph describing a process. Get students to look at the picture and see how many of the words they can match.

• Get them to ask you questions to find out about the words they don't know in English. Write the question *What's this in English?* on the board to help them. Tell them to use the questions in exercise 3a to find out more information about the words, for example, *How do you pronounce 'ground'?*

5b Students do activity as per Coursebook. If they can't find the answers, ask them to use the questions in exercise 3a to get the information they need.

> **1** heats; **3** forms; **4** move; **5** changes; **6** falls; **7** carry

6 Explain that sequencers show the order or 'sequence' that something happens in, and that they are very important in describing processes. Students do activity as per Coursebook.

It is important that students can use the sequencing phrases actively, i.e. they can understand them and use them. You might like to point out the grammatical structures needed: sequencer + subject + verb + object, for example *First of all, the sun heats the sea.* Note that *First of all,* and *Finally,* are both followed by a comma.

Tell students to be careful about capitalisation – the first word in a sentence has a capital letter.

> **1** First of all, **2** Next / Then / After that, **3** Next / Then / After that, **4** Next / Then / After that, **5** Next / Then / After that, **6** Finally,

7a Students do activity as per Coursebook.

> **2** they = the clouds; **3** it = the rain

7b Tell students that we use pronouns so we don't have to repeat the same things again and again, which makes our writing easier to read. Students do activity as per Coursebook.

> **1** The water vapour goes into the air and it forms clouds. **2** Animals go to the rivers and they drink the water.

8a Tell students that they are going to write a paragraph about the water cycle in the Antarctic, which is a different type of water cycle, and that the diagram and this exercise will prepare them to write it.

- Get them to look at the picture and to understand the process. Encourage them to use their questions about words to find out any extra information they feel they need.

- Students do activity individually as per Coursebook.

- You could tell students to check their answers with a partner first, before going through the answers together.

☀ Point out that the verb *become* means the same as *change into*, but that you cannot say *become into* …

> 2 evaporates; 3 becomes; 4 forms; 5 move;
> 6 become; 7 changes; 8 falls; 9 changes; 10 forms;
> 11 melt

8b Students do activity as per Coursebook.

> (clockwise) 2, 3, 4, 5, 6, 7, 8, 9, 10, 11

9 Write the first couple of sentences so that students have a model of what to do, e.g.:

First of all, the sun heats the sea. Then the water evaporates and it becomes water vapour. The water vapour …

- Tell students to copy down what you have written on the board and then to use their notes to continue writing the description. Remind them to use the sequencing phrases they covered in exercise 6.

- Monitor their writing and help if asked or if necessary.

- When most students are finished invite students to dictate part of their paragraphs to you. If there are any mistakes, tell the students. Give him/her the first chance to correct the mistake. If they can't, take suggestions from other students.

- Continue until the text is complete.

> **Model text:**
> This is a description of the water cycle in the Antarctic. First of all, the sun heats the sea. Then the water evaporates and it becomes water vapour. The water vapour forms clouds and they move over the ice. After that the clouds become very cold and the water vapour changes into snow. Next the snow falls to the ground and it changes into ice. Then the ice forms icebergs and finally, they melt and the water returns to the sea.

HOMEWORK OPTIONS

If students have finished their paragraphs, ask them to word-process them in English for next lesson.

Students do the exercises on page 23 of the Workbook.

Review

UNITS 1–3

GRAMMAR

1

> **1** lives; **2** is; **3** has; **4** produce; **5** does; **6** find;
> **7** carries; **8** are; **9** is; **10** need; **11** buy; **12** isn't;
> **13** need; **14** use

2

> **2** No, it isn't. **3** Yes, he does. **4** Yes, there are.
> **5** No, they don't.

3a

> **2** Which; **3** Where; **4** What

3b

> **1** (He needs a water pump) to carry water from a
> lake under the ground (for his fruit trees and cows).
> **2** India, China and Argentina.
> **3** (We buy our food) from a supermarket.
> **4** (They make) a litre of milk.

4

> **2**c; **3**i; **4**g; **5**b; **6**e; **7**f; **8**d; **9**a; **10**j

`1.26`

5a/b

> **b** 3; **c** 6; **d** 4; **e** 2; **f** 1; **g** 9; **h** 8

i The photograph shows the Old Town of Gdańsk at
night.

Track 1.26
Interviewer, Marek
1f
I: Who do you live with?
M: With my mother and father in Gda´nsk.
2e
I: Are you a student or do you work?
M: I'm a student.
3b
I: Is there a university in your city?
M: Yes. There is. It's famous in Poland.
4d
I: What do you study?
M: English and Art.
6c
I: Where exactly is your city?
M: Gdańsk is in the north of Poland.
continued…

8h
I: Does the city have an airport?
M: Yes, it does.
9g
I: When do tourists usually visit your city?
M: In the summer. The winter is very cold.
10a
I: Why do they visit the city?
M: They want to see the old town in the centre. It has
    beautiful buildings.

6 Get students to read each question again before they
ask their partners. Alternatively, if your students are
all from the same place, get them to think of another
town or city they know well. They can then answer
questions about that place.

VOCABULARY

7

> **2** restaurants; **3** bookshops; **4** park; **5** market;
> **6** festival; **7** tourist information; **8** bus tour;
> **9** museum; **10** car parks

8 Put students into pairs or groups. You could ask
them to quickly look at the Key Language (making
suggestions) on page 27.

KEY LANGUAGE

9 This section revises the Key Language sections from
Lesson 1.3 (saying where places are, page 11) and
Lesson 2.3 (asking for information, page 19). Students
do activity as per Coursebook.

`1.27`

10

> **1**a; **2**c; **3**b

Track 1.27
Fabio, Gill
F: Hello. Are you Gill?
G: Yes, that's right.
F: I'm Fabio. Is it your first day here?
G: Yes, it is.
F: What's your job?
G: I'm not sure exactly. I'm an assistant, with some
    computer work and filing, I think.
F: Well, don't worry. When do you have lunch?
continued…

> G: At 12 o'clock.
> F: That's now! Why don't we go together?
> G: That sounds good. Where do you usually eat?
> F: It depends. What do you want?
> G: Something small. And a coffee.
> F: OK. I know a quiet café. Let's go there.
> G: Good idea! Is it in the centre?
> F: Yes, it's next to the post office.
> G: OK. Let's go.

11a Students do activity as per Coursebook. Don't confirm the answers until after the listening in exercise 11b.

11b

> **b** 6; **c** 2; **d** 5; **e** 3; **f** 1

LANGUAGE CHECK

12

> **2** a lot/lots; **3** museums; **4** an; **5** pilots;
> **6** to (lunch); **7** often (uses); **8** (fish) every day;
> **9** I'd/I would (like); **10** (What) does 'glacier' mean?

LOOK BACK

13

> read an article about famous cities: 1.2, exercise 2; say where places are: 1.3, exercises 8 and 10; find out about two different jobs: 2.1, exercises 3 and 4; listen to an interview with a student: 2.2, exercises 7 and 8; write a CV: 2.4, exercise 11; ask about routines and habits: 3.2, exercise 11a; make suggestions: 3.3, exercises 11 and 12; describe a process: 3.4, exercises 5–9

Leisure time

4.1 SILVER SCREEN

IN THIS LESSON

Lesson topic and staging

The lesson looks at the topic of films. 'Silver Screen' originally referred to the type of projection screens used at the start of the film industry. Now it simply means the film industry in general. The lesson begins with students talking in general about films before looking specifically at types of film. This leads to reading a page from a fictional website, *World Cinema*. Students read two short articles: one about Iranian films and film directors, and the other a review of *Machuca*, a film set in Chile. The texts provide the context for the grammar focus – articles: *a/an, the* and no article. Students work with the articles in a number of ways before the final activity of the lesson: a speaking activity in which students talk about their favourite films, film stars and directors.

Objectives

By the end of the lesson students should have:

- learned more vocabulary to talk about types of film
- revised and extended their knowledge and use of articles: *a/an, the* and no article
- learned to talk about film in general and express their own personal tastes in film
- learned (more) about the world of film

Timings

If short of time, you could drop exercise 5 on page 33. Students could do this exercise for homework.

A possible lesson break would be after the reading and before the grammar focus on page 33.

WARM-UP

- This activity revises questions used to find out about words from Lesson 3.4, exercises 3a and 3b. Write the following answers on the board and ask students in pairs or small groups to write the questions.

  1 It's a large river of ice that moves down a mountain.
  2 /ˈɡlæsiə/
  3 G-L-A-C-I-E-R.
  4 It's a noun.
  5 It's on the first syllable.
  6 (Write the translation of 'glacier' in the language of your students if you have a monolingual class.)

- Give students a few minutes to write the questions before checking their answers.

VOCABULARY: types of film

1 Students do activity as per Coursebook
- When students are finished ask a couple of groups about their answers.

2a Students do activity as per Coursebook.
- Write the following prompts on the board: Name of film? Actors? Seen it? What think about it? Then get students to talk about the film posters and see if they can tell you anything about the films.

i **Film A – Pride and Prejudice**
The romance/drama was released in 2005 and stars Keira Knightley as the heroine, Lizzie (Elizabeth) Bennet. The film is based on the English novelist Jane Austen's story about five sisters: Jane, Elizabeth, Mary, Kitty and Lydia Bennet. It is set in Georgian England (1714–1834). Their lives change forever when a wealthy young man (Mr Bingley) and his best friend (Mr Darcy) visit their village.

Film B – The Fugitive
This action film / thriller was made in 1993 and stars Harrison Ford as Dr Richard Kimble. Wrongly convicted of murdering his wife, Dr Kimble escapes from a prison bus. He tries to find out why she was killed and who murdered her. Chasing him is Samuel Gerard, a US marshal. Kimble goes underground and cannot make contact with any friends or family. However, his determination and ingenuity soon produce results and he comes to the frightening realisation that he can trust no one.

Film C – Finding Nemo
This animation was released in 2003. Marlin (a clown fish) loses his wife and children, apart from his son, Nemo, in a shark attack. Years later, on Nemo's first day of school, he's captured by a scuba diver and taken to live in a fish tank in a dentist's office. Marlin and his new absent-minded friend Dory set off across the ocean to find Nemo, while Nemo and his tank mates plan how to escape before he becomes the dentist's niece's new pet!

Film D – Me, Myself and Irene
This crazy comedy came out in 2000 and stars Jim Carrey as Charlie, a kind and friendly Rhode Island State Trooper. Unfortunately, Charlie has a split personality. His other personality, Hank, is the complete opposite of Charlie; Hank is aggressive and crazy! Charlie has the simple job of taking Irene (Renée Zellweger), a suspected fugitive, back to New York. But Irene is wanted by a group of corrupt police officers who chase her and Charlie all the way to New York State. What should have been a routine job becomes a wild but hilarious escape movie!

Possible answers: A a love story; **B** a thriller;
C an animation; **D** a comedy

2b Get students to discuss the questions.

- Check students' answers to question 1.

- Ask a couple of students what they answered to
questions 2 and 3.

READING

3 Ask students to look at the text on page 33 quickly.
Ask them where they would see this kind of text and
what it is about.

- Get students to read items 1–5 before they read the
web page and then check their answers.

  2 ✓(*Country profile: Iran*); 4 ✓ (*This film is about
  two … boys in Chile …*)

4 Students do activity as per Coursebook.

  1d; 2e; 3b; 4c; 5a

5 Students do activity as per Coursebook.

  2 true (*Mohsen Makhmalbaf and his daughter,
  Samira*); 3 false (*they make films about the lives
  of ordinary people, and life in the city or in the
  country*); 4 false (*Gonzalo lives in a rich part of the
  capital city, Santiago …*); 5 ? text doesn't say; 6 true
  (*the excellent young actors Ariel Mateluna and
  Matías Quer*)

GRAMMAR: articles

⚠ Articles in English are a very tricky area for many
language learners. Here are some common errors.

Some languages use the definite article with nouns
when talking in a general sense: *I like the films.*

Some languages do not have articles, e.g. *What about
going to cinema?*

Many languages do not use the indefinite article with
jobs (see note b): *She's actor.*

Some languages only have one form of the article:
She wants to be the actor.

Go through the rules with the students and give more
examples of the rules if needed.

GRAMMAR TIP

If your students need more practice to clarify the rules,
write these words on the board and ask them to put *a* or
an in front of them. Some students may think the rule is
an + vowel not *an* + vowel **sound**, e.g.
an university ✗
a university ✓

(a) woman (a) house (a) university   (an) actor
(an) ice cream   (an) hour (a) car

For a full explanation and further practice activities, go to
pages 128–129 in the Language Reference.

6 Students do activity as per Coursebook. Do the first
sentence with the group to show them how to use the
rules to do the exercise.

- When you check students' answers ask them to
explain why they chose the answers they did by
referring to the rules a), b) or c) on page 33.

  2a; 3b; 4c; 5a; 6c

7 Students do activity as per Coursebook.

  1 an; 2 ∅; 3a; 4 a, a; 5 the

SPEAKING

8a Explain that this is a speaking activity and that
students should take the opportunity to use as much
English as they can.

- Get students to read the questions and think about
their answers.

- When they are ready let them start. As this is a
fluency-based activity you might prefer not to correct
students' English.

8b Get a few students to report to the class what their
partners said.

HOMEWORK OPTIONS

Students do/finish the extra practice activities 1, 2, 3 and
7 on page 129 in the Language Reference.

Students do the exercises on pages 24–25 of the
Workbook.

4.2 KEEP FIT

IN THIS LESSON

Lesson topic and staging

The lesson looks at leisure activities and sports in general and a health and fitness club in detail. Students begin by working with a vocabulary set on leisure and sports activities. They talk about what they personally like to do in their free time. The lesson moves on to a listening; students listen to two interviews with members of *Excel* – a health and fitness club. The listening provides the context for the main grammar focus of the lesson: *can* and *can't* for ability (for example, *I can swim*). Students then work with the meaning, form and pronunciation. In the reading that follows students find out more about the club. The meaning of *can/can't* is extended to the concept of possibility (for example, *You can buy sandwiches, fruit and drinks here*). The last activity of the lesson is speaking; students talk about what you *can* and *can't* do in certain places.

Objectives

By the end of the lesson students should have:

- learned more vocabulary to do with leisure activities and sport
- revised and extended their knowledge and use of *can* and *can't* to talk about ability and possibility
- learned to talk about their own abilities and interests in the area of leisure and sports
- learned about a typical British health and fitness club

Timings

If short of time, you could drop exercise 4b. Students could do this for homework.

A possible lesson break would be after exercise 6 and before the reading on page 35.

WARM-UP

This is an activity to revise the vocabulary set on types of films in exercise 2a on page 32. Students have to select a type of film and then draw it so that their classmates can guess the film type. There are two rules: the person drawing can only draw pictures, and mustn't write words or numbers; he/she cannot speak.

- Divide students into small groups and explain the activity, including the two rules.
- Tell students to turn to exercise 2a on page 32 and look at the box of vocabulary. They take it in turns to draw while the other students try and guess the type of film.

VOCABULARY: leisure activities, sports

1a

Preteach: *leisure time* (time when you are not working and can do things that you enjoy)

- Students work in pairs or small groups to read the vocabulary. If students don't know a word or phrase, encourage them to use the questions in exercise 3 on page 28 to find out the information they need.
- When you are confident that students understand the vocabulary, ask them to think about the question in exercise 1a.

1b Students do activity as per Coursebook.

- When they are finished you could revise third person singular forms and ask students to tell the group about their partner.

LISTENING

1.28

2a Students do activity as per Coursebook.

> Lisa can't swim; Dan can swim.

Track 1.28
Interview 1
Gym assistant, Lisa
GA: Hello. We're doing a survey of our customers. Can I ask some questions?
L: Erm, yes, that's OK.
GA: Thank you. First, what's your name?
L: Lisa. Lisa White.
GA: And how often do you come to the club, Lisa?
L: Three times a week, usually.
GA: Do you use the running machines?
L: Yes, I do.
GA: Right, can you run ten kilometres in an hour?
L: Oh no, I can't. Maybe in 70 or 80 minutes.
GA: That's good. And do you work out in the gym?
L: Yes, I do, twice a week.
GA: OK, and what weight can you lift?
L: Well, I don't usually lift a lot, but I can lift 35 kilos.
GA: Do you use the swimming pool?
L: No, I don't.
GA: Really? Why not?
L: Well, erm, I can't swim, so I don't use it.
GA: Can't you? We offer lessons here, you know.
L: I know, I know, but I'm scared of water.
GA: I see. Well, I'm sure our trainer can help you …
Interview 2
Gym assistant, Dan
GA: What's your name?
D: Dan. Dan Tobin.
GA: And how often do you come to the club, Dan?
continued…

D: Twice a week, usually.
GA: Do you use the running machines?
D: Yes, I do.
GA: Can you run ten kilometres in an hour?
D: Oh, yes, I can. Easy. I can run that in about 30 minutes.
GA: Really? That's fast! And do you work out in the gym?
D: Yes, but only once a week.
GA: OK. What weight can you lift?
D: I can lift 50 kilos.
GA: Mmm, that's good. And do you use the swimming pool?
D: Yes, I do. I usually swim two kilometres, but I can swim five kilometres.
GA: Really?
D: Oh yes, I'm super fit!
GA: Yes, clearly. Can we test your fitness today? We have a machine …
D: Oh, is that the time? I can't stay, I'm afraid, I have an important meeting. Bye.
GA: But I have … oh …

2b Give students time to look at the table before playing the recording.

> **Lisa: 1** three times a week; **3** yes, twice a week; **4** no
> **Dan: 2** yes; **3** yes, once a week; **4** yes

2c Let students read the sentences before playing the recording again and see if they can fill in the spaces. They may ask about *weight/lift*. If so, you could mime the action.

• Play the recording and let students check their predictions.

> **2** don't, can; **3** can't; **4** can; **5** usually, can

GRAMMAR: *can, can't*

3 Students do activity as per Coursebook. Check that they understand *can/can't*, giving extra examples if necessary.

> **1** can't; **2** can; **3** can't; **4** can

4a Check students understand these grammatical terms: *affirmative* and *main verb*.

• Students do activity as per Coursebook.

> **1** true (*He can swim.*); **2** false (*What weight can you lift?*); **3** true (*I can't swim.*); **4** false (*He can run.*)

4b Students do activity as per Coursebook.

> **1** She can ride a horse. **2** They can swim. **3** ✓; **4** ✓; **5** We can't ski. **6** Lisa can lift 35 kilos. **7** Can you ride a bike?

For a full explanation and further practice activities, go to pages 128–129 in the Language Reference.

pronunciation
1.29

5a Pronounce the two forms of *can*: /kən/ and /kæn/.

• Get students to pronounce the two forms after you.
• Tell students to write down numbers 1–6 and to tick the sentence with the strong form.
• Get students to listen and repeat the sentences. Play them one by one and pause the recording after each sentence. It may help your students to look at the audioscript for Track 1.29 on page 148.

> **4** Oh, yes, I can.

> **Track 1.29**
> **1** Can I ask some questions?
> **2** Right, can you run ten kilometres in an hour?
> **3** I can lift 35 kilos.
> **4** Oh, yes, I can.
> **5** I can run that in about 30 minutes.
> **6** I can swim five kilometres.

1.30

5b Point out that *can't* is always a 'strong' vowel before you play the recording.

• Tell students to look at the interviews from exercise 2a (the audioscript for Track 1.28 is on page 148) and practise the first dialogue with a student.
• Get students to read the two dialogues and then to practise them in pairs.

> **Track 1.30**
> **1** No, I can't.
> **2** I can't swim.
> **3** Can't you?
> **4** I can't stay, I'm afraid.

6 Model a couple of examples with a student before the other students do the activity, for example:
> *Can you drive a car? – Yes, I can.*
> *Can you lift 50 kilos? – No, I can't.*

READING

7a Ask students to read the questions. Then give them two minutes to quickly scan the text and find the answers.

> **1** Monday; **2** running, cycling and rowing machines; **3** 20 metres long and five metres wide; **4** sandwiches and fruit (drink is not a food); **5** yoga, aerobics, cycling and dance

7b Give students time to read the text more thoroughly before they answer the questions.

1 a trainer teaches you; 2 to the reception desk;
3 price, hours that the club can be used, access to
the clubroom and the health and beauty centre

8   Students do activity as per Coursebook.

1 You can buy sandwiches, fruit and drinks here.
2 Only full-time members can use the clubroom.
3 You can get a timetable for the classes from the
reception desk. 4 Part-time members cannot use
the health and beauty centre.

GRAMMAR TIP

The modal verb *can* has several different meanings. Here
the meaning of *can* is extended from ability/inability (*I
can/can't lift 50 kilos*) to something which is possible or
not possible: *Part-time members cannot use the health
and beauty centre.*

9   Students do activity as per Coursebook. Any 'new'
words like *borrow* should become clear when put in
the context of the sentences.

1 borrow books; 2 use a running machine; 3 find
information; 4 learn about the past
Other options are possible.

SPEAKING

10   Model the activity by playing the parts of teacher and
student, using the dialogue below:

TEACHER: You can walk.
STUDENT: Is it a park?
TEACHER: No, it isn't. You can stop and have lunch.
STUDENT: Oh, is it in the countryside?
TEACHER: No. You can ski.
STUDENT: Oh, right! Is it in the mountains?
TEACHER: Yes, yes, it is.

HOMEWORK OPTIONS

Students do/finish the extra practice activities 4, 5 and 8
on page 129 in the Language Reference.

Students do the exercises on pages 26–27 of the
Workbook.

4.3 SCENARIO: AT A
TRAVEL AGENT'S

IN THIS LESSON

Lesson topic and staging

The lesson looks at holiday destinations and develops
students' ability to ask for and give basic information
about holiday resorts.

Students begin by working with two groups of
vocabulary to talk about what they do on holiday and
what accommodation, sports, activities and evening
entertainment resorts offer. Students look at and talk
about a holiday advertisement before they listen to a
customer asking a travel agent for information about the
same resort. The listening provides the context for the
Key Language of the lesson: asking for information and
saying *no* politely. Students work with this functional
language and also focus on how words are linked in
pronunciation. They should then be ready for the main
focus of the lesson, the task. Students read two different
advertisements for resorts; these adverts are used as the
basis for two role-plays in which students take on the
role of customer and travel agent and ask for and give
information about one of the resorts. Students then swap
roles. After this they talk about which resort they prefer.
The lesson finishes with students deciding which would
be the best resort for the customer and her family.

Objectives

By the end of the lesson students should have:

*   learned vocabulary to discuss what people do on
    holiday
*   learned vocabulary to talk about what
    accommodation, sports, activities and evening
    entertainment resorts offer
*   learned functional language to ask for information
    and say *no* politely
*   improved their pronunciation by linking words within
    sentences and phrases

Common European Framework

Students can ask for and give basic information as well
as say *no* politely.

Timings

If short of time, you could drop exercises 1 and 10. These
could be done for homework or in the next lesson if
there is time.

A possible lesson break would be after exercise 7 and
before the task on page 37.

Make sure you leave sufficient time at the end of the
lesson to prepare for, complete and discuss the task in
exercises 8 and 9.

WARM-UP

This activity revises the vocabulary on leisure activities and sports from Lesson 4.2, exercise 1a.

• Get students into small groups. Tell them they have two minutes to write down as many leisure activities and sports (for example *ride a bike*) as they can.

• Stop the activity after two minutes and see how many activities the students have.

PREPARATION

1

Preteach: *beach* (an area of sand next to the sea), *campsite* (a piece of land where you can stay in a tent), *to try something*, e.g. food (to do, use or taste something in order to find out whether it is successful or good)

• Before students do the activity you might want to look together at the adverbs of frequency on pages 24–25.

2

Preteach: *entertainment* (things such as television, films, and shows that people like to watch or listen to), *chalet* (a wooden house in a mountain area), *hiking* (taking long walks in the countryside for pleasure), *kids' club* (a club for children)

• Students do activity as per Coursebook.

Accommodation	Sports and activities	Evening entertainment
a chalet, a sea view, satellite TV, a double room	mountain biking, scuba diving, wind-surfing, a hiking trip, a painting class, a kids' club, a museum visit	a concert, a dance show

3

Preteach: *all-inclusive resort* (a place where a lot of people go for a holiday and where everything is included in the price)

• Students read the ad and discuss the questions.

1.31

4a Tell students that they are going to hear a conversation between Sarah, who wants to go with her family to the Sarong Holiday Resort, and a travel agent.

Students should tick: the bedrooms, food, sports, children's activities
Sarah probably doesn't want to make a reservation because not all the rooms have a sea view, there are no family rooms, there are no other sports apart from water sports and finally, there is no kids' club.

Track 1.31
Sarah, Travel agent
S: Hello.
TA: Hello, can I help you?
S: Yes, please. Can you give me some information about the Sarong Holiday Resort?
TA: Yes, certainly. What would you like to know?
S: First of all, can you tell me about the accommodation, please?
TA: Yes, of course. All the rooms are double rooms. Some of the rooms have a sea view.
S: I see. Are there any family rooms?
TA: No, I'm afraid not. They can put extra beds in your room for children.
S: And what restaurants are there in the resort?
TA: There are five different restaurants – Thai, Chinese, Indian, Italian and American. You can eat breakfast, lunch and dinner in four of them. I'm afraid you can't have breakfast in the Indian restaurant.
S: The advert says that the resort offers water sports. Can I play other sports, tennis, for example?
TA: I'm sorry. I'm afraid you can't. They only have water sports at the resort.
S: I see. Finally, I've got two young children. Is there a kids' club in the day?
TA: No, I'm afraid there isn't. There's a babysitter service in the evenings. The babysitter looks after your children in your room and you can go to the cinemas and restaurants.
S: Right. Thank you very much for your help and the information.
TA: You're welcome, madam. Do you want to make a reservation?

4b Get students to read the questions so they know what to listen for.

1 no, just some; 2 in an extra bed in the room (with their parents); 3 yes, except for the Indian restaurant; 4 only water sports; 5 in the evening

KEY LANGUAGE: asking for information (2), saying *no* politely

1.32

5 Students do activity as per Coursebook.

1 Can, like; 2 tell; 3 not; 4 Can, can't; 5 Is, isn't

> **Track 1.32**
>
> **1**
> S: Can you give me some information about the Sarong Holiday Resort?
> TA: Yes, certainly. What would you like to know?
>
> **2**
> S: First of all, can you tell me about the accommodation, please?
> TA: Yes, of course. All the rooms are double rooms.
>
> **3**
> S: Are there any family rooms?
> TA: No, I'm afraid not.
>
> **4**
> S: Can I play other sports, tennis, for example?
> TA: I'm sorry. I'm afraid you can't.
>
> **5**
> S: Is there a kids' club in the day?
> TA: No, I'm afraid there isn't.

pronunciation

1.33

6a Students do activity as per Coursebook.

> **Track 1.33**
> TA: No, I'm afraid not.   TA: I'm afraid there isn't.
> TA: I'm afraid you can't.

6b Students do activity as per Coursebook.

> See the audioscript for exercise 5 (Track 1.32).

7 Students do activity as per Coursebook.

> See the audioscript for exercise 4 (Track 1.31).

TASK: exchanging basic information

8a Students read the adverts and answer the questions.

> **1** Scottish Dream (*Beautiful mountains and lakes*);
> **2** Club Mexico (*Kids' club*); **3** Scottish Dream
> (*Learn a new skill*); **4** Both would be suitable:
> Club Mexico (*Excellent water sports facilities,
> Great nightlife*), Scottish Dream (*Fantastic sports
> facilities*); **5** Club Mexico (the photo, *Beautiful
> beaches* and *Excellent water sports facilities*)

8b Students do activity as per Coursebook. Give them some guidance as to how many sentences to write.

> **Possible answers:**
> Scottish Dream has fantastic sports facilities but
> Club Mexico has excellent water sports facilities.
> Scottish Dream has wonderful food but Club
> Mexico has great nightlife.
> At Scottish Dream you can learn a new skill but
> Club Mexico has a kids' club.
> Scottish Dream has cottage-style accommodation
> but Club Mexico has hotel accommodation.

8c Give students time to read the ads, take notes and, if necessary, ask you any questions they need to.

9

Task summary: In the task students play the roles of a travel agent and a customer interested in buying a holiday. The customer asks for information from the travel agent, who has noted it in the table in the back of the Coursebook. Students then swap roles, and eventually have to decide which holiday they prefer. A successful task outcome is when students successfully ask for and give the required information, and can make and justify a decision about which holiday is best.

- Look at the OTHER USEFUL PHRASES with the students.
- Give them time to prepare for what they want to say. This rehearsal is important for the success of the task.
- If possible, get students to move the furniture so that they are sitting with a desk between them, the way they would in a travel agency. You could put the first two lines of the role-play on the board.
  Good morning. Can I help you?
  Yes, please. Can you give me some information about …
- Monitor the role-play and take notes. Remind students to use the Key Language on page 36.
- When the role-play is finished get students to swap roles. Give them time to prepare for their new roles.
- Start the role-play, monitor and take notes.
- Give students feedback on task achievement and language performance.

10a Get students to talk about this question together. Encourage them to justify their answers.

10b

- Ask students in pairs to think about which resort would be best for Sarah. Get students to look back at the conversation in exercise 5 to help them decide.
- When they are ready ask them to write down their reasons using one of the models.
- Get a couple of students to read their answers aloud.

> **Possible answer:**
> I think Club Mexico is a good place for her
> holiday because she can do water sports. She can
> swim and play on the beautiful beaches with her
> children. There is a kids' club and there are a lot of
> children they can play with.
> I don't think that Scottish Dream is a good place
> for her holiday because her two young children
> can't do anything. There isn't a kids' club and there
> are mountains and countryside and young children
> can't walk a lot.

HOMEWORK OPTIONS

If students wrote about the holiday which was good for Sarah and her family, get them to write about the one which is not good for her and vice versa.

Students do the exercises on page 28 in the Workbook.

4.4 STUDY AND WRITING SKILLS

IN THIS LESSON

Lesson topic and staging

In the first part of the lesson students study larger numbers, fractions and percentages and apply them to questions. In the second part of the lesson students learn to transfer information from a table and a graph to written form. They then complete a table about how often British adults go to certain leisure and cultural events such as exhibitions, dance events and pop and rock concerts. This table forms the basis for students interviewing and writing about how often their classmates go to certain leisure and cultural events.

Objectives

By the end of the lesson students should have:

- learned how to use larger numbers, basic fraction and percentages
- learned how to interpret and transform information in tables and bar graphs into written English
- revised and extended their knowledge of words to do with leisure and cultural events
- learned a basic set of expressions of approximation: *over, about, nearly* and *exactly*
- learned (more) about how often British adults go to certain leisure and cultural events
- written basic sentences to describe how often their classmates go to certain leisure and cultural events

Common European Framework

Students can express quantity using numbers, fractions and percentages. They can also interpret tables and bar graphs.

Timings

If short of time, you could do basic work on numbers (1–100), and move on to fractions and percentages in exercise 4a. Numbers are obviously an important part of any language so try to make time to come back to the topic later.

A possible lesson break would be after exercise 6 and before the work on the bar graph in exercise 7 on page 39.

WARM-UP

This is a quick activity to revise the functional work on asking for information and saying *no* politely.

- Write this conversation on the board if possible before students come into the lesson; alternatively prepare photocopies of it to give out to students.

- Tell students that C is the customer and TA is the travel agent. Ask them if the conversation is polite. Why? / Why not?
- Tell them to work in pairs and to make the conversation polite. They should talk and not write.
- Ask the whole group what changes should be made to make the conversation more polite.

C: Give me some information about the Sarong Holiday Resort.
TA: OK. What information?
C: First of all, tell me about the accommodation.
TA: Right. All the rooms are double rooms.
C: Are there any family rooms?
TA: No.
C: I want to play tennis.
TA: Well, you can't.
C: Is there a kids' club in the day?
TA: No.

STUDY SKILLS: working with numbers

1.34

1 Students do activity as per Coursebook.

(!) Many languages use full stops when writing numbers, but English uses commas. For example:
English – 2,300
German – 2.300

> **Audioscript and answers:**
> **Track 1.34**
> **1** The number of people in the UK is 60,500,000.
> **2** The number of people in Australia is 20,100,000.
> **3** The number of countries in the world is 192.
> **4** The number of languages in the world is 6,000.
> **5** The number of tigers in the world is 7,000.

1.35

2a Students do activity as per Coursebook.

(☆) You can help students by reminding them of the schwa sound /ə/, for example in *rock 'n roll*. Tell them to listen out for the weak form of *and*, which will sound like /dən/:

thousand and, hundred and

> **Students should tick: a** 140; **b** 2,345; **c** 5,670,000

> **Track 1.35**
> a) one hundred; a hundred
> b) a hundred and forty
> c) two thousand
> d) two thousand three hundred
> e) two thousand three hundred and forty-five
> f) five million
> g) five million six hundred thousand
> h) five million six hundred and seventy thousand

2b Students do activity as per Coursebook. Encourage them to try and produce the weak form and link the words, e.g. /dən/ in *140*.

3 Students do activity as per Coursebook. Monitor and correct them as they do it.

4a Students do activity as per Coursebook. Check they know and can pronounce *fraction* and *percentage* by asking: *What type of number is this?* Students may need help with the pronunciation.

> **1c; 2d; 3a; 4b**

4b Students do activity as per Coursebook.

> **1** 1/5; **2** 1/2; **3** 1/3; **4** 1/4

4c Students do activity as per Coursebook.

> **1** 10%; **2** 33.3%; **3** 50%; **4** 20%; **5** 15%; **6** 15%

WRITING SKILLS: a description of a table or bar graph

5 Make sure students understand *table* by pointing out the tables from the book.

• Students do activity as per Coursebook.

> **1** boys, girls; **2** boys, five hours; **3** percent; **4** girls, ten hours; **5** quarter; **6** girls, 15 hours

6 Explain the exercise to students. Divide then into As and Bs and give them time to read their part before you start the exercise.

	Men	Women
Never	4%	17%
Once a month	50%	46%
Once a week	27%	26%
Three times a week	19%	11%

7 Students do activity as per Coursebook.

> **1** 30; **2** 25; **3** 40; **4** 15

8 Students do activity as per Coursebook.

> **1c; 2a; 3b; 4a**

9 Students do activity as per Coursebook.

> **1** Over; **2** Exactly; **3** Nearly; **4** Exactly; **5** Nearly; **6** About/Over

10a

Preteach: *exhibition* (a collection of objects, paintings, photographs, etc. that are put in a public place so that people can enjoy looking at them), *ballet* (a type of dancing that dancers do on a stage in a theatre, which tells a story with music and actions but no words), *opera* (a play with music in which the words are sung), *classical music* (music by people such as Beethoven and Mozart, composed in Europe in the 17th–19th centuries)

• Give students time to read and think about their answers. You could get students to work in pairs. A useful phrase for this exercise would be: *I think …*

> Answers are on page 121 of the Coursebook.

10b Do the first couple of sentences with the whole class to model the exercise.

11a Draw the following table on the board, but substitute the names of five of your students:

Activities	Tomas	Carmen	Aysun	Gregor	Rahul	Total
Ballet and opera						

• Explain the activity to students and model it by asking five students the same question:

Do you ever go to the ballet and opera?

• Mark their answers on the table and complete the *Total* column.

• Get students to draw a similar table and complete the first column with four or five activities.

• Get students to stand up and move around the class, and ask ten other students if they do the different activities.

11b When most students are finished show them how to calculate the percentage and write a sentence about it, using the example on the board. For example:

20% of people go to the ballet and opera.
Only a fifth of people go to …

• Students should then be ready to write a short paragraph describing their results.

HOMEWORK OPTION

If students have written a couple of sentences, ask them to write three or four more based on the results of their interview.

Students do the exercises on page 29 of the Workbook.

5 Transport

5.1 SPEED

Lesson topic and staging

The lesson looks at the topic of transport. Students begin by doing some basic vocabulary work on forms of transport such as *lorry* and *ship*. Students then read an article on the speed of various forms of transport from a Lamborghini to the super fast Maglev train. The text contextualises the grammar and pronunciation work that follows on comparative forms such as *X is more comfortable than Y*. The lesson ends with a speaking activity where students compare two cars and decide which one to buy.

Objectives

By the end of the lesson students should have:

- revised and extended their range of vocabulary on types of transport
- learned (more) about some famous forms of transport around the world
- practised comparative adjectives to compare different forms of transport
- identified the vowel sound 'schwa' and practised the weak form of *than*
- compared different means of transport and expressed their preference for a certain type of car

Timings

If short of time, you could leave exercise 1 for students to do at home.

A good lesson break would be after exercise 4 and before the Grammar section and exercise 5 on page 41.

WARM-UP

- This activity revises numbers from Lesson 4.4. Dictate the numbers below and ask students to write them down:

  a) 200; b) 330; c) 676; d) 9,000; e) 10,333; f) 18,500; g) 24,670; h) 22,000,000; i) 12,600,000; j) 50
- Check students' answers and write them on the board.

VOCABULARY: transport

1a Get students to work in small groups when they do the exercise. Tell them to circle any words in the box they do not know.

> **1** to travel / go by *can be used with all these means of transport*; **2** to drive ... a bus, a car, a lorry, a taxi, a train, a tram; **3** to ride ... a bike, a motorbike; **4** to fly ... a plane
> **Note:** we 'sail' a boat or a ship.

1b Explain the task and give students a little time to think about their answers. Make sure they explain why they like or don't like a form of transport, e.g. *I like trams **because** they are clean*.

- Elicit a couple of answers from the class before students work in pairs.
- When most students are finished ask for a couple of responses before moving on to exercise 2.

READING

2

Preteach: *speed* (how fast something moves), *motorway* (a wide road on which you can drive fast for long distances)

- Students do activity as per Coursebook.
- Check answers and ask students which type of transport they would like to try.

> 1D; 2C; 3E; 4B; 5A

[i] The superjumbo: the Airbus A380 is the world's largest passenger plane. It is called the 'superjumbo' because it is even bigger than the Jumbo 747; its wingspan is the size of a football pitch! It was built by a European consortium, can carry 555 passengers and has a flight range of 15,000 km.

The Maglev train: invented and developed in Germany, this is the fastest train in the world and has reached speeds of 500 kph in tests. There is only one Maglev train in operation at the moment and that is in Shanghai, China. *Maglev* stands for 'magnetic levitation'; the train doesn't have any wheels and it hovers over the train tracks. Enormously powerful magnets are used to lift the train off the tracks, push it forward and make it brake. Because it doesn't have an engine it is completely pollution-free.

3 Students can do this matching activity in pairs. Tell them to read the article quickly and to only focus on checking their answers at this stage.

> b 1; c 2; d 5; e 4

4 Ask students to read the sentences first. Tell them that they should 'scan' the article to find what information is included.

☼ This task is specially designed to develop students' ability to scan texts for specific information, which is a very valuable skill for students who need English for personal, academic or professional needs.

2 ✓; 3 ✗; 4 ✗; 5 ✓; 6 ✓

GRAMMAR: comparative adjectives

5 Students do activity as per Coursebook.

1 slower; 2 faster; 3 nice; 4 easy; 5 modern;
6 more relaxing; 7 more comfortable

(!) Students may have trouble knowing when to form the comparative with -er and when to form it with more. For example they may make mistakes like:

That car is more fast that my car. ✗

That car is faster than my car. ✓

If this is a problem try to get them to work out the rules for themselves by looking at the examples in the article on page 40. The rules can be found in the Language Reference on page 130.

☼ When you check students' answers it is a good time to work on their pronunciation. It may be helpful for students if you treat the comparative forms as one chunk. Use the board to show students the stress patterns and drill the comparative forms that way. For example:

● ● ● ● ● ● ● ● ● ● ● ●
slower than   more modern than   more relaxing than

GRAMMAR TIP

Read through the grammar tip with students. Ask them if they know any more irregular forms.

For a full explanation and further practice activities, go to pages 130–131 in the Language Reference.

To extend this activity, if you feel that students need more practice manipulating form, divide students into teams. Write an adjective on the board and ask a team to give the comparative form (you could use regular and irregular comparatives). Students only get a point if they give the complete form, i.e. (more) + comparative adjective + than.

6 Students do activity as per Coursebook. Check students' answers and their spelling.

1 safer; 2 longer; 3 more expensive; 4 bigger;
5 busier

(i) The Panama Canal, in South America, is 80 kilometres long, whereas the Suez Canal, in Egypt, is 171 kilometres long.

Chicago O'Hare Airport is one of the busiest airports in the world. Paris Charles de Gaulle Airport is the second busiest airport in Europe.

pronunciation
1.36

7a Students do activity as per Coursebook.

The vowel sound in *than* is the schwa /ə/.

Track 1.36
1 Plane travel is safer than car travel.
2 The Suez Canal is longer than the Panama Canal.
3 Buses are more expensive in London than in São Paulo.
4 Lorries are bigger in the USA than in the UK.
5 Chicago O'Hare Airport is busier than Paris Charles de Gaulle Airport.

7b Students do activity as per Coursebook.

Suggested answers:
1 Trains are cheaper than planes. 2 Planes are noisier than motorbikes. 3 Motorbikes are more exciting than ships. 4 Cars are safer than bikes. 5 Buses are more common than trams.
There are a number of possible answers for this exercise. Accept all answers that are logical.

• If students need more practice of comparative adjectives, you could also drill those sentences.

SPEAKING

8 If you have brought a photo of a car with you, show it to the class and ask them for adjectives to describe the car. Alternatively, give them an adjective and ask for its opposite, e.g. *expensive – cheap; slow – fast; horrible – nice; uncomfortable – comfortable*, etc.

• Explain the task while students look at the photos.

• Provide a simple spoken model for the students by telling them which car you prefer and why.

• Ask students to work in pairs and complete the task. Monitor them and note down correct and incorrect examples of comparatives.

• When most students have finished, stop the activity and ask a few students which car they picked and why. Give feedback, using the notes you took.

HOMEWORK OPTIONS

Students do/finish the extra practice activities 1 and 6 on page 131 in the Language Reference.

Students do the exercises on pages 30–31of the Workbook.

Students could write a brief paragraph on a form of transport based on the text in exercise 3.

5.2 CITY TRANSPORT

IN THIS LESSON

Lesson topic and staging

The lesson looks at the topic of urban transport systems and how people get around their cities. Students begin by reading about urban transport systems around the world. The text contextualises the grammar that follows on superlative forms, for example *New York has the world's largest station*. After working on superlative adjectives students listen to three people talking about how they get around their cities. This leads into a speaking activity where students talk about using transport to move around their town/city. In the last activity of the lesson students write a paragraph about travelling in their town/city.

Objectives

By the end of the lesson students should have:

* developed their ability to skim and scan a reading text
* learned (more) about some of the most famous transport systems in the world
* analysed and practised using superlative adjectives to talk about transport systems
* developed their ability to listen for specific information
* written a basic paragraph about travelling around their town/city

Timings

If short of time, you could drop exercises 4 and 6b. Students could do these for homework.

A good lesson break would be after exercise 4 and before the grammar focus on page 43.

WARM-UP

Tell the students that this lesson is about different means of transport in their town or city. Revise the types of transport from the last lesson by putting the first letter of each one on the board and asking students in groups to write down the words: *b(ike), b(oat), b(us), c(ar), (t)ram, (u)nderground, (t)rain*.

READING

1 Get students to discuss the questions. Find out the most and least popular forms of transport where students are from.

2a Tell students that you want them to read the article quickly and answer ONLY ONE question: which means of transport does the article talk about? Tell them that they only have one minute to find the answer so they don't need to understand everything.

* Say 'Go!' and one minute later say 'Stop!' Check students' answers.

> metro / underground trains, trams, buses, trains

☼ Some teachers like to explain the principles behind how they teach. Research suggests that when students understand the logic of a task they are more likely to accept what they are asked to do. You might like to tell students that the purpose of looking at the text so quickly and only answering one question is to teach them a useful reading skill – reading a text quickly for gist, or basic meaning.

2b Students do activity as per Coursebook.

> **A** Moscow; **B** St Petersburg; **C** Tokyo; **D** New York; **E** London

ⓘ Picture A shows the interior of Komsomoloskaya metro station in Moscow.

Picture B shows a street with cars and a tram in St Petersburg. In the background you can see the Peter and Paul cathedral.

Picture C shows rush hour at Shinjuku metro station in Tokyo.

Picture D shows the interior of Grand Central Station in New York.

Picture E shows a famous 'double decker' London bus going past Big Ben.

3 Students do activity as per Coursebook.

☼ This exercise practises scanning skills. It is worth explaining to students, perhaps in their L1, that many of the activities in the book are designed to practise different ways of, for example, reading and listening. It is important, therefore, that they try hard to read or listen in this way. The result should be that they are stronger readers and listeners, although it may seem difficult and even frustrating at first!

> **1** 3.2 billion; **2** 720; **3** 468; **4** 4,300; **5** 3.2 million

4 You could ask students to do the task from memory, perhaps in pairs, and then to check their ideas by reading the text.

* Ask students where the biggest transport systems are in their country. Do they know any facts and figures about them?

> **1** true (… *it is the largest city in Europe*); **2** false (*It has the world's largest metro system …, the world's largest station … and the biggest bus system in the world*); **3** false (*London has perhaps the most famous buses in the world*); **4** false (*Unfortunately, it is also the most expensive in the world.*); **5** true (*It is certainly very busy and always crowded.*)

[i] Most countries (e.g. Italy, Turkey, Greece) refer to underground train systems as the 'metro'. However, the system in London is called 'the Underground' and is colloquially known as 'the Tube', while in American English the term 'Subway' is used rather than metro.

GRAMMAR: superlative adjectives

[!] Students may have problems with this structure, for example:

Heathrow airport is the busier airport of the world. ✗

Heathrow is the busiest airport in the world. ✓

This may be because many languages do not have different forms for comparative and superlative adjectives.

5a Students do activity as per Coursebook.

> 1c; 2a; 3b
> We use superlative adjectives to compare one thing (or person) with several things (or people) in a group. For example, *Cecylia is the tallest **woman in the class.***

5b Students do activity as per Coursebook.

- Check students' answers and pay special attention to their spelling. Point out that the last two forms are irregular.

> **1** oldest; **2** largest; **3** biggest; **4** busiest; **5** most famous; **6** most beautiful; **7** best

For a full explanation and further practice activities, go to pages 130–131 in the Language Reference.

6a Students do activity as per Coursebook.

> **2** the longest; **3** shorter; **4** the shortest

6b Students do activity as per Coursebook.

> **Possible answers:**
> **Price:**
> The metro system in New York is more expensive than the metro in Tokyo, but the London Underground is the most expensive system of the three.
> The metro system in New York is cheaper than the London Underground, but Tokyo has the cheapest metro system of the three.
> **Age:**
> The metro system in New York is older than the metro in Tokyo, but the London Underground is the oldest system of the three.
> The metro system in New York is more modern than the London Underground, but the Tokyo metro is the most modern of the three systems.

7 Students do activity as per Coursebook.

- Remind them of the rules for forming the superlative adjectives and get them to write out the examples. Tell them to write out the full form of the superlative adjectives, i.e. not *fastest* or *most comfortable* but *the fastest* and *the most comfortable*.

- When you check students' answers check their spelling too.

- Model the speaking activity by asking students the question in the book. Then ask them to give you the same question but using *comfortable* instead.

- Put students in pairs to do the activity.

> fast – the fastest; comfortable – the most comfortable; dangerous – the most dangerous; slow – the slowest; safe – the safest; exciting – the most exciting; busy – the busiest

LISTENING

1.37

8a Give students time to read the table before you play the recording. Check that students are clear on the difference in the stress patterns between *thirty* and *thirteen* when Mei talks about her journey time.

[🔧] If students are not very strong, you can divide the listening load up, e.g. some students listen to Mei, others to Fuad and others to Sandra. Alternatively, ask students to listen for the information on cities and length of journey on the first playing and for means of transport on the second playing.

> **1** Mei: motorbike, 30 minutes; **2** Fuad: Cairo, bus, 1 hour; **3** Sandra: Amsterdam, bike, 20 minutes

> **Track 1.37**
> **1**
> Hello. I'm Mei and I work in Beijing. I think the best way to get around Beijing is by motorbike. I've got a small motorbike and it's the quickest and cheapest way for me to travel. In Beijing, the buses are really crowded and I don't like them at all. The metro is the fastest way to travel, but it's not very large. Many people use bikes, but my motorbike is faster than a bike! It takes me 30 minutes to get to work.
> **2**
> Hi, my name is Fuad and I study at Cairo University. Travelling around my city is not very easy because the roads are very small and very busy. The metro here is quite small and my college isn't on a metro line. That's a pity because the metro is the most comfortable way to travel in Cairo. I travel by bus to college. It's the cheapest way to travel, but it's also the most popular, so the buses are very crowded. I never get a seat and it takes about an hour to get to my college!
>
> *continued…*

> **3**
> I'm Sandra, and I live in Amsterdam. Every day I cycle to university. It only takes me about 20 minutes. A bike is the cheapest way to travel, of course, and it's also very popular here, because the city is very flat. In the city centre, trams are the best way to get around – I always use them when I go shopping. Many tourists travel on the canal boats, but I don't because they're the most expensive way to travel.

8b Give the students the time to read the information and try to complete any gaps they can before playing the recording again.

- You could use the audioscript on page 149 to review answers.

- Ask students which city they prefer based on what they have heard.

> **1** Cairo and Beijing; **2** Beijing and Cairo; **3** Beijing and Amsterdam; **4** Cairo; **5** Amsterdam

SPEAKING

9 In pairs, students ask and answer the questions. This is more of a fluency-based activity so give students the opportunity to use the language they have seen in the lesson.

WRITING

10 Get students to look at the three audioscripts for Track 1.37 and to pick one as a model for their texts. Give them time to make notes and then to write their texts.

- Monitor while students are writing and help students when necessary.

HOMEWORK OPTIONS

Students do/finish the extra practice activities 2, 3 and 4 on page 131 in the Language Reference.

Students do the exercises on pages 32–33 of the Workbook.

5.3 SCENARIO: AT A TICKET AGENCY

IN THIS LESSON

Lesson topic and staging

The lesson looks at the topic of flying. Students do preparatory work on the topic of flying and the vocabulary associated with it. This is followed by work on stress in compound words connected to the topic. A reading on airline adverts sets the scene for Part one of a listening in which a person speaks to a travel agent about flights to New York. After some basic work on questions needed for booking flights, students listen to Part two of the conversation, in which the person books his flights. Students then do further work on question formation to prepare them for the main speaking task of the lesson: role-playing a phone call, in which they speak to a travel agent and book tickets.

Objectives

By the end of the lesson students should have:

- learned (more) words and phrases related to the topic of planes and flying

- learned (more) about how to find out about and book flights in English

- talked about food from different countries

- learned some functional language necessary for buying an aeroplane ticket

- improved their awareness of stress in compound nouns

Common European Framework

Students can ask for and give basic information about flying and booking flights.

Timings

If short of time, you could drop exercise 4 and come back to it later if you feel students need to do work on stress in compounds.

A good lesson break would be after exercise 6 and before the Key Language on page 45.

Make sure you leave sufficient time at the end of the lesson to prepare for, complete and discuss the task in exercise 10.

WARM-UP

This is a memory-test activity which revises superlative adjectives from Lesson 5.2.

- Write these prompts on the board:

  New York, London, Tokyo – metro systems

  Old:

  Long:

  Expensive:

5.3

- Ask students to write three sentences from memory using superlative adjectives comparing these metro systems. Which is the oldest, which is the longest and which is the most expensive? Give them an oral example with the adjective *cheap*: *New York has the cheapest metro system*.

- When they are finished get students to read out a few of their sentences to the whole class. Correct the sentences if necessary.

PREPARATION

1

Preteach: *duty-free* (duty-free goods are cheaper than normal goods because you do not pay tax on them), *hand luggage* (the bags that you carry onto a plane when you are travelling), *to board a plane* (formal – to get on a plane, ship, train, or bus), *aisle* /aɪl/ (a long space between rows of seats in a theatre, church or plane), *in-flight entertainment*, *food*, etc. (things such as television, films, radio programmes and food that an airline company provides for people when they fly), *departure* (when a person, plane, train, etc. leaves a place), *return flight* (a ticket for a plane journey to a place and back again)

- Ask students to complete the exercise on their own. If they have never flown before, ask them to imagine their answers.

  Get students to work in pairs to compare their experiences.

2 Students do activity as per Coursebook.

🔧 If students are not very strong, ask them to read sentences a–e first and then to match them with sentences 1–5.

> **1d; 2a; 3e; 4b; 5c**

`1.38`

3 Get students to work in groups to find out the answers together.

> **1** departures; **2** return; **3** standard, business; **4** in-flight, flight; **5** window; **6** aisle

---

Track 1.38
1 Check the departures board and see when the flight leaves.
2 I'd like a return ticket to Rio, please.
3 I usually travel in standard class, but sometimes my company pays and then I fly business class.
4 This airline has really good in-flight service. The flight attendants are really helpful.
5 I always ask for a window seat. I love the view of the clouds.
6 I always ask for an aisle seat because I've got long legs!

💡 Encourage students to record all 'new' vocabulary in the phrases or chunks they appear in, e.g. *window/ aisle seat* rather than just *aisle*. This will help them remember the phrases better, encourage them to start seeing words in chunks and make them more aware of the importance of collocation.

pronunciation
`1.38`

4a Tell students that most compound words they meet will have the stress on the first word.

- It may help them to say the compounds to themselves so they can 'hear' where the stress is.
- Get students to read and mark the stress on the phrases in 1–6 before they listen.
- Play the sentences so that students can check their answers.
- Write the phrases and the stress on the board.
- Play the recording again so that students can listen for the stress on the compounds again. You might also like to drill them from the board.

> **2** return ticket; **3** standard class, business class; **4** in-flight service; **5** window seat; **6** aisle seat

For the audioscript, see exercise 3.

4b Students do activity as per Coursebook.

5 Students do activity as per Coursebook. Ask students which airline they want to travel with.

> **1** International Budget Air; **2** Top Air; **3** Oz Air

`1.39`

6 Ask students who the people in the photos are and what they are talking about.

- Establish the situation and get students in groups to think of three or four questions that they think the person will ask the travel agent.
- Get students to tell you their ideas.
- Ask students to read the table before you play the recording.

🔧 If students are not very strong, ask half of the class to complete the information about Oz Air and the other half to complete the information about Top Air.

	Oz Air	Top Air
Departs	8 a.m.	6 p.m.
Arrives	7 a.m. (their / local time)	5 p.m. (their / local time)
Length	14 hours	14 hours
Price	$300 (Australian)	$600 (Australian)
In-flight service	very good	excellent

Track 1.39

Travel agent, Sasha.

TA: Hello.

S: Hello, it's Sasha Kaplinski here.

TA: Hello Sasha. I've got your email about New York.

S: Great! I'd like to book the trip now. Have you got some details for me?

TA: Well, I've got two flights for you, one is with Oz Air, the other one is with Top Air.

S: Can you tell me about the Oz Air flight first? When does it leave?

TA: OK. Well, the flight leaves at eight in the morning and it arrives at seven in the morning, their time.

S: OK. How long does that flight take?

TA: It takes 14 hours.

S: Fourteen, that's not bad. And how much does it cost?

TA: Erm, it costs 300 Australian dollars.

S: That's a good price. Is it a good airline?

TA: Oh yes. The in-flight service is very good.

S: Fine, and what about the second flight?

TA: The second one is with Top Air. This is a very good airline. Their in-flight service is excellent – it's better than Oz Air's. You can have a head massage and the food is great.

S: Sounds good. When does it leave? And when does it arrive?

TA: Well, it leaves at six in the evening and gets there at 5 p.m., their time.

S: How much does it cost?

TA: This one costs 600 Australian dollars.

S: I see. How long does it take?

TA: It also takes 14 hours.

S: Mmm, that's good, but it's expensive.

TA: Do you want to make a booking now?

S: Erm, I think so. Yes.

KEY LANGUAGE: buying a ticket

`1.39`

7   Check that all students are clear on the rules for forming basic questions with the verb *be* and other verbs.

- Elicit the answer for question 1 with the whole class, and ask the students to write the answers for questions 2–5 in pairs.

- Play the recording again so students can check their answers. Some students may still be having problems so check their answers carefully. You could also ask students what *it* refers to in each sentence.

> 1 does; 2 does; 3 long; 4 much; 5 Is

For the audioscript, see exercise 6.

`1.40`

8a Ask students to guess which flight Sasha takes.

- Play the recording so students can check their answers.

> The flight with Oz Air because it's half the price of Top Air.

Track 1.40

TA: Do you want to make a booking now?

S: Erm, I think so. Yes.

TA: OK. One moment please. Right, so, <u>can I have your full name, please?</u>

S: Sasha Andrei Kaplinski. That's K-A-P-L-I-N-S-K-I.

TA: Thank you. And <u>which airline would you like to travel with?</u>

S: I'd like to book the Oz Air flight, please.

TA: OK. <u>When do you want to travel?</u>

S: Next Tuesday.

TA: Next Tuesday, that's the 1st of October, and <u>what about the return flight?</u>

S: One week later, please.

TA: OK, on the 8th, that's no problem. So, <u>would you like business or standard class?</u>

S: Oh, standard class. The company doesn't want to spend a lot of money.

TA: Fine, and finally, <u>would you like a window or an aisle seat?</u>

S: Oh, can I book that now?

TA: Yes, you can.

S: Excellent. Can I have a window seat, please?

TA: Certainly. OK, that's all. <u>How would you like to pay?</u>

S: Oh, by credit card please, the company credit card.

TA: OK, can I have the card number, please? …

8b Ask students to complete any information they can before they listen again. This will prepare them for the new task.

> 4 Oz Air; 5 (Tuesday) 1st October; 6 (Tuesday) 8th October; 7 standard; 8 window; 9 credit card

9a Get students to work in pairs or small groups.

- Ask students to read the audioscript on page 149 to check their answers.

> See the audioscript for Track 1.40 (the answers are underlined).

🔧 With weaker students you could provide them with the seven questions but jumbled up. Alternatively, jumble up each sentence so that students have to reorder them. For example:

2 to travel with? / airline would / Which / you like
Which airline would you like …

9b Explain to students that this activity allows them the opportunity to prepare for the role-play that follows in exercise 10.

- Practise the dialogue with a student so that the other students have a model.
- Get students to practise the dialogue.
- Monitor their performance.

TASK: booking a travel ticket

Task summary: In the task students play the roles of a customer who needs to book a return flight to Moscow and a travel agent. Student A 'phones' the travel agent and asks questions to find the best flight they can. Student B is responsible for answering the customer's questions and helping him/her find the best flight possible. A successful task outcome is when Student A is able to book the best flight for him/her based on the information provided by Student B.

10 Explain the basic situation, task and task outcome.

- Give students their roles: Student A is the customer and Student B the travel agent. At this stage it is better for weaker students to be the travel agent even though they have more information to read.
- Give students time to read the description of their role, the email and, for Student B, the information on page 116.
- Get students to look at the OTHER USEFUL PHRASES box and to decide which of the sentences they could use in their conversation.
- Ask students if they want to clarify anything with you before they start. Establish that Chris (the travel agent) and Jo (the customer) have a relaxed, informal relationship. So students should be polite but not too formal. Write the opening lines of the conversation on the board to help students start.

  CHRIS: Good morning/afternoon, Speedy Travel. Chris speaking. How can I help?
  JO: Hi, Chris. This is Jo. Any news on my flight?
  CHRIS: Oh, hello, Jo. Yes, there are a number of possible flights …
- Once students have finished, get students' feedback on task achievement by asking how many customers booked flights, which flight they booked, if they had any problems, etc., and then ask the travel agents if they had any problems. Then give students feedback on the language areas needed to make basic enquiries in a ticket agency about flights.

HOMEWORK OPTION

Students could write a brief dialogue between a customer and a travel agent.

Students complete exercises on page 34 of the Workbook.

5.4 STUDY AND WRITING SKILLS

IN THIS LESSON

Lesson topic and staging

In the first part of the lesson students focus on planning written work. Students examine the normal stages in a piece of semi-formal writing and apply these stages in order to make notes on a transport system they know. In the second part of the lesson, students work on defining and identifying paragraphs and topic sentences. After some work on the conjunction *but* students combine what they have worked on in the lesson to write three paragraphs on the transport system in their country, city or area.

Objectives

By the end of the lesson students should have:

- recycled the grammar and vocabulary covered in the unit
- learned (more) about planning their written work
- learned to identify and use paragraphs topic sentences and the linking word *but*
- written a basic text on systems of transport

Common European Framework

Students can plan a piece of basic written work. They can write a basic description of transport in their country, area or city.

Timings

If short of time, you could drop exercise 9 and come back to it later if you feel students need to do work on using *but*.

A good lesson break would be after exercise 4b and before the Writing Skills section of the lesson on page 47.

WARM-UP

This is an activity which revises the vocabulary of flying from Lesson 5.3.

- Tell students to work in pairs. They have three minutes to write down as much vocabulary about flying as they can remember. They cannot look in their Coursebooks or notebooks.
- After three minutes tell students to stop.
- Write up all their vocabulary on the board.
- You could see which pair has correctly remembered the most words.

STUDY SKILLS: planning your written work

1a

Preteach: *draft* (a piece of writing, a drawing or a plan that you have not finished yet)

- Explain that it's important to have a structure for planning written work. Ask students if they make drafts of essays or assignments in their own language.

- Ask students to look at the stages and tell you which the first one is (it's c). Tell students to finish the exercise on their own.

If you allow use of the L1 in the classroom, you could ask students in the L1 why it is important to make a draft before you write.

> **Suggested answer: 1c; 2f; 3g; 4b; 5a; 6e; 7d**

1b Students do activity as per Coursebook.

1c This is an important stage. If possible, let students talk in their L1 so they can freely express themselves.

2

Preteach: *speed limit* (a limit on how fast you are allowed to drive), *tunnel* (a long passage through a hill, under the ground or under the sea, for cars or trains), *the Alps* (a range of mountains which go through France, Switzerland, Italy, Germany and Austria), *port* (an area / town where ships arrive and leave from), *motorway* (a wide road on which you can drive fast for long distances)

- Tell students to organise the information about transport in Italy into the five categories.

> **Air:** 4, 7, 11; **General information:** 5, 13;
> **Rail:** 2, 8; **Road:** 1, 3, 6, 10; **Sea:** 9, 12

3 Get students to look at the two examples in the mind map (*good system* and *excellent links*) and compare them to the corresponding sentences from exercise 2 (sentences 5 and 13). Point out that when we make notes we often drop some of the less important ideas and words, and that we don't use full sentences. Make a list on the board of the kinds of words we drop, e.g. verb *be*, articles, *there is/are*, etc.

- Look together at the first two sentences from exercise 2, and get students to make them into notes. Look together at their answers and give feedback.

- Get students to put the rest of the sentences into notes and use them to complete the mind map.

> **Suggested answers:**
> **Sea:** about six major ports; biggest sea port is Genoa.
> **Road:** drive on right; speed limit 50kph in towns; Fréjus tunnel under Alps; one of best motorway systems in Europe.
> **Rail:** modern, comfortable trains between big cities; metros in Rome and Milan.
> **Air:** about nine important airports; flights between most cities; airport in Rome: Leonardo da Vinci.

4a Agree on the area students will talk about, i.e. the town, city, area, their country or another country. It may be simplest if you make this decision.

- Ask students to discuss the questions in pairs. Tell them they can refer back to exercise 2 to help them.

- Get a couple of students to briefly tell you what they talked about.

4b This activity can be done in pairs or small groups providing that the students in each pair or group come from the same country.

- Get students to make a mind map using the questions and any other information they want to add.

- When students are finished get a couple of them to report back to the whole class. Alternatively, students could go up to the board and draw their mind maps as they talk to the class.

WRITING SKILLS: a description of a transport system

5 Students do activity as per Coursebook.

> **1** ✗; **2** ✓; **3** ✓; **4** ✓; **5** ✓; **6** ✗ (this is a *parachute*)

6 Tell students that they will read a text about transport in India. Ask them first to make as many guesses as they can about what transport systems are like in India. Refer them to the mind map about Italy.

- Tell students to read the text quickly and to match the paragraphs with the headings.

> **1** Introduction to the topic; **2** Rail transport;
> **3** Road transport

7a Students do activity as per Coursebook.

> Students should have underlined the first sentences of paragraphs 2 and 3.

7b Students do activity as per Coursebook. Ask students to tell you why the other sentences are suitable.

> c

8 Students do activity as per Coursebook.

> c, a, b

9 Introduce the idea of contrast by writing these incomplete sentences on the board about topics that your students are familiar with or that have been covered in the unit (e.g. *The Underground in London is good but …, Public transport in Tokyo is excellent but …*) and ask them to complete them (e.g. *… it's very expensive, … it's very crowded*).

- Students do activity as per Coursebook.

... over 3,300,000 kilometres of roads, but there are a lot of problems ...
Buses are very popular, but they are often very crowded.

10 Students do activity as per Coursebook.

1 Flights in India are expensive but they're cheaper ~~but~~ at night.
2 In Mexico, buses are cheap but long journeys can take ~~but~~ more than 24 hours.
3 On Italian motorways, ~~but~~ the speed limit is 130kph but it's 50kph in towns.

11 This task is the culmination of the work students have done in this lesson. Tell them that they are going to write three paragraphs on *Transport in my country* (*city/area*). Preteach: *traffic jam* (a long line of cars, etc. on the road not moving or moving very slowly), *air pollution* (harmful chemicals and waste in the air, and the damage they cause to the environment).

• Write the following paragraph prompts on the board:

   1 General introduction to the topic

   2 The most important type(s) of transport in my (country)

   3 Problems with transport in my (country)

• In pairs, students match these prompts to the paragraphs in the text on *Transport in India*.

• Tell students to use the text on India as a model and make notes for the three paragraphs about their country/countries (or city/area).

• Monitor and help students with any questions they may have.

• If there is time, get students to work on their own to write a draft. They could then work in pairs again to compare their work and to make changes and add new ideas to their drafts. You could also ask them to write topic sentences for each paragraph for you to check before they carry on writing.

• At this point they can continue to write, or if there is no time, they can write the final copy for homework.

🔧 If you feel students are not ready to write three paragraphs yet, use the text in exercise 6 as a model.

• Write the first paragraph on the board and working with the students, rub out and replace words and phrases that are not relevant to their context. For example,

Transport in _____

_____ is a _____ country with a population of _____ people. There are_____ distances between places. Different kinds of transport move people short/long distances every day.

• Get students in pairs to refer to the mind map they made in exercise 3 and to continue to use paragraphs 2 and 3 of *Transport in India* to write their text.

HOMEWORK OPTIONS

Students complete the written task.

If they have already finished, students could write about local transport instead.

Students do the exercises on page 35 of the Workbook.

6 Food

6.1 SUPER FOOD

Lesson topic and staging

This lesson looks at the topic of 'super food' – food which is particularly good for your health. The lesson begins with students working with a vocabulary set on food and drink. They then read a text, *Super Food*. The article provides the context for the grammar focus on countable and uncountable nouns plus *some* and *any*. After practising this language students talk about their diet: what they usually eat, what they like and dislike and what healthy and unhealthy food they eat. The lesson finishes with groupwork, in which they decide who has the healthiest diet.

Objectives

By the end of the lesson students should have:

* learned more vocabulary to talk about food and drink
* learned about the benefits of 'super foods'
* revised and extended their knowledge and use of countable and uncountable nouns and *some/any*
* learned to talk about their tastes in food and their diet

Timings

If short of time, you could drop exercise 4 on page 49. Students could do this exercise for homework.

A possible lesson break would be after exercise 4, before the grammar focus on page 49.

WARM-UP

This is a prediction activity to get students thinking about the content of the lesson.

* Write the unit title, *Food*, and the lesson title, *Super Food*, on the board.
* Ask students to write down what they think the lesson will be about and any vocabulary, in English, they think may come up.
* Get ideas from the whole group and then ask them to open their books up to pages 48 and 49 and check their ideas.

VOCABULARY: food and drink

1a Students do activity as per Coursebook. Check their pronunciation of the words when you check their answers.

> Students should be able to find bananas, bread, broccoli, carrots, garlic, milk, noodles, nuts, oranges, red peppers, rice, salmon, sardines, strawberries.
> Olive oil features at the bottom of the page.

1b Get students to do this activity in pairs but to note their own answers.

> **1** milk, green tea; **2** salmon, sardines; **3** broccoli, carrots, garlic, peppers; **4** bananas, oranges, strawberries

READING

2 Students do activity as per Coursebook. Ask students which super foods they eat.

3 Students do activity as per Coursebook.

> **1** broccoli, carrots; **2** nuts; **3** salmon, sardines; **4** blueberries, strawberries, broccoli, garlic

4 Students do activity as per Coursebook.

* You could also ask students a couple of questions about the text, e.g.

  1 Did you learn anything new from the text?

  2 Do you want to try any of these foods now? If so, which food?

> **2** vitamin A; **3** garlic; **4** heart; **5** a super drink

GRAMMAR: countable and uncountable nouns; *some* and *any*

⚠ Some words in English which are uncountable are countable in other languages and this can cause students problems. Some common examples are *advice, bread, English, furniture, news, information, travel, spaghetti* and *hair*. This can result in mistakes like the following:

I speak a very bad English.

Can you give me some advices about diet?

Spain produces a good wine.

Do you want some spaghettis?

Tell students to make a special note of any nouns in English that are used differently from nouns in their own language.

SUPER FOOD

6.1

5a Students do activity as per Coursebook.

> **1** Countable; **2** Uncountable

For a full explanation and further practice activities, go to pages 132–133 in the Language Reference.

5b Students do activity as per Coursebook.

> **1** some; **2** any; **3** any
> Note that there are exceptions to rule 3, an example of which is to be found in Lesson 3, exercise 5, number 4.

6 Students do activity as per Coursebook. Tell students to use the rules in 5a to help them answer.

> **Countable:** illnesses, orange, carrots, nuts, vitamins
> **Uncountable:** garlic, oily fish, olive oil, water

7 Students do activity as per Coursebook.

> **2** red pepper has; **3** Fruit is; **4** vegetables have; **5** food is; **6** Water doesn't have

GRAMMAR TIP

Read through the tip with students. Point out that *a tomato* means 'one tomato', *some tomatoes* means 'a number of tomatoes', but *some tomato* means 'a part of a tomato'.

Tell students that if they are not sure if a word is countable or uncountable, they can find out in a good dictionary. Uncountable nouns are marked in the *Longman WordWise* dictionary by *[no plural]*, for example:

> **food** /fuːd/ *noun [no plural]*
> things that you eat: *She was out buying food and drink for the party.*

In other dictionaries, nouns are often marked [C] for 'countable', [U] for 'uncountable' or [C/U] for 'countable' <u>and</u> 'uncountable', for example *salad*.

SPEAKING

8 Explain the task to students. You might want to write some useful language on the board to help them complete the activity, for example:

Do you have any X in your picture?

In my picture there are three Ys.

Is there any Z in your picture? – No, there isn't.

- While students do the activity monitor them and write down examples of correct and incorrect language.

- When students are finished check that they have found the differences.
- Spend some time looking at how students did the activity. You could read out the examples you noted of correct English. Write the examples of incorrect English on the board and see if students can correct them without your help.

> In Student A's picture there is some milk, bananas, garlic and nuts instead of the coffee, bottle of water, oranges, sardines and pasta (noodles) in Student B's picture.

9

Preteach: *cake* (a sweet food that is made by mixing flour, butter, sugar, eggs, etc. together, and baking it), *biscuit* (a thin dry sweet cake), *fast food* (hot food that a restaurant cooks and serves very quickly to customers), *meat* (the flesh of animals and birds that you eat)

- Check students know the words in the list and check their pronunciation. You could get students to work in groups to help each other with the words.
- Tell students to read the questions and think about their answers.
- Get students to discuss their answers in groups.
- When students are finished ask a few students to tell the whole class one or two things about one of their partners, for example:

Agata has a very unhealthy diet. She eats a lot of fast food and never eats 'super food'.

HOMEWORK OPTIONS

Students do/finish the extra practice activities 1, 2, 3, 8, 9 and 10 on page 133 in the Language Reference.

Students do the exercises on pages 36–37 of the Workbook.

6.2 THE 'HAVES' AND 'HAVE NOTS'

Lesson topic and staging

The lesson looks at people who have a lot of material comforts (the 'haves'), and those who have little or no material comforts (the 'have nots'). Students begin the lesson by talking about some serious world problems. They then read a leaflet about a 15-year-old boy called Fikru and his family, who live in Ethiopia. The focus of the lesson then moves to grammar: *much, many* and *a lot of*. Students work with this language in a number of different exercises. Next students listen to an interview with David, a 14-year-old boy in Scotland. David's lifestyle is obviously very unhealthy: he gets no real exercise, has a poor diet, watches too much TV and plays too many computer games! Students then personalise theses topics of diet, exercise and free time by writing questions and then interviewing each other. They use the results to write a simple paragraph about their partner's habits.

Objectives

By the end of the lesson students should have:

- learned about life for some people in Ethiopia and the common story of an overweight child in the West
- revised and extended their knowledge and use of *much, many* and *a lot of*
- learned how to ask and answer questions using *How much/many*
- learned to talk about their eating and drinking habits and how they spend their free time
- written a paragraph about their partner's eating and drinking habits and how they spend their free time

Timings

If short of time, you could leave exercise 12, the writing activity, for homework or until next lesson.

A possible lesson break would be after exercise 7 and before the listening on page 51.

This is an activity to revise the vocabulary set on food and drink from Lesson 6.1.

- Draw a two-column table on the board and label the first column *healthy food and drink* and the second column *unhealthy food and drink*.
- Elicit a couple of examples of vocabulary for each category and give students three minutes, working in pairs, to write down as many words or phrases as they can. Tell students they are not allowed to look at their Coursebooks or notebooks.

- After three minutes ask students to tell you what is on their list and write the language up on the board. Tell students to correct any spelling mistakes. If there are any disagreements about where words should go, e.g. *hamburgers*, encourage students to talk about them in English.

1

Preteach: *to waste* (if you waste something, you use more than you need to, or you do not use it in a sensible way), *overweight* (a person who is overweight is too fat and heavy)

- Explain the title of the lesson to students to contextualise things.
- Ask students to read the questions before they start to talk about them.
- When students have finished have a small class discussion of the issues. Students may find this challenging but encourage them to express themselves in English. Don't worry if the English is incorrect as the aim here is to communicate ideas successfully.

2 Students do activity as per Coursebook. Explain the meaning of phrases *I (don't) think …* and *Perhaps …* and drill them if necessary. They are very useful for students.

3 Ask students what ideas they had from exercise 2 and then get them to do the activity as per Coursebook. Make sure they read the leaflet quickly by only giving them a minute to read it.

It can help students if you give them time limits to complete such tasks. At first this may annoy them because they will want to read the text intensively. However, it's important to help them to read in different ways, for example here to scan the text for specific pieces of information.

4 Students do activity as per Coursebook.

> **1** any; **2** any; **3** some; **4** some; **5** some; **6** some; **7** any

5 Students do activity as per Coursebook.

> **1** He's 15. **2** There are eight members in his family, excluding him (his parents, brother and five sisters). **3** They live in the north of Ethiopia. **4** His father is a farmer. **5** Because there isn't enough / any rain. **6** They don't have any food and their animals die. **7** It runs a development project and gives families 15 euros a month. **8** Fikru has school books and his brother has a bicycle. **9** He wants to go to university, to learn and to help his country.

GRAMMAR: *much, many, a lot of*

(!) Some languages use the definite article with *most*, so students may make errors such as:

The most of my friends have part-time jobs.

(!) Students tend to overuse *much* and *many*. *Much* is rarely used in affirmative sentences, and *many* is also uncommon except in more formal speech or writing.

6 Students do activity as per Coursebook.

> 1 many, a lot of; 2 much, a lot of; 3 many, a lot of; 4 much

For a full explanation and further practice activities, go to pages 132–133 in the Language Reference.

GRAMMAR TIP

Read through the tip. Tell students that it is much more common to use *has/have got* in spoken English than *has/have*. However, it isn't wrong to use *has/have*.

7a Students do activity as per Coursebook. Remind students that it isn't very common to use *many* in affirmative sentences.

> 1 much/a lot of; 2 a lot of/many; 3 a lot of, a lot of; 4 a lot of/much; 5 a lot of/much

7b Get students to complete the questions and then check them.

* Get students to ask and answer the questions in pairs. Encourage them to talk as much as possible about the questions.

> 2 a lot of/much; 3 a lot of/many; 4 a lot of/much; 5 a lot of/much; 6 a lot of/many

LISTENING

8 You could do this activity as a whole-class discussion. Remind students of the phrase *fast food*.

> **Possible answers include:** Children eat too much food and don't exercise much. Children eat a lot of sweets, biscuits and crisps and fizzy drinks like cola and lemonade. Children eat a lot of fast food which has a lot of fat, salt and sugar in it; they don't eat any vegetables and fruit. Children watch a lot of TV and spend a lot of time playing video and computer games.

1.41

9a Students do activity as per Coursebook. When students tell you which topics he mentions ask them for more details about the topics.

> his family, exercise, the TV, food

Track 1.41
Interviewer, David

I: Hello, David. Before you can join the Kids' Fitness Club, we interview you about your lifestyle – about what you eat and what you do in your free time. OK?
D: Fine.
I: Right. Have you got a large family? Do your parents work?
D: Well, I've got a sister, she's two years older than me, and yeah, both of my parents work. Dad's a policeman and Mum's a teacher.
I: OK. How much exercise do you do in your free time?
D: Exercise?
I: Yes, do you play any sports, for example?
D: Oh, no, not really. At school we have one sports lesson a week, but in my free time I don't do much.
I: Do you walk to school or cycle?
D: No … Dad takes me to school in the car. I haven't got a bike.
I: Fine. So, how much TV do you watch?
D: I don't know, about four hours.
I: Four hours a week. That's good.
D: No, four hours a day.
I: I see. Erm, next, how many computer games have you got?
D: I don't know, a lot. I play them all the time. About 30.
I: OK, well, what about your diet? How much fruit do you eat? How many vegetables do you have each day?
D: Well, Mum gives me an apple every day, but sometimes I don't eat it. Vegetables? Perhaps one or two. I don't eat them at school, they're boring.
I: And how many pizzas or burgers do you eat?
D: Oh, I don't know. About three burgers and a pizza each week, sometimes more. I eat a lot of chocolate and sweets … oh, and I love crisps. Crisps are vegetables, aren't they?
I: Well, not really, but …
D: So, can I join the club?
I: Sure, but why do you want to join?
D: Well, I know I'm overweight and I want to change that. And the gym sounds fun – my friends say you can watch TV when you're on the bikes.
I: That's true. But you need to change your diet as well.
D: My diet?
I: What you eat. You need to eat more fruit and vegetables.
D: Yeah, whatever. Do the TVs show MTV?

9b Students do activity as per Coursebook.

(🔧) If your students are not very strong, you could divide the task into two parts and play the recording twice. For example, students complete questions 1, 3, 5, 7, 9 and 11 the first time and the other questions the second time.

> 1 three (excluding him); 2 policeman; 3 teacher; 4 not much (one lesson a week at school); 5 four a day; 6 about 30; 7 (perhaps) one or two; 8 about three; 9 chocolate; 10 crisps; 11 wants to lose weight, have fun and watch TV

10 Ask students to work in pairs or small groups and to see how many differences they can find between Fikru's and David's lives. Tell them to look at the leaflet in exercise 2 and the interview form in exercise 9b to do this. Use the example in the Coursebook as a model and ask someone to complete the example, e.g.:

David has got one sister, but Fikru has got five sisters and one brother.

- After a couple of minutes ask students to tell you how many differences they have found. Then ask them to give you some examples.

> **Suggested answers:**
> David has got one sister, but Fikru has got five sisters and a brother.
> David lives in Scotland and Fikru lives in Ethiopia.
> David has a lot of food, but Fikru doesn't have much – sometimes he doesn't have any!
> David eats chocolate, sweets, crisps and junk food, but Fikru doesn't have any of these things.
> David has probably got a lot of (pocket) money, but Fikru doesn't have any.
> There are probably a lot of shops and supermarkets where David lives, but there aren't any where Fikru lives.

`1.42`

11 Students do activity as per Coursebook. Remind students of how we use *much* with uncountable nouns and *many* with countable nouns.

> **Audioscript and answers:**
> **Track 1.42**
> 1 **How much** exercise do you do?
> 2 **How much** TV do you watch?
> 3 **How many** computer games have you got?
> 4 **How much** fruit do you eat?
> 5 **How many** vegetables do you have each day?
> 6 **How many** pizzas or burgers do you eat?

WRITING AND SPEAKING

12a Explain to students that they are going to write questions to interview their partners.

- Remind students of adverbs of frequency like *every week* that they studied in Lesson 3.2. Then write the answer *I watch TV every day* on the board. Ask students what the question is and elicit a few more questions to model the activity.

- Students do activity as per Coursebook.

- Check their answers carefully as some nouns need *much* and others *many*.

> **Possible answers:**
> **drink:** How many cups of coffee do you drink a/every day?
> **eat:** How many burgers do you eat a/every week?
> **do:** How much sport do you do a/every week?
> **spend:** How much time do you spend on the phone a/every day?
> **watch:** How many films do you watch a/every week?
> **read:** How many newspapers do you read a/every week?
> **waste:** How much food do you waste a/every day?

12b Provide a model for the writing activity as follows. Get a couple of students to ask you a few questions and note down your answers on the board. Tell them not to write full sentences but just to make notes, for example:

STUDENT: How much TV do you watch?
TEACHER: About an hour a day.

- Write *About an hour TV a day* on the board.

- Work with the whole class to use the notes the students made on the board to write a short paragraph about you on the board.

- Tell students to work in pairs and repeat the same steps used for the paragraph about you, i.e. questions → notes → full sentences to make a short paragraph.

- When students are finished ask a couple of students to read their paragraphs out to the whole group.

HOMEWORK OPTIONS

If there is no time to do/finish the writing, ask students to do/finish it for homework.

Students do/finish the extra practice activities 4, 5 and 6 on page 133 in the Language Reference.

Students do the exercises on pages 38–39 of the Workbook.

6.3 SCENARIO: AT A CONFERENCE

IN THIS LESSON

Lesson topic and staging

This lesson looks at catering within the context of an international conference on food and culture. Students begin preparing for the final task of the lesson by matching some famous dishes with their country of origin. This leads into a simple discussion on food from different countries. Students then read a leaflet advertising the international conference on food and culture. This contextualises a listening in which a conference organiser, Tariq, phones a catering company to order food for the conference. The conversation provides the context for work on requests and offers: *Could we have … ? Would you like some … ?*, etc. Students work with the form, meaning and intonation of this functional language. They should then be ready for the main focus of the lesson, the task phase. Students prepare themselves for a role-play in which a conference organiser telephones a supplier and orders food for a conference.

Objectives

By the end of the lesson students should have:

- learned (more) about the origins of certain famous dishes
- talked about food from different countries
- learned some functional language necessary for making requests and offers in the context of catering
- improved their awareness of intonation when making requests and offers

Common European Framework

Students can successfully make and respond to simple requests and offers.

Timings

If short of time, you could drop exercise 1. Students could do this exercise for homework.

A possible lesson break would be after exercise 7 or 8 on page 52.

Make sure you leave sufficient time at the end of the lesson to prepare for, complete and discuss the task in exercise 11.

WARM-UP

This quick warm-up activity gets students thinking about the topic of 'international' dishes such as *sushi* and *pasta*.

- Tell students to open their books at page 53 and see if they know any of the dishes pictured and where they traditionally come from.

- Then ask students which they have tried, which they like and which they want to try.

PREPARATION

1 Students do activity as per Coursebook.

1f; 2a; 3b; 4i; 5c; 6d; 7h; 8g; 9e; 10j

2 Students do activity as per Coursebook. Encourage them to use English. They will make mistakes but the focus here is on fluency and getting the message across rather than grammatical accuracy.

3 Students do activity as per Coursebook.

1a; 2b; 3b

1.43

4

Preteach: *to cater* (to provide a particular group of people with what they need or want), *first course* (the first of a number of different parts of a meal), *main course* (the most important part of a meal), *dessert* (something sweet that you eat after the main part of a meal)

- Students do activity as per Coursebook.

tomato soup: 50 cans; cheese salad: 50; vegetarian pizza: 50; lamb kebab: 40; ice cream: 100; apple pie: 50; still water: 50 large bottles; apple juice: 100 small bottles

---

Track 1.43
Jane, Tariq
J: Good morning, Event Catering Services. How can I help?
T: Hi, it's Tariq here, from the university.
J: Ah, hi Tariq. This is Jane. How are you?
T: Fine thanks. And you?
J: Great. So, how can I help you this time?
T: Well, there's a conference at the university next week and I'd like to order some food for the conference lunch.
J: OK, so, what would you like for the first course?
T: Well, have you got any tomato soup?
J: Yes, we have. How much would you like?
T: We'd like 50 cans, please.
J: That's fine. And for the main course?
T: Could we have 50 chicken salads, please, 50 vegetarian pizzas and 40 lamb kebabs?
J: Oh Tariq, I'm sorry. I'm afraid we haven't got any chicken salads at the moment. We can provide cheese salads.
T: OK, can we have 50 cheese salads then?
J: Sure, no problem.
T: Thanks. For dessert, we'd like 100 ice creams and 50 apple pies.
J: That's no problem. Would you like some water or fruit juice?
continued…

T: Yes, please. Could we have 50 large bottles of still water and some small bottles of apple juice?
J: How many bottles of juice would you like?
T: Oh, 100, please.
J: Fine, anything else? Would you like some coffee?
T: No, thank you.
J: Some tea?
T: No, thanks. That's everything.
J: OK. And when do you want the delivery?
T: Ah yes, well the conference is …

KEY LANGUAGE: requests and offers

5 Ask students to read the sentences and see if they can complete them before they listen.

> 1 have; 2 Can; 3 like; 4 like; 5 Could; 6 Would

6 Students do activity as per Coursebook.

> 1 sentence 1: request, sentence 2: request, sentence 3: request, sentence 4: offer, sentence 5: request, sentence 6: offer; 2 could; 3 We'd like; 4 some

1.44

7 Students do activity as per Coursebook.

> **Audioscript and answers:**
> **Track 1.44**
> 1 Could you send me some coffee? (*request*)
> 2 I'd like 50 lamb kebabs, please. (*request*)
> 3 Can we have 40 bottles of water, please? (*request*)
> 4 Would you like some bread? (*offer*)
> 5 We'd like some chicken salads, please. (*request*)

pronunciation
1.45

8a Students do activity as per Coursebook.

> 2 is more polite, because the voice has more range in it. It starts higher and falls and then rises on the main stress – coffee.

> **Track 1.45**
> 1 Could you send me some coffee?
> 2 Could you send me some tea?

8b Students do activity as per Coursebook.

We show politeness in intonation in a number of ways. One important way is to show a wide voice range. A narrow voice range can make the speaker sound bored, rude, tired or disinterested. Students may not have the same voice range in their language and it may feel uncomfortable to them to copy it. It can help to show voice range and the fall and rise of the voice with a drawing on the board like these.

1 Could you send me some coffee?
2 Could you send me some tea?

- Show students the voice range and rise and fall in intonation in the questions in exercise 7 on the board.
- Get students to repeat the sentences.
- Get students to listen and repeat the six sentences in exercise 5 (Track 1.43). Use the pause button between each sentence if it helps.

9 Students do activity as per Coursebook.

- After checking students' answers get them to repeat the replies after you.

> 1 reply to request; 2 reply to offer; 3 reply to request; 4 reply to offer; 5 reply to offer; 6 reply to request; 7 reply to request

10a Do a few examples with students to model the activity. Students do activity as per Coursebook.

10b Students do activity as per Coursebook.

TASK: talking about numbers and quantities

Task summary: In the tasks students play the roles of a conference organiser and catering supplier. The organiser has to 'phone' the supplier and make his/her order for food and drink for the conference. The catering supplier has to take down the order correctly and suggest alternatives if he/she can't provide certain things. Students then swap roles and repeat the activity. A successful task outcome is when both students have successfully placed and taken an order for the food and drink at the conference.

11a Explain the first part of the task as preparation for the role-play. Advise students to order a variety of food because it's an international conference; there will be people from different countries and religions and remind them they have to provide enough food for 100 people.

- Students prepare their order individually.

11b Check students understand the task and the task outcome. Tell Student Bs to look at their list of supplies on page 117. Tell them they may not be able to supply what the conference organiser wants but they can offer alternatives.

- While Student Bs do this tell Student As to plan what they want to say. They can look at the language in exercise 5 again.
- Write the opening of the conversation on the board to kick-start the conversation.

CATERER:	Good morning, Event Catering Services. How can I help?
CONFERENCE ORGANISER:	Hi, it's _____ here, from the university.
CATERER:	Ah, hi _____. How can I help you?

- Monitor students and take notes. You could ask them if they have any questions or had any problems so they can improve their performance in the next round of the role-play.
- Students swap roles and do the role-play again. When students are finished give feedback on how the task went and then look at how they did with their English.

HOMEWORK OPTION

You could ask students to write a short conversation between another conference organiser and a caterer.

Students do the exercises on page 40 of the Workbook.

DICTIONARY REMINDER

Ask your students to make a note to bring their dictionaries to class for the next lesson.

6.4 STUDY AND WRITING SKILLS

IN THIS LESSON

Lesson topic and staging

In the first part of the lesson students are asked to think about making mistakes. They then go on to correcting mistakes in the areas of grammar, vocabulary and spelling. They then apply a correction code (a shorthand system teachers use to indicate the type of mistake a student has made in written work) to a piece of work written by a student. In the second part of the lesson students analyse a simple review of a restaurant. They examine the structuring of ideas, the beginning of the review and the use of commas in making a list. At the end of the lesson, students write a short review of a restaurant they know. When they are finished they check their own work and their partner's work, looking for the types of mistake they worked with in the first part of the lesson.

Objectives

By the end of the lesson students should have:

- worked with some of the types of mistakes learners make when writing: mistakes in grammar, vocabulary and spelling
- learned how a correction code is used to highlight mistakes in grammar, vocabulary and spelling
- corrected a short piece of work written by a student
- examined how a review of a restaurant can be structured
- written a short, simple review of a restaurant they know
- corrected their review and the review of their partner

Common European Framework

Students can begin to correct the grammar, vocabulary and spelling elements in their written work.

Students can write a simple review describing a restaurant.

Timings

If short of time, you could drop exercise 5, which students can do for homework.

A possible lesson break would be after exercise 5 and before the Writing Skills section of the lesson on page 55.

WARM-UP

This is a quick activity to revise the topic of menus and food.

- Write up the following on the board and ask students to copy it into their notebooks and write down as many dishes and drinks as they can think of.

```
┌──────────────────────┐
│        Menu          │
│   First courses      │
│   Main courses       │
│   Desserts           │
│   Drinks             │
└──────────────────────┘
```

- Check their answers after a few minutes.

STUDY SKILLS: correcting your writing

1a Explain what the first part of the lesson is about and ask students to read and think about statements 1–4. You could discuss the statements with the whole group or let them discuss them in small groups.

💡 If your institution allows students to speak in their L1, you could have a quick discussion in their language. This will allow them to express their opinions and feelings about making mistakes much more easily.

1b Give students a moment to think about this before getting a show of hands on their answers.

2 Students do activity as per Coursebook.

> **1** ~~is~~ are; **2** ~~likes~~ like; **3** ~~more~~ most; **4** ~~many~~ much / a lot of / any

3 Students do activity as per Coursebook.

> **1** vegetables; **2** waste; **3** fat; **4** easy

4 Students do activity as per Coursebook.

> **1** often (note: some students may have a problem with the spelling of this word because most people pronounce it with a silent *t*, i.e. /ˈɒfən/); **2** heart; **3** brain – *Brian* is a boy's name; **4** glasses

5

Preteach: *to look* + adjective, e.g. *look happy, look nice, look tired, look dirty*, etc. (to have a particular appearance), *low* (something that is low is not high, or not far above the ground), *chopsticks* (a pair of thin sticks used for eating food in China and Japan)

- Students do activity as per Coursebook.

ℹ️ The pictures on page 54 show (clockwise from top left) a Vietnamese food stall, a very formal restaurant and a typical fast food restaurant.

💡 Correction codes are an effective way of providing feedback on written work. Research suggests that students learn better if they have to think for themselves, so many teachers simply indicate the type of mistake a students has made rather than correcting it. At this level it is probably enough to use these three symbols and to put the code above the word or phrase that is incorrect.

> Food in Vietnam <u>is</u> healthy. It's important for food to look <u>beautiful</u>, too. We sit at a low <u>table</u> and eat with chopsticks. Most people <u>eat</u> rice three or four times every day. Everywhere in Vietnam is near the <u>sea</u> or a river, so we eat a lot of fish. The fish markets <u>have</u> <u>different</u> kinds of fish. We often eat fish and meat together. We don't eat <u>much / a lot of</u> cheese or milk.

WRITING SKILLS: a restaurant review

6 Explain to students that they are going to write a *review*: a piece of writing about a new book, film or television show.

- Ask students to read the questions, think about their answers and then discuss them with their partners.
- When students are finished have a brief talk about their answers.

7 Get students to look at the photo of the restaurant. Ask if they know any restaurants like the *Corfu*.

- Students do activity as per Coursebook.

💡 When you go over the answers ask students to explain them by referring to the text. Teach them the chunk *The text says* + information. It is a useful piece of classroom language. So, for example:

STUDENT: The review is positive.
TEACHER: Can you give me some examples from the text?
STUDENT: The text says the place is clean and bright.

- Ask students to explain why they would or would not like to eat there.

> The review is positive.

8 Get students to read the list before they read the text again.

> 2e; 3g; 4f; 5b; 6a; 7d; 8i; 9h

9 Students do activity as per Coursebook.

> **Suggested answers:** 3 and 5 are the most interesting because they ask a question which pulls us in. The implication in 3 is that this restaurant is better than *Les Quatre Saisons* and that makes us curious to know more. In the same way, in 5, the writer suggests that this restaurant is the best in the world. We know that can't be true but the writer is trying to impress on us that this is an excellent restaurant. That makes us want to find out why.

10 Students do activity as per Coursebook.

> We write lists using commas and the word *and*, e.g. *V, W, X, Y and Z.*

11 Students do activity as per Coursebook.

> **1** I love chips, chocolate, pizza and ice cream.
> **2** My favourite cities are Venice, Kyoto, Edinburgh and Sydney.
> **3** My favourite subjects are History, French and English.
> **4** I like films, ballet, pop music and art exhibitions.
> **5** Our town needs a new shopping centre, a bus station, a car park, a cinema and a swimming pool.

12 Tell students that they are going to write a similar review to the one on *Corfu* but on a restaurant they know. Write this paragraph plan on the board and tell students to make notes based on it.

PARAGRAPH 1: name of restaurant, type of food and location
PARAGRAPH 2: basic description of the restaurant
PARAGRAPH 3: the food (good? bad?)
PARAGRAPH 4: the type of customers and the service/waiters (good? bad? friendly? unfriendly?)
PARAGRAPH 5: the price of the meal and finally, the writer's opinion.

- When students have made their notes, get them to connect their ideas and write a first draft.
- Then ask them to look for mistakes in their grammar, vocabulary and spelling.
- After that they should do a final copy.
- Finally, you could ask students to pass their review to a partner who decides if they would like to go to this restaurant. After that they could also see if they can help their classmate by suggesting any changes they can.

HOMEWORK OPTIONS

If students have not finished their reviews, ask them to do so for homework. Alternatively, you could ask them to write a short review of different restaurants they know.

Students do the exercises on page 41 of the Workbook.

Review

UNITS 4–6

GRAMMAR

1

> **1** A; **2** The; **3** an; **4** The; **5** a; **6** can't; **7** can; **8** can;
> **9** richest; **10** busier; **11** worst; **12** better; **13** many;
> **14** some; **15** a; **16** much

2a

> **A** comedy; **B** science fiction; **C** thriller; **D** action

VOCABULARY

3

> **1** yoga; **2** tennis; **3** ride; **4** weights; **5** drive;
> **6** speak; **7** CV

`1.46`

4a

	Interview 1	Interview 2
1	play football, run, use weights, teach aerobics.	use fitness machines, teach yoga, speak some Spanish, ride a bicycle
2	teach yoga	drive

Track 1.46

1

Interviewer, Man

I: Right, thank you for coming. First of all, what sports do you like?

M: Most sports really. I play a lot of football at the weekend and go running every morning.

I: That's good. And do you have any qualifications in fitness training?

M: No, but I'm good at using weights.

I: Can you teach yoga?

M: Erm … no, I can't but I can teach aerobics …

2

Interviewer, Woman

I: OK. I'd like to ask you some questions. First of all, do you often use a gym?

W: Yes, I use the fitness machines every week and I also teach yoga at a local college.

I: Great. We also have a lot of international clients. Can you speak any other languages?

W: Yes, I can. I can speak some Spanish.

I: OK. And can you drive?

W: No, I can't, I'm afraid. But I ride a bike everywhere and I go cycling every morning …

4b

> **Suggested answer:** The woman seems to be the better candidate because she can speak some Spanish and can teach yoga.

5 Students do activity as per Student's Book.

6

> **Across: 2** nuts; **6** tea; **8** underground; **11** no;
> **12** red; **14** worst; **15** oil
> **Down: 3** standard; **4** eat; **5** country; **7** go; **9** good;
> **10** city; **13** do

7 Write these two new words on the board: *Western*, *Ski*.

- Ask the whole group what crossword clues they could write for these words as a model for the activity.

- Get students to look for five new words from Units 4–6 and to write clues. Monitor if necessary.

- Move students into pairs to ask and answer the clues.

KEY LANGUAGE

`1.47`

8 This section revises the Key Language sections from Lesson 4.3 (asking for information, saying *no* politely, page 36), Lesson 5.3 (buying a ticket, page 45) and Lesson 6.3 (requests and offers, page 52). Students do activity as per Coursebook.

> **1** true (*The first train is at ten in the morning*);
> **2** false (*I'm afraid there isn't*); **3** true (*The first train is 34 dollars. The other trains are 40.*); **4** false (*That has only standard class seats, I'm afraid.*)

Track 1.47

Traveller, Employee

T: Hello, could you give me some information about trains to Seattle?

E: Yes, certainly. What would you like to know?

T: First of all, when do they leave?

E: The first train is at ten in the morning and the next train is at 12.

T: Is there a train in the afternoon?

E: I'm afraid there isn't. There's a train in the evening.

T: OK. How much does a ticket cost?

E: The first train is 34 dollars. The other trains are 40.

T: I'd like two tickets for the first train, please. First class, please.

E: That only has standard class seats, I'm afraid.

9a

> 2f; 3e; 4h; 5c; 6i; 7g; 8b; 9d

10 Tell students they will be in pairs, a traveller and employee. The traveller wants to but train tickets to Dallas in the USA.

- Get students to read about their roles.
- Put students in pairs to role-play the situation. Monitor the activity if necessary.

LANGUAGE CHECK

11 Students do activity as per Coursebook. If they can't find the mistake, tell them to check the sentences in the previous units in the Coursebook.

> **2** the; **3** do; **4** shop; **5** the; **6** than; **7** A; **8** got;
> **9** much; **10** to

LOOK BACK

12

> talk about your favourite film: 4.1, exercise 8;
> say what you can do: 4.2, exercise 6; ask for
> information: 4.3, exercise 9; read about speed 5.1,
> exercises 2, 3 and 4; listen to people talking about
> cities: 5.2, exercise 8; sell a flight: 5.3, exercise 10;
> find out about healthy food: 6.1, exercises 2 and
> 3; make a request: 6.3, exercises 10 and 11; write
> about a restaurant: 6.4, exercise 12

7 Shopping

7.1 CONSUMER HABITS

Lesson topic and staging

This lesson looks at the topic of shopping. Students begin to think about the subject by discussing how often they buy certain things. Then they read an article about different types of shopper like the *frequent shopper* and the *window shopper*. In the next part of the lesson students work with vocabulary to do with shopping. In the grammar section students study the form and the meaning of the present continuous for actions happening now. They continue working with this tense by listening to a number of extracts from mobile phone conversations using the present continuous and then completing a text about Christmas shoppers that contrasts the present simple with the present continuous. The lesson finishes with three conversations between shoppers and shop assistants.

Objectives

By the end of the lesson students should have:

- talked about their shopping habits
- found out about different types of shoppers by reading an article on the topic
- learned (more) vocabulary to talk about shopping
- revised and extended their knowledge and use of the present continuous to talk about actions happening now
- learned some useful language for shopping

Timings

If short of time, you could drop exercise 4 on page 59. Students could do this exercise for homework.

A possible lesson break would be after exercise 4 and before the grammar focus on page 59.

WARM-UP

This is a prediction activity to get students thinking about the content of the lesson.

- Write the unit title *Shopping* on the board.
- Ask students to write down the names of any shops they know, for example *bookshop*.

SPEAKING

1

Preteach: *furniture* (objects such as chairs, tables and beds), *make-up* (coloured creams and powders that a woman puts on her face to make herself look more attractive), *stationery* (things such as paper and envelopes that you use for writing)

- Students do activity as per Coursebook. You could write the question *What's 'X' in English?* on the board so that students can ask for help with words they don't know when they discuss the third question.
- When students have finished ask them to report back on the things they regularly buy.

READING

2

Preteach: *suit* (a jacket and trousers or skirt that are made of the same material)

- Students do activity as per Coursebook.

> **José:** The speed shopper; **Hiromi:** The frequent shopper; **Vince:** The window shopper; **Ulrike:** The careful shopper

3 Ask students to read the sentences before they read the text again.

> **1** false (*It's expensive but I can pay for it.*); **2** false (*a coat, a shirt … a pair of shoes and a belt*); **3** true (*I'm looking for a digital camera. I'm thinking about buying this one …*); **4** false (*I'm not looking for anything special.*)

VOCABULARY: shops and shopping (1)

4a Students do activity as per Coursebook.

> **1** to pay for; **2** to check; **3** to spend; **4** to spend; **5** to buy; **6** to try on
> **Note:** we use the verb *spend* for time and money.

4b Students do activity as per Coursebook.

- Get students to discuss the questions after checking them.
- Ask a couple of students to tell the class about their partner.

> **1** spend; **2** check; **3** try on; **4** pay for; **5** buy; **6** spend

GRAMMAR: present continuous (1)

(!) Some languages do not have a continuous form. Students may incorrectly use the present simple to talk about things happening now:

What do you read? What do you look at?

There are also verbs in English that are not used in the continuous form. This will cause the occasional problems, such as:

I'm not understanding.

5a Students do activity as per Coursebook.

(☼) If the concept and/or form is different in students' language, you could ask them to translate the sentences in the text into their language. Alternatively, talk about any differences in English by asking students: *Are these sentences the same or different in your language?*

> 1b – present simple; 2a – present continuous

5b Get students to look back at the text and circle or underline any other examples of the present continuous.

(☼) Draw students' attention to the adverbials of time that are used in the text with the present continuous, e.g. *at the moment, today, right now*. Knowledge of phrases like these is particularly useful in exam situations, where students may be required to provide the correct tense using such clues.

> **José:** At the moment, I'm looking for a new suit.
> **Hiromi:** Right now, I'm carrying five new things …
> **Vince:** I'm not looking for anything special. Right now, I'm waiting for my friend. She's trying on a pair of jeans.
> **Ulrike:** Today, I'm looking for a digital camera. I'm thinking about buying this one …

5c Students do activity as per Coursebook.

> 1 'm; 2 are; 3 is; 4 'm not; 5 he/she/it; 6 is not

For a full explanation and further practice activities, go to page 134 in the Language Reference.

`2.2`

6 Get students to complete these sentences before they listen. You could ask them how *can* is used in sentences 1, 3 and 4 (1 to mean 'not possible'; 3 idiomatic, with verbs of perception such as *see* or *hear*; 4 as a request).

> 1 'm trying on; 2 'm driving; 3 'm standing; 4 's waiting; 5 're, arriving; 6 'm putting

Track 2.2
1 I can't talk now, I'm trying on some trainers.
2 Call me back later. I'm driving.
3 Can you see me? I'm standing at the corner, opposite the bank.
4 Can I call you back? The waiter's waiting for me to order.
5 We're just arriving at the bus station. See you in five minutes.
6 I'm in the car park. I'm putting the food in the car.

7 Students do activity as per Coursebook.

(!) Some students may confuse the present simple and present continuous because in certain languages the present simple is used for both concepts. You could write these two examples on the board and ask students: *Which sentence means 'All the time. It is my home.'? (b) Which sentence means 'At the moment. It's only temporary.'? (a)*

1 I'm living in Canada.
2 I live in Canada.

> 2 'm looking for; 3 'm looking at; 4 listens; 5 don't live; 6 is; 7 'm having; 8 'm wearing

LISTENING AND WRITING

`2.3`

8 Ask students to read the list of phrases. Students do activity as per Coursebook.

> **Possible answers: 1** … on shoes; **2** He's in a bookshop. He's ordering a book. **3** She's in a clothes shop. She's buying a shirt.

Track 2.3

1

Shop assistant, Customer

SA: Do they fit?

C: Yes, they feel fine.

SA: Walk around the shop and check they're OK. There's a mirror over there. How do they feel?

C: OK, but perhaps the left one is a little small.

SA: Right, well, try a bigger size.

2

SA: Can I help you?

C: Yes, I'm looking for *Birds Without Wings*.

SA: I'm afraid we don't have that one in the shop.

C: Oh, I see. That's a pity. I really want to read it.

SA: We can order it for you.

C: Really? Great! Thanks very much.

SA: That's fine. Can I have your name …

3

SA: OK, so that's 15 pounds. How would you like to pay?

C: By credit card, please.

SA: Fine.

C: Here you are.

SA: Thank you. Can you enter your number please?

C: Of course.

SA: Great. Here's your receipt, and here's your shirt. I've only got a large bag, I'm afraid.

C: That's fine. Thank you very much. Bye.

9 Ask students to read the dialogues on pages 150–151.

• Get students to write a similar dialogue in pairs.

• Tell them to practise the dialogue. You could ask one or two pairs to act out their dialogues in front of the class.

HOMEWORK OPTIONS

Students do/finish the extra practice activities 1, 2, 6 and 7 on page 135 in the Language Reference.

Students do the exercises on pages 42–43 of the Workbook.

7.2 SHOPPING TRENDS

IN THIS LESSON

Lesson topic and staging

This lesson looks at the topic of shopping at supermarkets and then shopping on the Internet. The lesson begins with students covering key vocabulary that appears in an article on the British supermarket giant, *Tesco*. In the second half of the lesson, students listen to an interview that explores the rising popularity of online shopping. The listening provides the context for the grammar focus of the lesson – the present continuous for actions happening around now. After working with this tense the lesson finishes with a discussion on the changing face of shopping in town centres and on the Internet.

Objectives

By the end of the lesson students should have:

• talked about their shopping habits

• learned more about British shopping culture, supermarkets and online shopping

• learned (more) vocabulary to talk about shopping

• revised and extended their knowledge and use of the present continuous to talk about actions happening around now

• discussed shopping in their country

Timings

If short of time, you could leave the discussion in exercises 10a and 10b until the beginning of the next class.

A possible lesson break would be after exercise 5 and before the listening on page 61.

WARM-UP

This warm-up activity gets students thinking about the differences between shopping in the past and shopping today.

• Write the title of the lesson, *Shopping Trends*, on the board. Explain that it means the way that shopping is changing or developing. Then ask students how shopping in the past is different from shopping today. For example, in the past people went to a shop to buy things. Today people can buy things on the Internet.

VOCABULARY: shops and shopping (2)

1

Preteach: *discount* (a lower price than usual), *hypermarket* (a very large shop outside a town that sells many different kinds of food and other things), *product* (something that is made and sold by a company), *service* (providing help or doing a job for people), *supermarket* (a large shop that sells food, drink, cleaning products, etc.), *online shopping* (using a computer that is connected to the Internet to buy things)

• Students do activity as per Coursebook.

> discount and price; hypermarket, supermarket and store; Internet shopping and online shopping

2 Ask students to work in pairs or small groups to talk about the questions.

• Get a couple of students to share their answers with the whole group.

READING

3 Explain that this is a speed reading activity. Students have 30 seconds to decide if the text is about 1, 2 or 3. Say, 'Go!'

• Stop them after 15 seconds and check their answers.

> 2 a growing supermarket

4a Check students understand all the words in the headings.

• Get students to read the first paragraph and ask them which heading is correct. Then get them to continue reading on their own and matching headings in the right places.

> **A** A success story; **B** Number and location of stores; **C** Products and services; **D** The effects of supermarkets

4b Students do activity as per Coursebook.

> **1** £1; **2** 1,000; **3** 30 percent; **4** 15 million

5 Students do activity as per Coursebook.

> **1** false (*… makes about 100 euros a second*);
> **2** false (*Tesco has over are 1,000 stores in the UK and about 600 in countries in Central/Eastern Europe and East Asia.*); **3** false (*The non-food business is growing very quickly …*); **4** true (*… a lot of small independent shops are closing down*);
> **5** doesn't say; **6** true (*As a result, some town centres are dying.*)

To extend this activity, write the following questions on the board. Discuss the questions as a whole-class activity or get students to work in small groups to discuss them.

1 What do you think about the success of supermarkets like Tesco?

2 What can governments do to help small stores?

3 What can ordinary people do to help small stores?

GRAMMAR TIP

Read through the grammar tip together and make sure students understand the idea of *a changing situation*. Point out that sentences 3 and 5 in exercise 5 both show situations that are changing.

LISTENING

6 Students do activity as per Coursebook. When students are finished ask a couple of people to tell the whole group what they discussed.

`2.4`

7a Ask students to read the topics before you play the recording. You might want to clarify the meaning of *get business*, i.e. 'find business/customers'.

> 1c; 2d; 3e; 4a; 5b

> **Track 2.4**
> *Presenter, Linda*
> P: Good afternoon and welcome to our weekly shopping programme *Shopaholic*. Now, are you an online shopper? Or do you prefer to queue at the supermarket? Linda Stanley of *Consumer World* magazine is with us in the studio to talk about Internet shopping. Hello, Linda.
> L: Hi there!
> P: First of all, Linda, is Internet shopping becoming really popular now?
> L: Yes, it is. It's becoming part of our lives. More and more people are buying online.
> P: Mmm, so what are they buying?
> L: Books and CDs are the most popular things, and then travel. People are also spending a lot of money on health and beauty, and food and drink. For example, they're using the online services of supermarkets for big or heavy things like bottles of water.
> P: Interesting. And <u>how</u> are people using the Internet to shop? I mean, how do they start?
> L: Well, people are usually online for 12 to 18 months before they try online shopping. They usually start with something simple like books.
> P: Yes, it's great for books. Are people comparing prices on the Internet now?
> L: Yes, they are. It's easy to compare prices – there are special websites for this. So the Internet is giving people a lot of power.
> *continued…*

> P: I see. I guess men enjoy using the Internet. What about women? Are <u>they</u> using the Internet for shopping?
>
> L: Yes, they are. Definitely. More and more women are shopping online. The great thing about the Internet is this: it's 24/7. You can shop online all day, every day. This is very good news for busy women with jobs and children.
>
> P: Of course. And what are companies doing to get business on the Internet?
>
> L: Well, some companies are offering big discounts to get new customers. You can get a Harry Potter book, for example, for half price.
>
> P: Is this the end of traditional shopping – you know, people going to shopping centres and supermarkets?
>
> L: No, I don't think so – not just yet, anyway. Perhaps in the future. Right now, people are moving between the Internet and real shops to save time and money.
>
> P: Well, it all sounds very exciting. Thanks for coming in and telling us about it, Linda.
>
> L: My pleasure.

7b Get students to try to read through the notes and complete any gaps they can in pairs from memory before you play the recording again.

> **1** books, CDs, travel, health and beauty, food and drink; **2** books; **3** prices; **4** women; **5** discounts; **6** time, money

GRAMMAR: present continuous (2)

8a Ask students to read and complete the sentences and then check their answers with the audioscript on page 151.

> **1** Internet shopping; **2** What; **3** using; **4** Are

📝 To extend this activity, and emphasise how we use the present continuous to talk about a changing situation, write the following sentences on the board:

MOTHER:	What are you doing?
SON:	I'm buying a present for Dad online.
FRIEND ON MOBILE:	Where are you and what are you doing?
FRIEND ON MOBILE:	I'm in a shop. I'm buying a CD.
MOTHER:	Anna is on the phone for you.
DAUGHTER:	I can't speak to her now. I'm sending an important email.

Ask students what the difference is between the sentences you've written on the board and the sentences in exercise 8a. (All the actions on the board refer to *actions happening as we speak*. In contrast, all the sentences in exercise 8a refer to *changing situations, over a period of time*.)

8b Students do activity as per Coursebook.

> **1** *to be*, question; **2** subject; **3** after

For a full explanation and further practice activities, go to pages 134–135 in the Language Reference.

9 Students do activity as per Coursebook.

❗ Students may have problems with the spelling of the present participle. For example, in *travel* the consonant *l* is doubled to become *travelling*. The main focus here is on understanding the tense but if students make spelling mistakes, correct them. You don't need to go into the spelling rules yet.

> **1** Are you travelling; **2** Are you learning;
> **3** Are you going out; **4** are people reading;
> **5** are people watching

SPEAKING

10a Ask students to rearrange the questions on their own.

• Allow students some preparation time before they talk about the questions with their partners.

> **1** How are people's shopping habits changing?
> **2** What are young people buying these days?
> **3** How much money are big supermarkets making?
> **4** What are stores doing to get business?
> **5** What changes are happening in town centres?
> **6** How are people using the Internet?

🔆 Preparation or 'Rehearsal' time is very important to the quality of students' responses. Research has shown that when students are given time to prepare themselves for a role-play or a discussion by thinking about what they will say, they almost always do better. In teaching terms this simply means giving them time to think about an activity before they do it. If it helps students, they can make notes, ask you or their classmates for help or just sit and think about what and how they will say something.

10b Students do activity as per Coursebook.

HOMEWORK OPTIONS

Students do/finish the extra practice activities 3 and 4 on page 135 in the Language Reference.

Students do the exercises on pages 44–45 of the Workbook.

7.3 SCENARIO: AT A MEETING

Lesson topic and staging

Students read about an American city, Charleston, and then look at differences between some British English and American English vocabulary. Next, students listen to two people, Brad and Zara, talking about their plans to open a bookshop and the advantages and disadvantages of opening it in the town centre. This language is drawn out of the listening and is the focus of the Key Language section of the lesson. Students work on the meaning, form and pronunciation of this functional language and are then ready for the main focus of the lesson, the task phase. In the task students have to help Brad and Zara with their bookshop plans. Students have to find out about different parts of the city and then report back to their partners. They then decide which is the best shopping area for the bookshop. The lesson finishes with a writing stage in which students write a short paragraph explaining their choice of location for the bookshop.

Objectives

By the end of the lesson students should have:

- learned about Charleston in the USA
- learned how to talk about the advantages and disadvantages of doing something
- learned how to describe places
- learned to identify word stress in simple sentences
- discussed and come to an agreement about the best place to locate the bookshop
- written a short, simple paragraph explaining their choice of location for the bookshop

Common European Framework

Students can describe the advantages and disadvantages of doing something.

Timings

If short of time, you could drop exercise 7a. This exercise on sentence stress is important and should be covered at some future point.

A possible lesson break would be after exercise 6b and before the focus on pronunciation on page 63.

Make sure you leave sufficient time at the end of the lesson to prepare for, complete and discuss the task in exercise 9.

This is an editing task in which students have to correct the grammar, spelling, vocabulary and punctuation.

- Write the conversation below on the board before the lesson begins if possible. Tell students that there are six mistakes. There are mistakes in grammar, spelling, vocabulary and punctuation.
- Tell students to find and correct the mistakes.

PABLO: So what changes happen in the town centre?
JOANNA: Well, they build a new supermarket.
PABLO: A new soopamarket! That's good.
JOANNA: No, I'm afraid not. Much small shops are worried about the future.
PABLO: Why?
JOANNA: Because supermarkets sell a lot of different things: books DVDs food clothes.
PABLO: Oh, and is that a problem?
JOANNA: Yes! Supermarkets are cheaper as small shops!

Corrected conversation:

PABLO: So what changes <u>are happening</u> in the town centre?
JOANNA: Well, they <u>are building</u> a new supermarket.
PABLO: A new <u>supermarket</u>! That's good.
JOANNA: No, I'm afraid not. <u>Many/A lot of</u> small shops are worried about the future.
PABLO: Why?
JOANNA: Because supermarkets sell a lot of different things: <u>books, DVDs, food and clothes</u>.
PABLO: Oh, and is that a problem?
JOANNA: Yes! Supermarkets are cheaper <u>than</u> small shops!

1   Make sure students understand the task; it encourages a personal response to the text.

- Ask a few students what they think of Charleston. Ask if they would/wouldn't like to visit the city and why / why not.

2   Tell students that there are some differences between British and US English in vocabulary, grammar and pronunciation. Ask if they know of any differences, and then get them to do the activity.

> 1c; 2d; 3b; 4e; 5f; 6a

3   Get students to try to describe the pictures as well as match them to the sentences. This will revise some of the language from exercise 2 as well as introduce new language and prepare students for what follows in the lesson.

> 1B; 2A; 3C; 4D

4   Check that students understand the meaning of *advantage* and *disadvantage*. Use examples relevant to the students if necessary.

> **1** advantages: 1, 2, 3, 4, 5; **2** disadvantages: 6, 7;
> **3** students' own opinions

2.5

5

Preteach: *rent* (money you pay to live in a place or to use something such as a car)

- Make sure students read the sentences carefully before they listen.

> All of the points except 4 are mentioned.

> **Track 2.5**
> *Brad, Zara*
> B: So, what advantages does downtown have?
> Z: Well, first of all, I think it's a nice place for people to visit, and there are some interesting local shops.
> B: Oh yeah? What are they?
> Z: Well, there are some cafés and there's a music shop, and also an art shop. This means that people there are interested in the books we sell.
> B: OK. Are there any more advantages?
> Z: Yes, another advantage is that the area is safe – crime is low. And, of course, there's a bus station.
> B: Right. What about the disadvantages?
> Z: I think there are two main disadvantages. One disadvantage is that the rent is high and the other is that a lot of people go to the shopping mall outside the town. This means that sometimes there aren't very many customers downtown.
> B: I see. So, the area is a nice one, but the rent is expensive and most people go to the mall.
> Z: Yes.
> B: Mmm. What do you know about the shopping mall?
> Z: Well, it's …

KEY LANGUAGE: giving advantage and disadvantages

6a Ask students to read through the sentences and complete any gaps they can in pairs before you play the recording again.

> **1** have; **2** first; **3** think; **4** more; **5** another; **6** about; **7** main; **8** disadvantage; **9** other; **10** means

6b Students do activity as per Coursebook.

> **1** 1, 3 and 5; **2** 2, 4, 6, 7 and 8; **3** 9

pronunciation

2.6

7a Students do activity as per Coursebook.

> **Track 2.6**
> 1 Well, first of all, I think it's a nice place for people to visit.
> 2 Yes, another advantage is that the area is safe.
> 3 I think there are two main disadvantages.
> 4 One disadvantage is that the rent is high …
> 5 … and the other is that a lot of people go to the shopping mall outside the town.
> 6 This means that sometimes there aren't very many customers downtown.

7b Students do activity as per Coursebook.

Stressed words in English are sometimes called 'content' words because they carry the important content or information. These words tend to be nouns, adverbs, adjectives and main verbs. The other words in a sentence or phrase are unstressed. These tend to be 'grammar' words, i.e. words that hold a sentence together like articles, prepositions, conjunctions and auxiliary verbs. By not stressing these words they become 'reduced' and are said more quickly. This allows the speaker to maintain a stress pattern that is, more or less, regular.

You can show students the effect of 'content' versus 'grammar' words quite easily. Draw three columns on the board. In the middle column write this simple dialogue and ask students to tell you which words are stressed (they are underlined below).

PEDRO: <u>Hello</u>. <u>What's</u> your <u>name</u>?
JOHN: Oh, <u>hi</u>. I'm <u>John</u>. And <u>you</u>? <u>What's</u> <u>your</u> <u>name</u>?
PEDRO: My <u>name's</u> <u>Pedro</u>. <u>Where</u> are you <u>from</u>?
JOHN: <u>Manchester</u>. And <u>you</u>? Are you from <u>Spain</u>?
PEDRO: <u>No</u>, I'm from <u>Venezuela</u>.

When you are finished, write all the words that are not stressed in the first column. Ask students if they could understand this conversation if they had not heard it before – they should say *no*. Then ask students to write down in their notebooks the conversation with only the stressed words in it. Could they understand this one if they had not heard it before? This somewhat simplified version of the effects of stress helps students to see how the concept works.

8 Students do exercise as per Coursebook.

If you feel your students are not ready to move straight into exercise 8, you could do the following:

- Get students to read through the audioscript (page 151) first.

- Then divide the class into 'Brads' and 'Zaras'. They have to say their parts at the same time as the recording is playing.

- Get students to swap and play the other person as you replay the dialogue. This will prepare them for exercise 8.

TASK: describing places

Task summary: In the task students work in groups of three. Each one reads about a different potential location for the bookshop. They then exchange information, talking about the advantages and disadvantages of each location. A successful task outcome is when the group is able to discuss the advantages and disadvantages of each shopping area and to decide on the best location for the bookshop.

9a Explain the task and task outcome to students.

- Divide students into As, Bs and Cs and get them to read about their locations.

9b Students do activity as per Coursebook.

9c Get students to look at the OTHER USEFUL PHRASES and practise the phrases if necessary.

- Let students discuss the situation and monitor them. Remind students to try to use the Key Language on page 62 (giving advantages and disadvantages) as well as any other language that you feel is important.

- When most students have finished ask a group to report their decision. See if the rest of the class agrees.

- If you feel it's necessary, spend some time looking at examples of correct and incorrect English.

WRITING

10 Ask students to provide endings for all the OTHER USEFUL PHRASES and write them on the board to model how they can be used.

- Then write up this framework to help students structure the paragraph.

  I think the best shopping area for the bookshop is _____. There are _____ main advantages. The first is that _____. That means _____. The second advantage is _____. That means _____. I don't think _____ is the best shopping area because _____.

- Ask students to use their notes from exercise 9b plus their discussion in 9c to write the paragraph.

HOMEWORK OPTIONS

You could ask students to write a short paragraph about where to open a bookshop, or a shop of their choice, in their town or city.

Students do the exercises on page 46 of the Workbook.

7.4 STUDY AND WRITING SKILLS

IN THIS LESSON

Lesson topic and staging

In the first part of the lesson students look at the stages in preparing a talk. They then listen to a short talk about the famous British department store, Harrods, and take notes. They listen again and note down useful language for giving talks. After discussing the problems people can have when giving a talk, students practise giving a talk by repeating the one on Harrods. This is a rehearsal for giving a very short talk on their favourite shop or the best/worst/most unusual shop in their town. The second part of the lesson begins with a discussion about buying books. This leads into reading two informal emails in which a woman asks her brother for advice on which book to buy for his partner. Students are then given a problem-solving task: they have to pick a book for that person based on the information in the emails and the 'blurb' written on the back covers of three books. Students analyse the emails for certain words and phrases used in greetings, opening phrases and endings. Then some work on the linking words *because* and *so* prepares students for the final task: emailing a classmate to ask for and give advice on which music CD or film DVD to buy for another classmate.

Objectives

By the end of the lesson students should have:

- learned a set of stages for preparing a talk
- learned useful language for giving a talk
- thought about common problems people have giving talks
- given a simple talk about a shop they know
- learned about the British department store, Harrods
- analysed how greetings, opening phrases and endings are expressed in informal emails
- written two simple, informal emails asking for and giving advice

Common European Framework

Students can write a simple, informal email asking for and giving information/advice.

Timings

If short of time you could drop exercise 8.

A possible lesson break would be after exercise 7 and before the Writing Skills section of the lesson on page 64.

WARM-UP

This is a quick activity to revise the British versus American English vocabulary in Lesson 7.3.

- Tell students that you are going to test their American English.

- Ask students to write the numbers 1–6 in their notebooks.

- Read out the British English words in column 2 of exercise 2 on page 62. Students have to write the equivalent word or phrase in American English.

- Check students' answers, including their spellings.

STUDY SKILLS: giving a short, informal talk

1a Students do activity as per Coursebook. Do the first item with students so they understand how the activity works.

> 1d; 2e; 3f; 4a; 5c; 6b

1b Students do activity as per Coursebook.

> **Suggested answers:**
> 1 Find out some interesting information. 2 Put your ideas in the best order. 3 Prepare some pictures or tables to make your points clearer. 4 Make some notes to help you remember things in the talk. 5 Check the pronunciation of difficult words. 6 Practise the talk.
> Accept all answers that are logical.

`2.7`

2

Preteach: *department store* (a large shop that sells many different types of things)

- Ask students if anyone recognises the shop in the picture, and if they know anything about it. Tell them that they will hear more about it in the listening exercise.

- Get students to read the topics and then play the recording.

> **Students should tick:** 1, 3 and 4

> **Track 2.7**
> *Teacher, Nicolas*
> T: Are you ready to give your talk, Nicolas?
> N: Of course.
> Good afternoon everybody. In this short talk, I'd like to tell you about my favourite store – Harrods, the huge department store in London. The building is beautiful, especially at night, when there are hundreds of lights outside. It's open every day of the week, including Sundays. There are seven floors, I think. You can find everything in Harrods: clothes, watches, books and DVDs, children's toys, things for your home and sports equipment. You can even buy a famous green Harrods shopping bag. And Harrods can order anything you want! It's famous for its fantastic food halls, and there are about 25 cafés and restaurants. One of the most interesting things is that there's even a doctor in the store – as well as a bank. To finish, I think Harrods is the best department store in the world! That's all. Thank you.

3 Ask students how they make notes. Do they use sentences, words, pictures, mind maps?

- Get students to complete the notes with words from the box.

> 1 department; 2 building; 3 every; 4 floors; 5 food

4 Students do activity as per Coursebook.

> a tell you; b famous; c most interesting; d finish

5 Students do activity as per Coursebook.

> **Additional possible answers:** the person speaks in a very low voice; the person has a very flat voice which sounds boring; the person moves a lot or doesn't move at all; the person keeps repeating the same information; the person stops all the time and looks at their notes; the person reads from a script rather than from notes, and never looks up; the information in the talk is boring, etc.

6 This exercise gives students a chance to rehearse a talk based on a model they have already heard. Students do activity as per Coursebook.

7 Students do activity as per Coursebook. Stress that they must make notes first and that they have to talk for one minute.

WRITING SKILLS: an informal email

8 Students do activity as per Coursebook.

9 Students do activity as per Coursebook. Get students to justify their opinions by referring to evidence in the text (see answers below).

Nick and Miranda are probably brother and sister. They have the same surname, *Jones*.
Nick is probably Paula's boyfriend or husband. This is clear because Nick knows her taste in books very well and they are going to South America or Japan the following year.

10 Get students to look at the three book covers and see if they know anything about the books or the authors.

- Ask them to read the information about each book and say which, if any, they are interested in.

- Get students to do the task and ask them to explain why they think the book they've chosen is the best for Paula.

The best book for Paula is *Of Love and Shadows* by Isabel Allende. It's 'a great love story' and she likes love stories. It is set in South America and Paula and Nick want to go to South America.
My Name is Red would be second choice because it's a thriller and a love story, and it's historical in a sense. However, it is set in Istanbul, not South America or Japan.
Black Rain isn't a good choice even though it is set in Japan because it is about Hiroshima and Paula doesn't like war books.

11 Students may not know the meaning of *Greeting, Opening phrase* or *Ending* but the terms should be clear from the examples. Students do activity as per Coursebook.

Greeting: Dear …, Hi
Opening phrase: How are things? How are you? Hope you're OK.
Ending: Bye for now, Love, Take care
Note: *Dear …* is normally used in neutral or formal emails when the writer doesn't know the reader (very well). *Dear …* would normally be an inappropriate greeting in an informal email.

12 Write these sentences on the board and ask students to complete them with a word.

James likes books about history, Japan and war ____ I want to buy him Black Rain.

I want to buy him Black Rain *____ he likes books about history, Japan and war.*

- If they can't complete the sentences, tell them the missing words are *because* and *so*. If they still can't do it, complete the sentences for them and ask them two questions:

  1 Which word answers the question *Why*? (*because*)

  2 Which word means *because of that*? (*so*)

- Get students to look for examples in the emails, and then complete the sentences.

First email: Just a quick message *because* I'm very busy today.
Second email: We want to go to South America … *so* maybe you can get her …
1 so; **2** because; **3** so; **4** because

If your students are strong, you could get them to transform the sentences from *so* to *because* and vice versa. For example, *Books are very expensive in my country so I don't buy many.* → *I don't buy many books because they are very expensive in my country.*

13a Explain the task to students and tell them to get into pairs.

- Draw a piece of paper on the board and write the following on it: *My name is ____ and my partner's name is ____.*

- Tell each student to rip out a piece of paper and complete it with their name and their partner's name.

- Collect in all the pieces of paper, check you have as many as there are students and then redistribute them, one piece per student.

- Tell students to write to the first person on the piece of paper and ask him/her about what music CD or film DVD to buy for his/her partner.

- When students are ready, tell them to deliver their 'emails' by hand.

13b Get students to read their 'emails' and to reply using the second email in the Coursebook as a model. They then deliver their replies to the original writers.

- Ask students to read the replies.

- Finally, ask students to tell the person in the class they wrote about the birthday present they planned to buy. Was it something they would like?

If your class is too big to do the last step, ask students to pass the emails to the person they wrote about. They should enjoy reading the questions and answers. Ask a few students if they are happy with their proposed birthday present.

HOMEWORK OPTIONS

If students have not finished their emails, ask them to do so for homework.

Alternatively, you could ask them to write another email suggesting ideas for someone else in the class, or even for you, the teacher!

Students do exercises on page 47 of the Workbook.

History and culture

8.1 PAST TIMES

IN THIS LESSON

Lesson topic and staging

This lesson looks at the ancient city of Çatal Hüyük in Turkey and the ancient Mayan, Inca and Aztec civilisations. Students learn some basic vocabulary about buildings in preparation for a reading on Çatal Hüyük, one of the world's first cities. The reading provides the context for the grammar focus, the past simple of *to be*, and for the pronunciation of the weak (unstressed) forms of *was* and *were*. Students then combine this with work on common past time phrases like *six weeks ago* and *last week*. The lesson finishes with a speaking and a writing activity. Students find out and exchange information about the Mayas, Incas and Aztecs. They then use this information and write a few sentences about one of the cultures.

Objectives

By the end of the lesson students should have:

- learned (more) about the ancient city of Çatal Hüyük and the Mayan, Inca and Aztec civilisations

- learned a basic set of vocabulary to describe parts of buildings

- learned (more) about the use of the past simple of *to be*: affirmative, negative and question forms

- improved their awareness and pronunciation of the weak forms of *was* and *were*

Timings

If short of time, you could drop exercise 3 on page 67. Students could do this exercise for homework.

A possible lesson break would be after exercise 3 and before the grammar focus on page 67.

WARM-UP

This is a revision activity which recycles *so* and *because* from Lesson 7.4.

- Write these sentences on the board:

  Ana likes classical music so we want to buy her a CD by Mozart.

  We want to buy a DVD of The Incredibles *because Tomas likes comedy and animation films.*

- Ask students in small groups to see how many sentences they can write about the birthday presents from last lesson (exercises 13a and 13b).

- Get some students to tell the group what they have written.

VOCABULARY: buildings

Preteach: *courtyard* (an outdoor area surrounded by walls or buildings), *entrance* (the way into a place)

You should be able to preteach the rest of the words through the context of the picture or the classroom.

1a Students do activity as per Coursebook.

> Students may be able to identify some or all of the following: courtyard, door, entrance, garden, gate, ladder, roof, wall. There is also a picture of a painting at the bottom of page 66.

1b You might want to do this as a whole-class activity. Ask for or elicit an example and write it on the board to model what students could say. For example:

The houses are smaller than my home. There aren't any roads.

To extend this activity, you could ask students to explain why they like or don't like these buildings. This would recycle the use of *because* and *so*.

I don't like the building because there are no windows.

READING

Preteach: *BC* (an abbreviation for 'Before Christ', used in dates to mean before the birth of Christ), *peaceful* (not violent), *trade* (the business of buying and selling things, especially between countries), *goddess* (a female god), *community* (a group of people who live in the same town or area)

2a Tell students that they are going to read about the city where the people in the picture in exercise 1 lived. Make sure they understand that they only need to read the first paragraph to answer the questions.

> 1c; 2b

2b Students do activity as per Coursebook. Make sure students quickly skim the text to answer the questions, rather than read it in detail.

> 2C; 3A; 4B

3 Students do activity as per Coursebook.

> 1 place; 2 population; 3 farming; 4 good; 5 unusual

GRAMMAR: past simple of *to be*

4a Check students know that there are two forms of *to be* in the past simple form (*was* and *were*) before they do this activity.

> There are many examples in the text.

4b Students do activity as per Coursebook.

> **1** was; **2** were; **3** was; **4** wasn't; **5** weren't; **6** weren't; **7** weren't; **8** were; **9** was

For a full explanation and further practice activities, go to pages 136–137 in the Language Reference.

5 Students do activity as per Coursebook.

> **1** were; **2** were; **3** was; **4** Were; **5** wasn't; **6** was, was; **7** weren't, were, were

pronunciation

`2.8`

6a Remind students of weak and strong forms (as covered in Lesson 4.2, exercises 5 and 6). Ask them first to mark the stresses in sentences 1 and 2; they should mark them as follows:

    •   •

1 The city was lovely.

    •   •

2 There were gardens everywhere.

• Ask students to listen for the vowel sound in *was* and *were*.

> In both words the vowel sound is the schwa /ə/.

Track 2.8
1 The city was lovely.
2 There were gardens everywhere.

`2.9`

6b Let students listen to the sentences.

• Play the sentences one by one and get students to repeat after each one by pausing the recording.

Track 2.9
1 The city was lovely.
2 There were gardens everywhere.
3 It was very safe, too.
4 The people were kind.
5 The women were beautiful.
6 The streets were busy.
7 There was an interesting market.

7a

⚠ Check that students know the position of these past time phrases. *Last* + time can go at the beginning of a sentence, but it normally goes at the end of a sentence. *Ago* always goes at the end of a sentence:

I was in London ago three years. ✗

I was in London three years ago. ✓

Also, point out that we don't use *last* with time periods smaller than a week (so we can say *last year*, *last week*, but we don't say *last day, last hour, last minute*, etc.).

> two hours ago, yesterday, the day before yesterday, last week, last month, six weeks ago, last year, 1,000 years ago

7b Check students' answers before they begin to discuss the questions with their partners.

• Ask a few students the first question to model different answers.

• Get a few students to report back something about their partner: *Umay's birthday was last week.*

> **2** When was your last holiday? **3** When was your last school exam? **4** When was your last visit to a museum?

SPEAKING AND WRITING

8a

ℹ The Mayas were an Indian group that lived in Meso-America (or Middle America). They lived in modern-day Mexico, Guatemala, Honduras and Belize. They were astronomers and mathematicians who introduced the concept of zero to mathematics as well as a solar calendar of 365 days. We actually base our calendar on this one. When the Spanish arrived in 1517 the Mayas were already in decline.

The Incas were an Indian group which lived in the Andes mountain chain that runs along the west coast of South America. The Incas created a powerful and sophisticated empire that grew out of their capital city Cuzco and lasted for a century until the arrival of the Spanish in 1532.

The Aztecs were originally a wandering Indian tribe from Northern Mexico. They settled in what is now Mexico City in 1325 where they built the magnificent city of Tenochtitlan. The Aztec empire grew but in 1519 the Spanish *Conquistadores* defeated the Aztec emperor Montezuma II and the empire came to a sudden end.

• Ask students what they know about the three civilisations. Don't spend too long on this activity because students will find out more in the next stage of the lesson.

8b

Preteach: *modern-day* (used, for instance, for the name we now give to a place), *AD* (an abbreviation for 'Anno Domini', used in dates to mean after the birth of Christ)

- Explain the task to students: they each have a table with information about the three civilisations, but with different bits of information missing. They have to ask each other questions to find out the missing information.

- Divide students into As and Bs, and let them read the information on pages 112 and 117. When students are ready get them to work together to complete their tables. You might want to give or elicit the questions they will need, i.e.

  Where was the civilisation?

  When was the main period of the civilisation?

  What was the capital city?

  What were the abilities and skills of the people?

  When was the end of the civilisation?

9 Get students to write about one of the civilisations. You could work with the whole group and use the information in the tables to write sentences about the Mayans on the board as a model for students.

  The Mayans were in modern-day Mexico, Guatemala, Honduras and Belize.

  They were important between 600 BC and AD 250.

  There were many important cities. Chichén Itzá was the most important (city).

  The Mayans were writers, astronomers, mathematicians and builders.

  The end of the Mayan civilisation was about AD 900.

HOMEWORK OPTIONS

You could ask students to write about an old civilisation they know about.

Students do/finish the extra practice activities 1, 2, 3 and 7 on page 137 in the Language Reference.

Students do the exercises on pages 48–49 of the Workbook.

8.2 THEN AND NOW

IN THIS LESSON

Lesson topic and staging

This lesson looks at how the world is changing by examining the stories of people from China, Afghanistan and Northern Canada.

The lesson begins with a reading about people living in these countries and how their worlds have been changed by economics, government and climate change. The reading contextualises the grammar focus on *could* and *couldn't* to express possibility, impossibility, permission and ability in the past. Students work with this and contrast it with *can/can't*. Students then listen to a talk given by two students on how technology has 'made our world smaller' and changed culture. The impact of improved transport, TV and the Internet has shrunk our world and made things possible that weren't so two generations ago. The next stage of the lesson examines verb and preposition combinations (for example *to focus on a topic* and *to move onto another topic*). The final activity allows students to talk about their own personal experiences of change by saying how their lives compare to the lives of their grandparents.

Objectives

By the end of the lesson students should have:

- learned (more) about China, Afghanistan and the Inuits who live in Northern Canada
- extended their knowledge and use of *could* and *couldn't* to talk about possibility, impossibility, permission and ability in the past
- learned some common verb and preposition combinations
- discussed the differences between their way of life now and their grandparents' when they were young

Timings

If short of time, you could drop exercise 10b and ask students to do it for homework.

A possible lesson break would be after exercise 7 on page 69, before the listening.

WARM-UP

This activity revises some vocabulary and information students learned about the ancient civilisations of the Mayas, Incas and Aztecs.

- Tell students that you want to see how much they remember about the civilisations they studied last lesson.

- Tell them to work in pairs or small groups and write two sentences about each civilisation. Write this sentence on the board to show them the type of thing you expect:

The Mayan civilisation was in Mexico, Guatemala, Honduras and Belize.

READING

Preteach: *to go abroad* (to go to a foreign country), *economy* (the way that money and business are organized in a country or area), *can afford to do something* (have enough money to buy something), *air conditioner* (a machine that controls the temperature in a building), *laws* (rules that people in a country must obey), *Inuits* (a group of people who live in the very cold northern areas of North America and parts of Siberia)

1 Get students to read through the sentences and mark them true or false. Encourage them to write more sentences if they can.

- Discuss students' answers with the whole group. Encourage them to say more about their ideas if they can.

2a This exercise develops students' ability to get the gist or general idea of a text, so encourage them to read the article quickly by setting them a time limit of 30 seconds.

> **1** China; **2** Afghanistan; **3** the Inuits, who live in Northern Canada

2b

Preteach: *economics* (the study of the way that a country produces money and things to sell)

- Students do activity as per Coursebook.

> **1** economics; **2** government; **3** climate

3 Students do activity as per Coursebook

> **1** P; **2** P; **3** P; **4** N

4 Explain to students that they have to imagine from the context who says these things.

- Ask students if any of the information in the article surprises them. Are any of the changes happening in their families, towns/cities or countries?

> **1**d; **2**a; **3**e; **4**b; **5**c

GRAMMAR: *could, couldn't*

⚠ *Can* and *can't* refer to the present and *could* and *couldn't* to the past. Some students may ask why we use *Could* for requests in the present if it refers to the past. Explain that in English we usually use *Could* when the situation is formal, e.g when we speak to an older person we don't know, or when the request

is for a big favour. The form *Could* is past but the meaning is present. Compare:

Could I borrow £10,000, please? = a big request to a bank manager.

Can I borrow your dictionary? = a small request to a classmate.

5a Students do activity as per Coursebook.

> **1** drive; **2** travel; **3** travel; **4** learn

5b This exercise focuses on the form of *could* and *couldn't*. Get students to underline all the examples in the text.

> c

For a full explanation and further practice activities, go to pages 136–137 in the Language Reference.

6 Ask students to see if they can complete the sentences without looking at the text. They can then check their answers by looking at the article.

> **1** could; **2** couldn't; **3** can, couldn't; **4** can't, could

7 Ask students to look at the list and give them time to think about their answers.

- Get students to talk about the prompts in pairs.

- Invite a few students to tell the whole class one thing about their partner (perhaps something that surprised them).

LISTENING

[2.10]

8

Preteach: *pollution* (harmful chemicals and waste, and the damage they cause to the environment), *stranger* (someone who you do not know)

- Tell students to listen carefully for the title. It comes at the beginning of the recording.

> **1** A Smaller World; **2** car, plane, television, the Internet

> **Track 2.10**
> *Tutor, Nathan, Marjorie*
> T: OK everyone! Today's presentation is by Nathan and Marjorie. Start when you're ready, Nathan.
> N: OK. Hello everyone. Our presentation is called *A Smaller World* and it's about technology and cultural change. The talk focuses on technology that makes the world smaller, for example television.
>
> *continued…*

(Track 2.11)

M: First of all, can you imagine life without cars and planes? Before the invention of these means of transport, people could only travel by train or boat, and they couldn't travel very fast. Now, with cars and planes, we can travel further and faster. Some people even live in one country and work in another because they can fly to work. Fifty years ago, people certainly couldn't do that. And of course, many people fly thousands of miles to go on holiday, and while their grandparents could only read about distant places, they see them. Before we move onto the next type of technology, it is important to remember that planes and cars do have their negative points. They can be dangerous and they cause a lot of pollution, and this also changes the way we live.

(Track 2.12)

N: OK. Second, communications technology, like television and the Internet, certainly makes the world smaller. We stay in our house or office, but we can see news and shows from all around the world. With the Internet, we can write and chat to people all over the world. This is an incredible invention. We can find anything we want in seconds. It makes the world smaller, and it makes it faster! But do these things have any negative points? Well, yes, they do. Nowadays, people spend more time using the technology than they do meeting other people. We're spending more and more of our time in our houses, talking to strangers in other countries, than we are with our friends and neighbours. My grandmother could name all the people in her street, but I don't even know the names of my neighbours!

M: So, you can see that technology changes our way of life and culture, in both positive and negative ways. A lot of technology makes the world a smaller place, but does it make it a better place?

T: OK. Thank you Nathan and Marjorie, that was great. Are there any questions?

2.11

9a Make sure students read the sentences before they listen again to the first part of the presentation by Marjorie.

> 1, 2, 4 and 5

2.12

9b Give students time to read the questions first and then play the second part of the presentation.

- Encourage students to justify their opinions when they answer the third question.

1 We can stay in our house or office and see news and shows from all around the world. With the Internet, we can write and chat to people all over the world. We can find anything we want in seconds.

2 People spend more time using the technology than they do meeting other people. We're spending more and more of our time in our houses, talking to strangers in other countries, than we are with our friends and neighbours.

VOCABULARY: verbs + prepositions

10a Students do activity as per Coursebook. Play the recording again and get students to check their answers with the audioscript on pages 151–152.

> **2** holiday; **3** places; **4** the next type of technology; **5** our house; **6** people; **7** strangers

10b Students do activity as per Coursebook.

> **1** focuses on; **2** reading about; **3** move onto; **4** chat to / talk to; **5** go on; **6** stay in; **7** talk to / chat to

SPEAKING

11 Students do activity as per Coursebook.

🔧 If you feel your students will find this difficult, write some or all of the topics below on the board to guide them. Tell them they can talk about these or other ideas.

transport TV the Internet telephones clothes food music dance sport school work religion marriage

- Give students time to think about ideas and to ask you any questions they may have, for example about vocabulary.

- Get one or two students to give you their ideas about the differences as a model for the other students.

- Allow students sufficient time to talk as much as they can about the topics.

- Get some of the students to tell the whole group one of the things they talked about.

HOMEWORK OPTIONS

Students do/finish the extra practice activities 4 and 8 on page 137 in the Language Reference.

Students do the exercises on pages 50–51 of the Workbook.

8.3 SCENARIO: AT A MUSEUM

Lesson topic and staging

This lesson looks at the British Museum in London. Students begin with a brief discussion about the museum, and then match examples of *can* and *can't* for permission to notices that you might find in a museum. This leads into a listening in which two people working in a museum answer questions from six visitors. The listening contextualises the Key Language focus on polite requests. Students work with the meaning, form and pronunciation of this language before moving on to the main focus of the lesson: the task. Students study general information about the British Museum, such as opening and closing times. They then use this information to role-play a visitor and someone who works at the museum by asking and answering questions about the museum.

Objectives

By the end of the lesson students should have:

- learned about the British Museum in London
- learned to recognise common notices such as 'Way Out' and 'Do not touch'
- learned how to make and respond to polite requests
- developed their awareness of linked sounds in phrases and sentences
- role-played the parts of a museum visitor and a person who works at a museum and made and responded to polite requests to find out about important information

Common European Framework

Students can make and respond to polite requests.

Timings

If short of time, you could drop exercises 7 and 8. These exercises are important and should be covered later.

A possible lesson break would be after exercise 6b and before the focus on pronunciation on page 71.

Make sure you leave sufficient time at the end of the lesson to prepare for, complete and discuss the task in exercise 10.

WARM-UP

Tell students they are going to look at a famous museum in the UK. Get them to talk about their opinions and experiences of museums by discussing these questions in pairs/small groups:

1 How many museums can you name in your town or city?

2 When did you last go to a museum? Which one was it?

3 Do you have a favourite museum? What do you like about it?

4 Is there a museum you don't like? Why don't you like it?

PREPARATION

1 Students do activity as per Coursebook.

i The British Museum is one of the most famous museums in Britain. It has hundreds of collections from different cultures and periods, for example the Egyptian, Mayan and Japanese civilisations.

The Great Court, also called the Queen Elizabeth II Great Court, was completed in 2000. It was designed by the architect Sir Norman Foster and cost £100 million to build. It includes the inner courtyard of the British Museum and is covered by a glass and steel roof, which was designed by computer.

> 1 The British Museum is in London.
> 2 Hundreds of collections from different cultures and periods in history.

2

Preteach: *lift* (a machine that takes you up and down in a building)

- Students do activity as per Coursebook.

> 2E; 3I; 4G; 5C; 6B; 7H; 8F

2.13

3 Make sure students read the topics before they listen; they have to order them according to the recording.

Stop the recording after every conversation so students have enough time to find and number the right topic.

> 2a; 3d; 4c; 5b; 6e

Track 2.13
1
Visitors, Richard, Jessica
V1: Excuse me.
R: Yes, madam. How can I help you?
V1: Could you tell me where the cloakroom is, please?
R: Certainly, madam. Can you see those stairs over there?
V1: Yes, I can.
R: Well, go down those stairs and then turn left. The cloakroom is next to the toilets.
V1: Thank you.
R: You're welcome.
2
V2: Excuse me, could you help me, please?
J: Yes, of course. What would you like?
V2: Well, I'd like to go on a guided tour. Could you tell me how much it costs?
continued...

J: Certainly, sir. Are you interested in the long or the short tour?

v2: Oh, the short one, please.

J: OK, well a short tour costs two pounds.

v2: Oh that's cheap, could you tell me how much the long one costs?

J: Yes, of course. That's five pounds. Which would you like?

v2: Erm, the short one please.

3

v3: Excuse me.

R: Yes madam, how can I help?

v3: Well, I'd like to see a film about the Egyptian Mummies. Could you tell me when the next film starts?

R: Of, course, let me just check … erm, yes, it starts at 2.30.

v3: At 2.30?

R: Yes, madam. That's right.

v3: OK. Isn't there one before that?

R: I'm afraid not, madam. We only show the film in the afternoon.

v3: OK, thank you.

R: You're welcome.

4

v4: Excuse me.

J: Yes, sir, how can I help?

v4: I'm really interested in this statue. Could you tell me how old it is?

J: Mmm, let me see … Yes, this is a Roman statue, it's about 2,000 years old. It's a statue of Venus, the goddess of love.

v4: I see, it really is lovely. Thank you.

J: Not at all.

5

v5: Excuse me.

R: Yes, madam?

v5: We're visitors. Could you give us a map of the museum, please?

R: Of course, madam. Where do you come from?

v5: Italy. Why?

R: Well, would you like the map in Italian or English?

v5: Oh, could you give us both please, so we can practise our English?

R: Certainly. There you are.

v5: Thank you very much.

R: Not at all. Enjoy your visit!

6

v6: Excuse me.

J: Yes, sir?

v6: I'm here with my friends. Could you take a photo of us? Next to the mummy?

J: Oh. I'm afraid not, sir. You can't take photographs in the museum.

v6: Really? Oh dear, I only want you to take one quick photo.

J: I'm afraid I can't do that. Why don't you take one outside, after your visit?

v6: OK, we can wait.

J: Thank you. Enjoy the rest of your visit.

v6: Thank you.

4 Students do activity as per Coursebook. Pause the recording after every conversation to allow students time to write their answers.

> **1** down the stairs, on the left, next to the toilets; **2** £5; **3** 2.30; **4** 2,000 years old; **5** two (one in English and one in Italian); **6** outside the museum

KEY LANGUAGE: polite requests

5 Students do activity as per Coursebook.

> 2a; 3c; 4e; 5g; 6h; 7d; 8b

6a Students do activity as per Coursebook.

(!) Students may have problems with the word order in the embedded questions *Could you tell me + how much it is?* and *Could you tell me + where the cloakroom is, please?* They may try to invert the second clause and say:

Could you tell me how much is it?

Could you tell me where is the cloakroom, please?

Point out how the question is inverted in the first clause and so is NOT inverted in the second part of the question. Don't go into further detail at this stage.

> **1** help; **2** give; **3** take; **4** how; **5** costs; **6** where; **7** is; **8** when; **9** starts; **10** how; **11** is

6b Students do exercise as per Coursebook.

> **Saying *yes* politely:** That's no problem. Certainly. (Yes,) of course. Yes, sir/madam.
> **Saying *no* politely:** I'm sorry, I'm afraid … I'm afraid not. I'm afraid I can't do that.

pronunciation
`2.14`

7 The focus here is on the linking between *could* and *you*. Show students on the board like this.

Could you …

- Play the recording. See if students can pick out the sound used when the two words are linked.

> *Could* and *you* combine to make the sound /dʒ/ where they join, i.e. /kʊdʒʊ/.

> **Track 2.14**
> 1 Could you help me, please?
> 2 Could you tell me when the next film starts?
> 3 Could you give us a map of the museum, please?

`2.15`

8 Students do activity as per Coursebook. Get students to listen and repeat the requests.

Audioscript and answers:
Track 2.15
1 Could you open the door, please?
2 Could you take my coat, please?
3 Could you tell me when the museum closes?
4 Could you tell me what this means, please?
5 Could you tell me where the shop is?

9 Students do activity as per Coursebook.

TASK: finding out important information

Task summary: In the task students work in pairs. Firstly, Student A plays the part of someone who works at the British Museum. He or she has to answer the visitor, Student B's questions about the museum. Students then reverse the roles and ask and answer new questions. A successful task outcome is when 'visitors' have asked polite questions and the people who work in the museum have given clear, polite responses.

Preteach: *senior citizen* (a person who is over the age of 65), *souvenir shop* (a shop that sells something you keep to help you remember a place), *hot meal* (hot food that you eat at lunch or dinner time), *afternoon tea* (a light meal of tea and cake or biscuits).

10 Explain the task and task outcome to students, and look at the OTHER USEFUL PHRASES with them.

- Divide the students into As and Bs. Tell As to study the information about the museum and ask Bs to turn to page 117 and prepare their questions. Remind them to think about the OTHER USEFUL PHRASES.

- Pair up As with Bs, remind them to try to use the Key Language on page 70 and let them role-play the situation. Monitor the activity and take notes.

- When the students are finished see if they have any questions before they swap roles and do the role-play again as per Coursebook.

- When the students are finished look at task achievement by asking these questions: were all their questions answered? Were the people in the museum polite? Did the visitors use polite requests to find out information? See if students have any questions.

- Move on to language performance and give students feedback on how they did.

HOMEWORK OPTIONS

You could ask students to find out information about a local museum to tell their classmates about next class.

Students do the exercises on page 52 of the Workbook.

DICTIONARY REMINDER

Ask your students to make a note to bring their dictionaries to class for the next lesson.

8.4 STUDY AND WRITING SKILLS

IN THIS LESSON

Lesson topic and staging

In the first part of the lesson students look at a list of different ways to record vocabulary and they say which techniques they use. They then go on to examine five different ways of working with words, such as putting words into categories or making mind maps. Students are then encouraged to think about which of these ideas they personally find useful when they learn vocabulary. The second part of the lesson is about learning how to write a simple description of an object. Students begin by matching pictures to a category, followed by matching a description to a picture. After completing a gap-fill exercise, students analyse how the pronouns *it* and *they* and the determiners *this* and *these* are used to link references in a text. Students then study a text, a model for the final task of using notes to write a simple paragraph describing an object.

Objectives

By the end of the lesson students should have:

- reviewed and extended their knowledge of ways of recording and learning new vocabulary

- reviewed and extended their knowledge of ways of working with new vocabulary in order to learn it better

- analysed basic descriptions of objects

- written a simple description of an object

Common European Framework

Students can write a simple description of an object.

Timings

If short of time, you could drop exercises 3 and 10.

A possible lesson break would be after exercise 6b on page 72.

WARM-UP

This is a quick activity to revise vocabulary introduced in Lesson 8.3. Tell students that you are going to test them on vocabulary from pages 70 and 71. Give students three minutes to look at these pages. While students are doing this write the following gapped words up on the board. If you can, cover them up so students can't see them.

Stop the students after three minutes and ask them to work on their own and write down the complete words.

1 _u_eum	2 _hee_ _hair
3 l_ ft	4 sou_e_ir
5 e_hibi_ion	6 _ame_a
7 sh_p	8 _loak_oo_
9 _ _atue	10 _ _stairs

> 1 museum; 2 wheelchair; 3 lift; 4 souvenir;
> 5 exhibition; 6 camera; 7 shop; 8 cloakroom;
> 9 statue; 10 upstairs

STUDY SKILLS: learning new words

1 Ask students what techniques they use to write down new vocabulary, for example writing the word in a sentence or translating it into their language.

- Students do activity as per Coursebook.
- Have a brief class discussion about the things students do. You could suggest that they pick two ways that are new to them and try them for a week or two.

Many students tend to think that learning a language is about learning more words and more grammar. Just as important is learning how to learn, i.e. learning strategies that make you a more effective learner. Effective students develop a range of strategies for different situations. Encourage students to see the type of activity that follows as a shortcut to learning more quickly. Encourage students to try out new strategies. It is best to be systematic about this. For example, at the end of this part of the lesson ask students to circle all the new strategies. Tell them to pick three they want to try and to use them every time they learn new vocabulary. In two weeks' time, allow 10 minutes at the beginning of the lesson to talk to students about what they think of these new techniques. When teachers give time to study skills and stress the value of them, students see the importance of them. Hopefully, as a result, they will see their learning become more effective.

2 You may prefer to do the exercises one by one, checking with all the group after each exercise.

a Students do activity as per Coursebook.

> Materials: leather, metal, plastic, wood
> Shapes: circle, rectangle, square

b Students do activity as per Coursebook.

> The adjective for *circle* is *circular*.
> rectangle – rectangular; square – square; wood – wooden
> 1 width; 2 widen; 3 lengthen; 4 long; 5 weight

c Students do activity as per Coursebook.

> Possible answers: orange, yellow, green, blue, white, pink

d Students do activity as per Coursebook.

> heavy – light; long – short; narrow – wide

e Students do activity as per Coursebook. You may want to limit the words students use in order to help you check their answers.

> Accept all logical answers.

3 Students do activity as per Coursebook. You may want to limit the words students use in order to help you check their answers.

> Accept all logical answers.

4 This activity is a review of the strategies students use when learning new vocabulary. Get students to read exercises 1 and 2 again and to circle the activities they think could be useful for them.

- Discuss their answers. Naturally, students will have different answers as they have different learning styles.

WRITING SKILLS: a description of objects

Preteach: *Internet auction site* (a place on the Internet where people sell things to the person who offers the most money, e.g. the website *ebay.com*), *antique* (an old and unusual piece of furniture, jewellery, etc. that costs a lot of money)

5 Ask if your students have ever bought or sold anything on an Internet auction site. Do they think it's a good way to shop? Students do activity as per Coursebook.

> A Antiques: games; B Antiques: Asia;
> C Collectables: North America

6a Students do activity as per Coursebook.

> Photo B

6b Students do activity as per Coursebook.

> 1 unusual; 2 musical; 3 rectangular; 4 yellow;
> 5 red

7 Students do activity as per Coursebook. You may want to point out that *it* is used as a substitute for a noun. The determiners *this* and *these* combine with a noun to identify something, e.g. *I like these colours / this colour.*

> it = the photograph album; it = the photograph album; it = the photograph album; these pages = the ten pages; it = the wonderful picture

8

Preteach: *scratch* (a long thin cut on something)

- First ask students to read the text and match it to one of the three photos. They should ignore the missing words for the moment.

> The description goes with picture C.
> **1** This; **2** It; **3** it; **4** It; **5** It; **6** it; **7** This; **8** These; **9** they

9a Use photo A to preteach the word *dominoes*. Ask students if they play dominoes and tell them they are going to write a description of a box of dominoes.

- Get students to use the notes in the box to complete the first sentence of the description.

> **1** China; **2** 90; **3** a/one

9b Divide students into As and Bs. Ask As to write about the box and Bs to write about the dominoes. Tell them to use the model text in exercise 8 to help them.

- Monitor students and answer any questions they have as well as pointing out any problems individual students are having.

- When students are finished ask them to swap their work and read and check their partner's work.

- If you have a strong group of students, you could ask them to write both paragraphs of the description.

- To extend this activity, you could recycle correction codes with students.

- Write the correction code letters on the board and ask students to tell you what they mean.

Gr = _____ Sp = _____ Cap = _____

(*Gr* = grammar; *Sp* = spelling; *Cap* = capitalization)

- Write the following sentence on the board. Tell students to copy it down and to use the correction code to show where the mistakes are.

These photograph is of a beuatiful mountain in japan.

- Ask students what codes they used and then ask them to correct the mistakes.

- If appropriate, you could also use the codes *P* for punctuation and *WW* for wrong word.

> These photograph is of a beuatiful mountain in japan.
> (Gr) (Sp) (Cap)
> This photograph is of a beautiful mountain in Japan.

- Tell students to help their partners by correcting any mistakes they find with a pencil. They should use a pencil in case they actually make a mistake when correcting.

- When students are finished they should hand their partners' paragraphs back to them and discuss any corrections.

- Ask students if they have any questions.

> **Model texts:**
> This description models the text in exercise 8. Students may organise their descriptions differently. Accept all descriptions that are logical and grammatically correct.
> **The box**
> The wooden box is square and it is 20cm wide. It is red and it has a picture of flowers on it. This box is in good condition and the picture is in excellent condition.
> **The dominoes**
> In the box there are 28 plastic dominoes. They are rectangular and they 4cm long and 2cm wide. The dominoes are white with black spots and they are in very good condition.

10 Use this last activity as a brief discussion which ties up the lesson.

HOMEWORK OPTION

If students have not finished their descriptions, ask them to do so for homework. Alternatively, you could ask students to write the description of another simple object.

Students do the exercises on page 53 of the Workbook.

Inventions

9.1 MARVELLOUS MINDS

IN THIS LESSON

Lesson topic and staging

This lesson examines the work of the famous inventors Alfred Nobel, Levi Strauss and in particular Leonardo da Vinci. Students find out about the life and work of da Vinci and his inventions such as the precursors to the robot, the car and the helicopter. The text contextualises the grammar focus on the past simple (affirmative). Students work with the tense including the pronunciation of the regular verb endings: /d/, /t/ and /ɪd/. Students then broaden their knowledge of the tense by looking at irregular past tense forms such as *went, had* and *got*. After personalising the language in a speaking activity about their last weekend, students read and write a short text about Alfred Nobel or Levi Strauss.

Objectives

By the end of the lesson students should have:

- learned (more) about the life and work of Leonardo da Vinci, Alfred Nobel and Levi Strauss

- learned (more) about the use of the past simple of regular and irregular verbs in the affirmative

- improved their awareness and pronunciation of the endings of regular verbs in the past simple: /t/, /d/ and /ɪd/

- learned to talk about how they spent their last weekend

- read and written a short text about Alfred Nobel or Levi Strauss

Timings

If short of time, you could drop exercise 8 on page 75. Students could do this exercise for homework.

A possible lesson break would be after exercise 4 and before the Grammar section.

WARM-UP

This is a prediction activity.

- Write the unit and lesson titles up on the board: *Inventions* and *Marvellous Minds*.

- Ask students what they think the lesson will be about.

- Let them check their predictions by looking at pages 74 and 75 for a couple of minutes.

- Answer any questions they may have.

READING

ⓘ Alfred Bernard Nobel was born in Sweden in 1833. He studied chemistry in Paris and then went on to work on explosives, especially nitroglycerin. Sadly, an explosion at a factory he built specially for producing nitroglycerin safely led to the death of his brother and four other workers. Nobel worked hard and in 1866, he produced a safer explosive, dynamite. During his lifetime he invented a number of other things and became a rich man. Before he died he set up the Nobel Prize, which is given to individuals and organisations whose work helps humanity in some way.

Levi Strauss was born in Germany in 1829. When Strauss was 16 he decided to emigrate to the USA. He began to work there with his two brothers in the textile and tailoring business. When he heard that people were making money from gold in California he decided to move there. He wanted to make tents for workers but nobody wanted to buy tents so he used the material to make trousers for workers. A little later he changed the material to a strong cotton from France called *serge de Nîmes*. *De Nîmes* soon became *denim* and *denim trousers* became popularly known as *blue jeans*. Levi Strauss's jeans were very popular and made him a fortune. He was a generous man and gave a lot of his money away to help others. He died in 1902.

1

Preteach: *to invent* (to think of or to make something completely new), *inventor* (someone who thinks of or makes something completely new), *invention* (a completely new thing that someone thinks of or makes)

- Students do activity as per Coursebook. Have a brief discussion with the whole group about what they know.

2

Preteach: *high heels* (women's shoes with high heels), *parachute* (a large piece of cloth that people use when they jump out of a plane, to make them fall through the air slowly and come to the ground safely), *robot* (a machine that can move and do jobs like a person), *telescope* (a piece of equipment like a long tube that you use to look at things that are far away)

- Students do activity as per Coursebook.

the robot, the car, the helicopter, the diving suit

3 Students do activity as per Coursebook.

> **1** false (*He studied at home …*); **2** false (*he moved to the city of Florence for art classes … He then worked in Milan as an engineer …*); **3** true (*he had the first ideas for many machines that we use today …*); **4** false (*The robot … held things in its arms.*); **5** true (*It travelled 40 metres at a time.*); **6** false (*This is different from the modern design …*); **7** true (*Today, divers use them on their feet!*)

4 Students do activity as per Coursebook. You could use the activity to recycle comparatives by writing an example sentence on the board, for example *I think the car is more important than gloves because we use cars much more than gloves.*

GRAMMAR: past simple (affirmative)

5a Students do activity as per Coursebook. When you check students' answers teach them the spelling rules page 138.

Infinitive	Past simple
live	lived
study	studied
enjoy	enjoyed
want	wanted
move	moved
finish	finished
work	worked
start	started
return	returned
travel	travelled
stay	stayed

For a full explanation and further practice activities, go to pages 138–139 in the Language Reference.

`2.16`

5b Students do activity as per Coursebook.

> **Audioscript and answers:**
> **Track 2.16**
> 1 Leonardo started his studies of art in 1468.
> 2 He finished these studies in 1472.
> 3 He wanted money so he started work as an engineer.
> 4 Leonardo worked as an engineer for 32 years.
> 5 He lived in Milan from 1472 to 1500. / He stayed in Milan from 1472 to 1500.
> 6 He returned to Florence after 28 years in Milan. / He moved to Florence after 28 years in Milan.

`pronunciation`

`2.17`

6a Students do activity as per Coursebook.

> **Track 2.17**
> enjoyed, helped, needed

You might want to teach students the rules for the pronunciation of past simple *-ed* endings:

1 They are pronounced /d/ after voiced consonants (/b/ /ʒ/ /dʒ/ /g/ /l/ /m/ /n/ /ŋ/ /r/ /z/ /v/ /w/) and all vowel sounds, for example *played* and *cal**led***.

2 They are pronounced /t/ after unvoiced consonants (/p/ /s/ʃ/tʃ/ /k/ /f/ /s/), for example *finis**hed*** and *tal**ked***.

3 They are pronounced /ɪd/ after the sound /t/ or /d/, for example *wan**ted*** and *nee**ded***.

To help students with the idea of 'voiced' versus 'unvoiced' sounds write these verbs on the board in two columns.

/t/	/d/
talk → talked	live → lived
watch → watched	study → studied
stop → stopped	move → moved

- Ask students to put their hands firmly on their throats and get them to try the two exercises below.

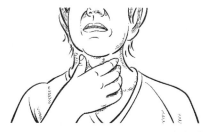

- Get them to repeat the last sound in *talk*, /k/. Ask them if they can feel movement under their hands or not. They shouldn't feel any movement. Explain this is because the sound /k/ is a 'voiceless' sound.

- Compare the 'voiceless' sound of /k/ with the last sound in *live*, /v/. Ask students to put their hands on their throats again and pronounce /v/. Can they feel any movement? They should do. Explain that this is because /v/ is a 'voiced' sound.

- Get students to repeat /k/ and /v/ as many times as they like until they feel the difference in the two sounds.

6b

- Ask students to write the three symbols in their notebooks and then to put the verbs in exercise 5b in the correct column.

- Students check their answers and repeat the sentences.

/d/	/t/	/ɪd/
lived	finished	started
stayed	worked	wanted
returned		
moved		

GRAMMAR TIP

Look at the box with students and point out that some past simple forms are irregular.

7   Students do activity as per Coursebook.

> 1 stood; 2 sat; 3 held; 4 drove; 5 made

For a full explanation and further practice activities, go to pages 138–139 in the Language Reference.

8   Explain the task to students. Point out that some of the verbs are regular and others are irregular. See if they can complete the sentences without looking at the irregular verb list first.

• Let students check their answers by looking at the irregular verb list on page 159. Make sure they look at the past simple, not past participle forms in the list.

> 1 saw; 2 went; 3 visited; 4 stayed; 5 got; 6 studied;
> 7 lived; 8 came

SPEAKING

9   Explain the task to students and ask them what verbs they need. Write the infinitive forms on the board. Elicit the past simple forms and put them on the board too.

• Elicit a couple of examples of things students did the previous weekend and give students time to prepare their conversation.

• Get students to tell their partners what they did.

• Ask a number of students to tell the whole group one thing their partner did. Note any mistakes they make.

• Give feedback on students' mistakes by asking them to correct the mistake orally or by writing any mistakes on the board and getting students to correct them.

WRITING

10a

Preteach: *explosive* (a substance that can cause an explosion), *experiment* (a scientific test that you do in order to discover or prove something), *dynamite* (a substance that can cause powerful explosions), *miner* (a person who works underground in order to find coal, gold, etc.), *equipment* (the things that you use for a particular activity)

• Tell students to turn to page 121 and match the description of the inventor with their name.

• Check their answers and any language they have a problem with.

• Tell students to write a short text about the inventors based on the notes. They need to use the past simple form of the verbs given.

• Monitor students while they write and help them when they need it.

🔧 If your students are strong, ask them to write both descriptions. If they are not very strong, divide them into two groups and get one group to write about Nobel and the other to write about Strauss.

2.18

10b Students do activity as per Coursebook. They may want to listen more than once so they can correct their work as they listen.

> **Track 2.18**
> Alfred Nobel was born in 1833 in Sweden. He studied chemistry but he also wrote poetry, novels and plays. He tried to make a safe explosive, but, unfortunately, he killed his brother in an experiment in 1864. He invented dynamite in 1866. In 1895 he started the Nobel Prize Foundation.
> Levi Strauss was born in Germany in 1829. He travelled to New York in 1846 and moved to San Francisco in 1853. He started a shop for gold miners: he sold equipment and clothes. In 1873 he invented jeans – he used a material from Nîmes in France and called it 'denim'.

HOMEWORK OPTIONS

Students do/finish the extra practice activities 1 and 2 on page 139 in the Language Reference.

Students do the exercises on pages 54–55 of the Workbook.

DICTIONARY REMINDER

Ask your students to make a note to bring their dictionaries to class for the next lesson.

9.2 WHITE COATS

IN THIS LESSON

Lesson topic and staging

This lesson looks at the world of medical science. The title is a reference to the idea that doctors in hospitals and scientists in particular are famous for wearing 'white coats'. Students begin by reading about four famous medical inventions: the scalpel (a small, light and very sharp knife), acupuncture needles, false teeth and the microscope. The reading text contextualises the grammar focus on the past simple negative form. After some work on this students listen to a text about the invention and use in medicine of the MRI (magnetic resonance imaging) scanner. The listening text contextualises the next grammar focus: the past simple question form. Students work on the question form in the context of science and inventions before personalising the language in a speaking activity; students talk about their first experiences in life, for example the first time they ate foreign food or travelled alone.

Objectives

By the end of the lesson students should have:

- learned (more) about a number of important medical inventions such as the scalpel and the MRI scanner

- learned a set of vocabulary to talk about some basic medical science

- extended their knowledge and use of the past simple negative and question forms

- learned how to talk about some of their first experiences in life, such as flying and moving to a new house

Timings

If short of time, you could drop exercise 1 and ask students to do it for homework.

A possible lesson break would be after exercise 5 on page 76 and before the listening on page 77.

WARM-UP

This activity revises the pronunciation of the regular past simple verbs.

- Draw three columns on the board and label each with one of the three pronunciations of the simple past, /d/, /t/ and /ɪd/. Tell students to put the following verbs into the correct column, according to their past tense pronunciation: *live, finish, want, travel, talk, need, study, watch, visit, return, like, invent.*

Answers:

/d/	/t/	/ɪd/
lived	finished	wanted
travelled	talked	needed
studied	watched	visited
returned	liked	invented

VOCABULARY: medical science

1 Get students in pairs to choose the best words to complete the sentences without a dictionary.

- Let them use a dictionary to complete the sentences they couldn't do.

- Check answers with the whole group.

1 Medicine, treatment; 2 Teeth, bones; 3 scientist, laboratory; 4 equipment, experiments

READING

2 Use the photos to preteach the words they illustrate and then get students to match the pictures with the appropriate paragraphs.

A 3; B 4; C 2; D 1

3 Students do activity as per Coursebook.

1 Iraq; 2 4,000; 3 2000 BC; 4 China; 5 China; 6 false teeth; 7 Italy; 8 1770; 9 microscope; 10 1590; 11 small

To extend this activity, write the following questions about the text on the board and ask students to discuss them in small groups.

1 Which is the most important invention?

2 Which invention is important in your life?

3 Do any of your friends or family have acupuncture? Why?

4 Do you like the idea of acupuncture? Why? Why not?

5 Do you know anything about 'alternative medicines'?

- Ask the groups to report back their discussion to the whole group.

GRAMMAR: past simple (negative)

Students may have problems with the negative form of the past simple because the auxiliary *did* does not exist in other languages. As a result students may say things like:

I no went to the cinema last weekend.

I no goed to school last Friday.

Help students by pointing out the auxiliary and prompting them if they leave it out by saying *Auxiliary?* or *did?*

4 Students do activity as per Coursebook.

> **Students should underline:** did not make, did not change, did not give, did not use, did not want
> Rule: subject + *did* + *not* + infinitive without *to*

For a full explanation and further practice activities, go to pages 138–139 in the Language Reference.

5 Explain that the sentences are based on the text. Students do activity as per Coursebook.

> **1** used; **2** didn't invent; **3** didn't wear; **4** didn't change; **5** made; **6** didn't show

LISTENING

6a Get ideas from the whole class. It is important that students say something about the photograph so that they can manage the listening that follows. If students say very little, help them with questions. For example, *What type of machine is this? What does it do? When was it invented? What happens to the patient?*

`2.19`

6b Students do activity as per Coursebook.

> an MRI (magnetic resonance imaging) scanner

> **Track 2.19**
> *Presenter, Stephen Bayley*
> P: Welcome to this week's edition of *Understanding Science*. With me in the studio is Professor Stephen Bayley of Nottingham University. Professor Bayley, I'd like to start by asking you this question: what is the most important medical invention of the last 30 years?
> SB: Well, that's a difficult question because there are a lot of important inventions. Certainly, one of the most important is the MRI scanner.
> P: The scanner? Can you tell us something about it?
> SB: Yes, well, basically it's a big box with a hole in the middle …

7a

Preteach: *dangerous* (likely to harm you)

- Get students to read the sentences and guess the answers.

> **1** true (*Like an X-ray machine, the MRI scanner can look into our bodies …*); **2** false (*It can take a picture of the whole body …*); **3** false (*It's not dangerous, either, like X-ray machines.*); **4** false (*Another American, Raymond Damadian, and his team built the first full-body MRI scanner.*); **5** true (*In 1984, hospitals around the world bought their first MRI scanners.*)

`2.20`

7b Students do activity as per Coursebook.

> **Track 2.20**
> P: … And how does it work?
> SB: Well, you lie in the hole and the scanner takes pictures of you. Like an X-ray machine, the MRI scanner can look into our bodies, but normal X-ray machines can only show the hard parts of our bodies, the bones and teeth for example, while the MRI scanner can show both the hard and soft parts of the body, so it's more useful. It can take a picture of the whole body and you get the pictures very quickly. It's not dangerous, either, like X-ray machines.
> P: That's good. When did scientists invent it?
> SB: Well, it didn't happen overnight. In 1945, scientists discovered NMR – Nuclear Magnetic Resonance. In the 1950s an American scientist named Felix Bloch did some experiments in the lab and understood the importance of NMR for looking inside the human body.
> P: So did Felix Bloch invent the MRI scanner?
> SB: No, he didn't. Another American, Raymond Damadian, and his team built the first full-body MRI scanner.
> P: When did they do that?
> SB: In 1977.
> P: And when did doctors start to use this new machine?
> SB: A few years later. In 1984, hospitals around the world bought their first MRI scanners.
> P: It all sounds fantastic. Are there any problems with the scanner?
> SB: Well, it isn't good for people who don't like small spaces!

8 Get students to read the sentences before they listen again.

> **2** whole; **3** understood; **4** 1977; **5** 1984; **6** small spaces

GRAMMAR: past simple (questions)

[!] Students may have problems with the question form of the past simple, because the auxiliary *did* does not exist in other languages. As a result students may say things like:

Felix Bloch invented the scanner? If they make this common mistake, prompt them to correct themselves by saying, *Did?* or *Auxiliary?*

Another common mistake is when students put the auxiliary verb *did* after the subject of the sentence, for example

Felix Bloch did invent the scanner?

If students make this mistake, you can correct them by saying,

Is 'did' before or after the subject?
Alternatively, try saying, *Did Felix Bloch invent …?*

9 Students do activity as per Coursebook.

> **1** do; **2** before; **3** after; **4** the infinitive without *to*

GRAMMAR TIP

Study the grammar tip with the students. Get students to repeat the forms after you if they need accuracy practice.

For a full explanation and further practice activities, go to pages 138–139 in the Language Reference.

10 Students may not be familiar with some of these people. They can still do the activity though and can check their answers at the end of the exercise.

[!] Tell students that when we add a question word or phrase (*When, How long*, etc.) to a past simple question we put it in front of the auxiliary, as we do with present simple. For example:

Did Leonardo da Vinci live in Italy?

Where did Leonardo da Vinci live?

Did Leonardo da Vinci draw the first helicopter?

When did Leonardo draw the first helicopter?

- Check students have ordered the questions correctly before they talk about the answers.

> **1** Did Thomas Edison invent TV? **2** Did Europeans make the first paper? **3** What did Wilhelm Röntgen invent? **4** When did the Americans land on the moon? **5** Where did Christopher Columbus first arrive in America?

- Get students to discuss the questions in pairs before they check the answers on page 121.

SPEAKING

11 Look at the list of phrases and clarify any questions students have about meaning and pronunciation.

- Ask a few questions to different students to model the activity. Encourage students to extend the conversation as much as they can.

- Get students to pick a number of experiences that interest them and to think about the questions they want to ask their partner.

- Get students to talk to their partner and monitor and make notes if appropriate.

- Ask a few students to tell the whole class one thing about their partner.

- If necessary, look at students' language performance with the past simple.

HOMEWORK OPTIONS

Students do/finish the extra practice activities 3, 4, 5, 8 and 9 on page 139 in the Language Reference.

Students do the exercises on pages 56–57 of the Workbook.

9.3 SCENARIO: ON THE RADIO

IN THIS LESSON

Lesson topic and staging

This lesson continues with the theme of inventions: not inventions that have changed the world but everyday ones instead like the umbrella. Students discuss some everyday inventions like chewing gum and lipstick before listening to a radio programme about the invention and history of the umbrella. The listening provides the context for the Key Language focus on giving reasons. Students work with the meaning, form and pronunciation (sentence stress) of this language before moving on to the main focus of the lesson, the task. The task is to give a short presentation on an everyday object: the tin can, chewing gum, lipstick or the Post-it® note. Students prepare their talks and give them to small groups of classmates. At the end of the lesson, students vote for their favourite invention.

Objectives

By the end of the lesson students should have:

- learned about the history of the umbrella

- learned how to give reasons, e.g. *the umbrella is a great invention because …* and *the main reason is …*

- developed their awareness of sentences stress

- learned how to use sequencers when giving a talk

- learned how to prepare and give a short, simple presentation about an object

Common European Framework

Students can prepare and give a short talk on a simple object.

Timings

If short of time, you could drop exercises 7b and 7c.

A possible lesson break would be after exercise 7 on page 78.

Make sure you leave sufficient time at the end of the lesson to prepare for, complete and discuss the task in exercises 9 and 10.

WARM-UP

This activity revises key vocabulary from Lesson 9.2.

Write three headings, *Parts of the body, People* and *Equipment* on the board. Read out the following words randomly and ask students to write them under the correct heading: *bones, head, heart, teeth; doctor, engineer, inventor, scientist; acupuncture needles, microscope, MRI scanner, robot, scalpel, telescope, X-ray machine.*

PREPARATION

1 Students do activity as per Coursebook. You could use the photos to preteach the words and phrases for exercise 1.

> **A** chewing gum; **B** tin cans; **C** umbrellas; **D** lipstick; **E** Post-it® notes

2.21

2a

Preteach: *everyday* (ordinary, usual, or happening every day)

- Students do activity as per Coursebook.

☀ This is an intensive listening activity. Students have to listen for very specific information: the name of a programme and a telephone number. Explain this to them and be prepared to play the recording two or even three times.

> **1** favourite, invention; **2** 40 50 60

Track 2.21

Hello and welcome to *The nation's favourite everyday invention*, the show that tells you the story behind the everyday objects that we use in our daily lives. Each week, we tell you some key facts about the inventions and I tell you why I think they are wonderful or important. At the end of each programme, you can vote for your favourite invention. Simply send a text message to 0810 40 50 60, giving the name of your personal choice. So, vote for an invention and let's find our national favourite.

2b

Preteach: *texting* (sending a text message on a mobile phone)

- Get students to read the description first and try to complete any gaps they can before they listen again.

> **1** history; **2** normal; **3** information; **4** opinion; **5** choose; **6** texting

3a Students do activity as per Coursebook.

2.22

3b Students do activity as per Coursebook.

> **1** true (*in hot countries such as China, India and Egypt …*); **2** true (*First, many hundreds of years ago, rich and important people … used umbrellas; poor people… didn't have umbrellas*); **3** false (*Secondly, the Chinese invented the first umbrellas for use in the rain.*); **4** false (*Thirdly, umbrellas reached Britain about 400 years ago, but, at first, only women had umbrellas: men didn't like them.*); **5** true (*… the first umbrella shop, James Smith and Sons, opened in London in 1830 …*)

Track 2.22

The first of today's everyday inventions is that classic symbol of the English businessman – the umbrella. Nowadays, everyone has got one, but before 1750, men never carried umbrellas. So, what's the story of the umbrella, or brolly? Here are today's four facts.
First, many hundreds of years ago, rich and important people in hot countries such as China, India and Egypt used umbrellas. These rich people did not use their umbrellas in the rain, they used them in the sun. Of course, poor people worked in the sun, but they didn't have umbrellas.
Secondly, the Chinese invented the first umbrellas for use in the rain. They put oil and wax on their paper umbrellas.
Thirdly, umbrellas reached Britain about 400 years ago, but, at first, only women had umbrellas: men didn't like them. In 1750, Jonas Hanway, a British traveller, was the first man to use an umbrella on the streets of England. Other men followed his example and the umbrella at last became very popular in Britain.
And finally, the first umbrella shop, James Smith and Sons, opened in London in 1830, and it's still open today. And did you know that over 7,000 people lose an umbrella on London Transport every year, and all these umbrellas go to the Lost Property office. That's a lot of umbrellas!

2.23

4 Ask students to discuss the sentences in pairs before they listen to check their answers.

> 1, 3, 4, 5

Track 2.23

So, why vote for the umbrella?
Well, the most important reason is that it's one of the oldest inventions in the world. People found it very useful thousands of years ago, and we still find it useful today.
Secondly, the umbrella is a great invention because it's got several different uses. We can use it in the rain, we can use it in the sun and we can use it as a walking stick.
Thirdly, vote for the umbrella because umbrellas bring colour to our grey, rainy streets.
My final reason is that umbrellas are very cheap to make and cheap to buy.
So, that's the wonderful umbrella. When it rains, the rich and the poor can all stay dry. It's an invention for everyone. If you think this is the greatest everyday invention, vote now by sending a text message to …

KEY LANGUAGE: giving reasons

2.24

5 Students do activity as per Coursebook.

🔧 If your students are not very strong, write the answers on the board but jumble them up. Ask students to complete the sentences and then listen to check their answers.

1 most, is; 2 because; 3 because; 4 final, is

Track 2.24

1 Well, the most important reason is that it is one of the oldest inventions in the world.

2 Secondly, the umbrella is a great invention because it's got several different uses.

3 Vote for the umbrella because umbrellas bring colour to our grey, rainy streets.

4 My final reason is that umbrellas are very cheap to make.

---

6 Students do activity as per Coursebook.

Another / One / The main reason is (that) …
People buy umbrellas / Umbrellas are useful / Buy an umbrella because …

pronunciation

7a Students do activity as per Coursebook.

2 A good reason is that …
3 The second reason is that …
4 One reason is that …
5 Another reason is that …
6 The main reason is that …

`2.25`

7b Students do exercise as per Coursebook.

1 important; 2 good; 3 second; 4 one; 5 another; 6 main

Track 2.25

1 An important reason is that …
2 A good reason is that …
3 The second reason is that …
4 One reason is that …
5 Another reason is that …
6 The main reason is that …

7c It might help students to listen and repeat the phrases in the recording before they say them to their partner.

8 Ask students to look at the reasons given for learning English. Tell students to use the phrases and see how many other reasons they can add, for example *Another reason is that I like English pop music*.

- Get students to work through the other questions.

- When students have finished get them to give you one reason for each of the questions. Acknowledge good ideas first and correct the grammar second.

TASK: giving a short presentation

Task summary: In the task students work in pairs: pair A, B, C and D. Each pair reads notes about a different everyday invention: the tin can, chewing gum, lipstick or the Post-it® note. Students prepare the presentation in pairs. When they are ready they regroup and present their inventions to each other. A successful task outcome is when each student has managed to give a simple but well-structured presentation that their classmates can understand and learn from.

9a Explain the task and task outcome to students.

- Go over the stages of the preparation stage and make sure students are clear about exactly what to do.

- Draw their attention to the OTHER USEFUL PHRASES and tell them to use the phrases in their presentations. Also remind students to try to use the Key Language on page 78.

- Point out that they can use the audioscript for Tracks 2.22–2.23 on page 153 to help them structure the presentation.

- Put students into pairs and give the pairs a letter, A, B, C or D. As look at page 113, Bs look at page 118, Cs and Ds look at page 120.

- Allow students plenty of time to prepare for the task. They may want to ask you for help.

☀ Recent research has shown the positive effects of allowing students to 'rehearse' a task. This simply means that they try out the task with their partner or group before the 'real' performance. 'Rehearsal time' has been shown to produce much greater accuracy in students' language performance.

9b Regroup students and let them present their everyday objects to their group. Monitor the presentations and take notes.

- When the students are finished see if they have any questions.

10 Students do activity as per Coursebook.

- Then look at task achievement by asking these questions: *What did you learn from the presentations? What did you find most interesting? How clear were the presentations? How could the presentations be clearer?*

- Move on to language performance and give students feedback on how they did.

HOMEWORK OPTIONS

You could ask students to prepare another presentation at home.

Students do the exercises on page 58 of the Workbook.

9.4 STUDY AND WRITING SKILLS

IN THIS LESSON

Lesson topic and staging

The first part of the lesson focuses on study skills involved in taking notes while reading. Students talk about when and how they normally take notes before looking at two alternative methods for note-taking: a mind map and more conventional notes. Students then apply one of these note-taking styles to the text on Leonardo da Vinci from Lesson 9.1. The second part of the lesson focuses on writing a short biography. Students order events in the life of the inventor, Hedy Lamarr. They then listen and check their answers. The listening then provides some work on linking words for time such as *during, later* and *after that*. Students practise using these words in a text about Lady Ada Lovelace, the world's first woman in computers. Finally, students use information about the first African-American woman millionaire, Madam CJ Walker, to write a biography.

Objectives

By the end of the lesson students should have:

- reviewed and extended their knowledge of techniques for taking notes, including use of abbreviations
- revised and extended their knowledge and use of linking words for time such as *at that time*, *later* and *then*
- analysed the structure of a short biography
- written a short biography about a famous person

Common European Framework

Students can write a short biography describing a person's life. ·

Timings

If short of time, you could drop exercise 3 on page 80.

A possible lesson break would be after exercise 5 on page 80.

WARM-UP

This activity revises the past simple. It also tests students on how much they can remember about four everyday inventions from Lesson 9.3.

- Tell students that you are going to give them a test on how much they remember of the presentations from last lesson. Get students into small groups and tell them to write the numbers 1–10 on a piece of paper.

- Explain that you will ask 10 questions (although you could ask fewer), and they have to discuss the answer in their group and write down ONE answer only. They should appoint a group secretary who writes down answers and gives answers at the end of the quiz.

- Use the following information at the back of the Coursebook to ask your questions: tin cans on page 113; chewing gum on page 118; lipstick and the Post-it® note on page 120. For example, you could ask *When did the Englishman Peter Durand make the first metal can?* (Answer: 1796)

- When you are finished ask the group secretaries to give you their answers. Give a point for answers that are reasonably close (for example if students answer *1782* to the question above, give them a point.)

STUDY SKILLS: taking notes while reading

1 Students do activity as per Coursebook. Discuss some of the students' answers with the whole group so that students are exposed to other ideas.

2 Get students to look briefly at the two sets of notes before they do the activity.

> **1** paper; **2** travellers; **3** 6th c.; **4** Silk; **5** 9th c.; **6** northern Africa; **7** 1661
> **1** paper; **2** 6th c.; **3** Silk; **4** Gulf; **5** travellers

3 Students do activity as per Coursebook. Point out that abbreviations like those in question 2 also save time and space when taking notes.

> *A, the* and *in* are not normally used because they don't carry the key meaning most of the time, and leaving them out also saves times and space.
> **a** to; **b** and; **c** same word or phrase as above; **d** century

4 Students may not be used to discussing this type of question. Encourage students to explore this question. If your institution accepts use of the first language in the classroom, you could have this discussion in the students' language.

5 If students normally make conventional notes, encourage them to experiment by making a mind map of the text on da Vinci on page 75.

> Students' notes will differ, but should contain the main facts.

WRITING SKILLS: a short biography

6 Students do activity as per Coursebook.

i Some important women inventors are as follows:

Marie Curie (1867–1934)
Curie (born Maria Skłodowska) is famous for her work on radioactivity. She won the Nobel Prize twice, first in 1903 (with her husband, Pierre Curie, and her university tutor, Henri Becquerel) for the discovery of radium and polonium, and again in 1911 for the isolation of pure radium.

Evelyn Boyd Granville (born 1924)
Granville was one of the first two black women to obtain a Ph.D. in Mathematics. She wrote computer programs to follow vehicles in space and made important contributions to the US space program including Vanguard, Mercury and Apollo. She also worked at Space Technology Laboratories as a mathematical analyst studying rocket trajectories.

Grace Hopper (1906–1992)
Hopper was a mathematician and the driver for modern US computer technology. She used (but didn't invent), the term 'computer bug' after discovering that a moth had shorted out two tubes when she was working with the first electronic computers.

Gertrude Belle Elion (1918–1999)
She invented cancer drugs and drugs used for organ transplants. In 1988 she won the Nobel Prize for Medicine along with her colleagues George Hitchings and Sir James Black.

Stephanie Louise Kwolek (born 1923)
Kwolek's inventions focus on polymers and fibres. Her most famous invention is 'Kevlar'. Kevlar's fibres are stronger than steel and it is used to make bullet-proof vests, fibre-optic cables, outdoor clothing, radial tyres and aeroplane fuselages.

7a

Preteach: *submarine* (a ship that can travel under water), *to grow up* (to gradually change from being a child to being an adult), *composer* (someone who writes music, especially classical music)

- Ask students to look at the picture of Lamarr and ask them what she was famous for (she was a famous actress but she was also an inventor).
- Get them to order the events of Lamarr's life. Don't correct students' answers until after the listening in 7b.

`2.26`

7b Students do activity as per Coursebook.

2h; 3d; 4b; 5i; 6e; 7a; 8f; 10g; 11c

Track 2.26
Hedy Lamarr was very famous in the years before the Second World War. She was born in Vienna, Austria, in 1913. As a child, she grew up in Vienna. Later, when she was a teenager, she went to acting school in Berlin. Then, in 1932, she acted in the European art film *Extase*, and she became famous. The next year, she married Fritz Mandl, the first of her six husbands. Mandl sold weapons to Adolf Hitler in the years before the war. During her marriage, she learnt many things from her husband, but after four years, she left him and she went to London. After that, she went to America and she became a Hollywood star. At that time, people called her the most beautiful woman in the world. In the summer of 1940, she met George Antheil, a composer. She and George developed a radio communications system for submarines in 1942. In 1966, she wrote a book about her life, *Extase and Me*. She died in 2000.

8 Look at the definitions of *during* and *later* and show how the words link events:

During her marriage, she learnt many things from her husband.

As a child, she grew up in Vienna. Later, when she was a teenager, she went to acting school in Berlin.

At the same time	Next
At that time	Then The next year after After that

9 Students do activity as per Coursebook.

1 after; 2 later; 3 Then; 4 after that; 5 After

10

Preteach: *cotton fields* (the place where cotton grows; African-Americans were forced to work in these fields as slaves)

- Get students to look at the photo of Madam CJ Walker and see if anyone knows anything about her.
- Students do activity as per Coursebook.
- Ask students if anything surprises them about Walker's life.
- Tell students that they are going to write a biography of Madam CJ Walker. Remind them to use the linking words for time and to use the text about Lady Ada Lovelace to help them write the biography.
- Work with students to write the opening line of the biography:

Madam CJ Walker, born Sarah Breedlove, was born in 1867 in Louisiana, USA.

- Monitor students while they are writing and help them if asked to.

Model answer:

Madam CJ Walker, born Sarah Breedlove, was born in 1867 in Louisiana, USA. In 1874 her parents died and Sarah went to work in the cotton fields. Seven years later, she married Moses McWilliam and in 1885 she had a daughter, Lelia. In 1887 her husband died and she got a job washing clothes. During the 1890s she lost some of her hair so in 1905 she developed some new hair products and changed her name to Madam CJ Walker. Three years later Walker opened a training college in Pittsburgh and two years later she built a factory in Indianapolis. In 1916 she started to give money to help African-Americans. Three years later she died in New York State. She was the richest African-American woman.

HOMEWORK OPTIONS

Students finish their descriptions; alternatively, you could ask students to write another simple biography of someone that interests them.

Students do the exercises on page 59 of the Workbook.

DICTIONARY REMINDER

Ask your students to make a note to bring their dictionaries to class when you start Lesson 10.1.

Review

GRAMMAR

1

> **1** wasn't; **2** was; **3** were; **4** travelled; **5** built; **6** were; **7** used; **8** traded; **9** controlled; **10** couldn't; **11** left; **12** had; **13** lived; **14** gave; **15** came; **16** left; **17** became; **18** could

2

> **Suggested answers:**
> 1 … get to/travel to Malta?
> 2 … were the other early visitors (to Malta)?
> 3 … did they come to the island?
> 4 … long did the Romans control the island?
> 5 … did the Arabs give the modern Maltese language?
> 6 … did Malta become independent?

3 Explain to students that they are going to share information about another island, Mallorca. Mallorca is an island in the Mediterranean Sea off the southeast coast of Spain.

- Ask students if they know anything about the island.
- Get students into pairs. Student A reads the questions and information about Mallorca on page 114 and Student B on page 119.
- When students are ready let them ask and answer the questions. Monitor and help if necessary.

4 Students can discuss these questions in pairs, or you can have a class discussion.

`2.27`

5

> 1a; 2c; 3b; 4c

Track 2.27
Manager, Customer
M: Hello. I'm the manager of this supermarket and today we're talking to some of our customers. Do you have five minutes?
C: Yes, OK.
M: Great. What are you buying today? Food or clothes?
C: Food and clothes. I always buy food on Mondays and today I'm also looking for some clothes for my children.
M: OK. And do you usually pay by credit card?
C: Yes, I do but I'm using cash today.
M: I see. And on average how much do you spend here every week – under or over 100 pounds?
C: Oh, probably over 100 pounds.

6a Students do activity as per Coursebook. Don't check their answers until after the listening in exercise 6b.

6b

> **1** I'm; **2** we're talking; **3** Do you have; **4** are you buying; **5** I always buy; **6** I'm also looking for; **7** do you usually pay; **8** I'm using; **9** do you spend

VOCABULARY

7

> 1c; 2b; 3b; 4c; 5a; 6c; 7a; 8c; 9a

KEY LANGUAGE

8 Remind students to use capital letters where needed.

> **a** Could you show me some mobile phones please?
> **b** That's no problem.
> **c** Can I help you?
> **d** I'm afraid not.
> **e** Which phones would you like to see?
> **f** It has two main advantages.

9a This section revises the Key Language sections from Lesson 7.3 (giving advantages and disadvantages, page 62) and Lesson 8.3 (polite requests, page 70).

> 1c; 2a; 3e; 4f; 5b; 6d

`2.28`

9b You may want to pause the recording to help students.

> 15 designs (*not* 50); this one is the best (*not* popular); you can watch TV on it (*not* listen to music); I'd like something simpler (*not* cheaper); Does it have games? (*not* Does it play music?)

Track 2.28

Shop assistant, Customer

SA: Hello, can I help you?

C: Yes. Could you show me some mobile phones, please?

SA: Certainly. We have over 15 different designs. Which phones would you like to see?

C: I don't know. There are so many!

SA: This one is the best.

C: Why?

SA: Well, it has two main advantages. The first advantage is the camera and the second is that you can watch TV on it.

C: Yes, but that means it's the most expensive. Sorry, but I'd like something simpler.

SA: That's no problem. This model is half the price.

C: Does it have games?

SA: No, I'm afraid not, but it has a camera.

LANGUAGE CHECK

10 Get students to try and write in all the missing prepositions before they check with the previous units in the Coursebook.

2 (pay) for; **3** (business) on; **4** (first) of; **5** (day) before; **6** (go) on; **7** (chat) to; **8** (go) down; **9** (studies) in; **10** men (during).

LOOK BACK

11

discuss your shopping habits: 7.1, exercise 1; learn American English: 7.3, exercise 2; give a short talk: 7.4, exercises 6 and 7; read about one of the world's first cities: 8.1 exercise 2; compare your grandparents' way of life with yours: 8.2, exercise 11; ask politely for something: 8.3, exercise 9; find out about the first helicopter: 9.1, exercises 2 and 3; say what you did last weekend: 9.1, exercise 9; listen to a radio programme: 9.2, exercises 6b and 7b

Money

10.1 KEEPING IT SAFE

IN THIS LESSON

Lesson topic and staging

This lesson looks at the topic of money, particularly from the perspective of a foreign student studying at a British university. Students begin the lesson by learning a vocabulary set on money. Students personalise this language in a speaking activity. The lesson then shifts to the topic of foreign students and advice on how to stay safe while at university. Students read a poster advertising a talk on the subject and then listen to the talk. This leads into the grammar focus of the lesson: *should* and *shouldn't*. Students first work with the meaning and form of the modal. A longer speaking activity then gets students to read a letter from a university student who is having problems with money. Students discuss the letter and offer advice to the student. In the last stage of the lesson students write replies offering advice to other university students who are also having money problems.

Objectives

By the end of the lesson students should have:

- learned about how to keep money safe while studying in the UK
- revised and extended their knowledge and use of *should* and *shouldn't*
- read about typical money problems for students
- written a letter to a student offering advice on how to deal with a money problem

Timings

If short of time, you could drop exercise 6 on page 85. Students could do this exercise for homework.

A possible lesson break would be after exercise 5 on page 85.

WARM-UP

This is a prediction activity.

- Write the following words and phrases on the board and tell students that they all come from this lesson. What do they think the lesson will be about?

  *keeping it safe   university   credit card
  the city is dangerous   carry a lot of cash*

- Check students' ideas and then tell them to have a very quick look at pages 84 and 85 to check.

VOCABULARY: money

1a In this activity students are encouraged to find answers from a dictionary so it is better not to preteach any vocabulary if possible. Remind them of the questions about words on page 28 of their Coursebook. If they can't understand any words tell them to use their dictionaries.

> coin, note

1b

Preteach: *to destroy* (to damage something very badly, so that people can no longer use it, or it no longer exists)

- Students do activity as per Coursebook.

> Students' answers will differ.

To extend this activity, write these questions on the board and ask students to discuss them:

1 Have you got a credit card? If you do, what do you normally use it for?

2 If you have a credit card, do you ever forget your PIN number?

3 Do you ever write cheques? If so, what for?

4 What is the biggest note in your country?

5 Do you normally carry a purse or a wallet?

READING

Preteach: *to worry about something* (to keep thinking about something bad that might happen so that you do not feel happy or relaxed), *safe* (not likely to be hurt), *to steal* (to take something that belongs to someone else), *Welfare Officer* (the person responsible for students' health, comfort and happiness), *to look after* (to do things to make sure that someone or something is safe and well)

2 Students do activity as per Coursebook.

> In a university café, arts centre, bar, laundry, etc.

3 Students do activity as per Coursebook.

> **1** false (*International Students!*); **2** false (*looking after yourself*); **3** true (*Sue Cutler, Sheffield Met International Student Welfare Officer*); **4** false (*4 p.m.*); **5** false (*Tea and biscuits from 3.30 p.m.*)

LISTENING

2.29

4 Check students understand who is giving the talk and what the talk is about.

- Give students time to read the sentences before playing the recording.

2

Track 2.29
Sue Cutler

Good afternoon, everyone. How are you today? My talk this afternoon is about how to stay safe in the city. First of all, let me tell you that the city of Sheffield is actually one of the safest cities in the UK. Most other big cities are much more dangerous than here. So don't be scared! But we should always be careful and look after ourselves and our possessions.
We can talk about our personal safety later, but let's start by saying something about looking after our money. Here are a few things you should and shouldn't do. A lot of this is common sense, of course, and I'm sure you already do most of these things in your own countries.

2.30

5

Preteach: *crowded* (full of people), *pickpocket* (someone who steals from people's pockets in public places), *thief* (someone who steals things)

- Get students to read the statements before they listen. Students may ask about the meaning of *should* and *shouldn't*. Don't focus on the meaning too much yet and simply tell them they mean the right or wrong thing to do in a situation.

1 crowded; **2** PIN number; **3** wallet; **4** cash; **5** busy public

---

Track 2.30
Sue Cutler, 3 Students

SC: Anyway, here goes, starting with the things you <u>should</u> do. Number one – you should be careful in crowded places. By this, I mean on trams, on buses, in busy markets and shopping streets. Pickpockets – that's people who steal your wallets, purses, cameras and so on – pickpockets love crowded places. So take care.
The next thing is about cards, credit cards and debit cards. You should keep your PIN number safe and secret – only you should know it. Cashpoints are usually outside banks. When you use them, have a look at who is behind you. Are they too close? Are they interested in what you're doing? Don't let anyone see you put in your PIN number.
Another important point. If you carry a bag, carry your bag carefully. Make it difficult for someone to take it off you. And if you carry just a wallet, you should keep it in your jacket, in an inside pocket, not in the back pocket of your trousers.
Now, that brings us to some things you <u>shouldn't</u> do. You shouldn't carry a lot of cash about with you. By that, I mean lots of big notes, and coins. You can replace traveller's cheques and credit cards. But you can't replace lost cash.

continued…

Next, you should never take your money out of your wallet or purse in busy public places. This one is obvious, isn't it? Don't attract the attention of thieves by counting your money on a busy street! OK. Any questions so far?
s1: Should I wear a money belt when I go out?
SC: Well, most people here don't wear money belts. Also, money belts are often uncomfortable so I don't think that it's necessary, but it's up to you, I suppose.
s2: Last night, some of us went out to a café. One of the girls had her mobile phone on the table all the time. Is that OK?
SC: Well, no, she shouldn't do that. That's really not a good idea. She should keep it in her bag.
s3: Should I leave money in my university room?
SC: The rooms are generally very safe, but, no, you shouldn't really have a lot of cash in your room, just in case. Any other questions? OK, now let's move on to talk about personal safety …

6 Students do activity as per Coursebook.

1 no; **2** yes; **3** no; **4** no

GRAMMAR: *should, shouldn't*

7 Students do activity as per Coursebook.

1 no; **2** can

For a full explanation and further practice activities, go to pages 140–141 in the Language Reference.

8 Students do activity as per Coursebook.

2 You shouldn't go; **3** He should be; **4** She shouldn't buy; **5** You should tell; **6** Should we spend

9 Students do activity as per Coursebook. Note: this is a speaking activity but could be used as a writing activity if you feel students need more controlled written work with *should/shouldn't*. Encourage students to use *should/shouldn't* in their answers.

- Check the answers in a group. You could use the answers to drill the structure.

1 You should join a sports club. **2** You should watch TV and practise listening. **3** You should go out in a group. **4** You shouldn't use your computer late at night.

SPEAKING

10a Ask students to read the letter and ask them if they know anyone who has or had similar problems.

- Get students to work in pairs and give Nadia some advice. Remind them to use *should* and *shouldn't*.

10b Get students to compare their answers with the first letter on page 121.

• Students read the other letters and give advice.

WRITING

11 Write the beginning of the letter on the board:

Dear

I'm sorry to hear about your problem(s). I think that you …

• Tell students to work in pairs, pick a letter that they find interesting and write a reply to the person.

• Remind them to use the key language *should* and *shouldn't* and tell them to use the letter to Nadia on page 121 to help them.

• Monitor and help students when needed.

🔧 If your students are strong, ask them to write two or three letters. If they are not very strong, work with students to write a reply to one of the letters on the board as a model. The second letter would be a good choice because it recycles all the ideas on working with new words from Lesson 8.4 on page 72.

> **Model answer:**
>
> Dear Li,
> I'm sorry to hear about your problem. You shouldn't be afraid. I think that you should speak to your teachers or the Welfare Officer at the university. They can tell you about your part of the city. You can also talk to other students that live near you.
>
> Dear Veronica,
> I'm sorry to hear about your problem. I think that you should read your vocabulary notes every day. Once a week you should test yourself on new vocabulary – that helps memory.
>
> Dear Klara,
> I'm sorry to hear about your problem. I think that you should talk to your friends about the situation. You should tell them that you can't afford to eat in expensive restaurants and go to the theatre. I think you shouldn't go out so much, and you should look for a better job.

HOMEWORK OPTIONS

Students could finish their letters at home or write another letter.

Students do/finish the extra practice activities 1, 2 and 3 on page 141 in the Language Reference.

Students do the exercises on pages 60–61 of the Workbook.

DICTIONARY REMINDER

Ask your students to make a note to bring their dictionaries to class for the next lesson.

10.2 MICRO-CREDIT

IN THIS LESSON

Lesson topic and staging

This lesson looks at how an organisation called Credit Aid helps poor people who want to set up their own businesses. Students start the lesson by learning a vocabulary set on phrases connected with money like *borrow money from, get a loan* and *earn money*. This vocabulary prepares students for the reading that follows on Credit Aid. Students explore the idea of organisations that help people to help themselves by lending them small sums of money to set up their own businesses. The reading contextualises the grammar focus of the lesson: *have to, don't have to.* Students work with the meaning and form of the language. Students then read about Jane, a widow from Rwanda who has benefited from a loan from Credit Aid. Students finish the lesson with a problem-solving activity; they read about four people who want a loan and have to pick two people to give the loan to.

Objectives

By the end of the lesson students should have:

• learned a set of vocabulary to talk about money such as *borrow money from* and *lend money to*

• learned about the concept of micro-credit

• extended their knowledge and use of *have to* and *don't have to* to talk about what is necessary and unnecessary

• solved a problem by choosing two people to give a micro-credit loan to

Timings

If short of time, you could drop exercise 6 and ask students to do it for homework.

A possible lesson break would be after exercise 6 on page 86 and before the Reading section on page 87.

WARM-UP

This activity revises vocabulary on money from Lesson 10.1.

• Draw a mind map like the one below on the board and ask students to complete it without looking at their Coursebook or their notes.

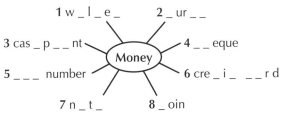

• Ask students to check their answers on page 84 of the Coursebook.

> **1** wallet; **2** purse; **3** cashpoint; **4** cheque; **5** PIN number; **6** credit card; **7** note; **8** coin

VOCABULARY: phrases connected with money

(!) Students often have trouble with the verbs *borrow from* and *lend to*. You can help students by drawing this picture on the board to illustrate the meanings:

Person A lends money to Person B.

Person A borrows money from Person B.

1   Students do activity as per Coursebook. Tell them to use their dictionaries for any words they don't know.

> **1** earn money; **2** borrow money (from someone); **3** pay back; **4** lend money (to someone); **5** get a loan; **6** charges you interest

To extend this activity, write these questions on the board and ask students to discuss them.

1   Do you ever lend money to people? Who?

2   When was the last time you borrowed money? What for?

3   How much does a waiter or waitress earn in your country?

4   What do people in your country get loans from a bank for?

5   How much interest do banks charge in your country?

READING

(i) Micro-credit programmes give small loans to poor people who want to start up a business but who have no capital. Most of these people live in developing countries. Micro-credit is not a new concept but it started to really gain momentum in the 1970s and today there are some 7,000 microfinance institutions working with 16 million people.

2

Preteach: *developing country* (a poor country that is trying to build up its industry and improve the living conditions of its people)

• Students do activity as per Coursebook.

> **1** poor people who want to start their own businesses; **2** It works with poor people in poor or developing countries by lending them small amounts of money for their own businesses.

3   Students do activity as per Coursebook.

> **1** false (*has to be over 21 years old*); **2** true (*doesn't have to be in work*); **3** true (*doesn't have to own a house*); **4** false (*has to have a good business idea*); **5** false (*has to earn less than one dollar a day*)

GRAMMAR: *have to, don't have to*

4   Students do activity as per Coursebook.

> **1**b; **2**a; **3**a; **4**b

GRAMMAR TIP

Read the tip with students. Make sure they know all the forms for question form; you could also drill the forms.

For a full explanation and further practice activities, go to pages 140–141 in the Language Reference.

5

Preteach: *foreign currency* (the money another country uses, e.g. the pound, dollar, yen, euro, etc.)

• Get students to check they remember what the verbs mean before they start the exercise.

> **2** don't have to pay; **3** don't have to use; **4** has to keep; **5** Does, have to check; **6** do, have to pay; **7** doesn't have to give

6   Do another example with all the class to show them that you want them to use *have to* and *don't have to*, for example *A footballer has to train. A footballer doesn't have to work from nine to five.*

• Students do activity as per Coursebook.

> Accept all answers that are logical.

READING

Preteach: *widow* (a woman whose husband is dead), *easy to run* (easy to manage or control a business, organization or country), *war* (a period of fighting between two or more countries or states), *single* (not married), *an iron* (a piece of electrical equipment that you heat and press onto your clothes to make them smooth), *a sink* (the thing in a kitchen or bathroom that you fill with water to wash dishes or wash your hands), *to look smart* (if you look smart, you are dressed in a neat and attractive way), *school fees* (the money you pay to go to a school)

7a Students do activity as per Coursebook.

	Jane	Maya
1	Rwanda	The Philippines
2	yes	yes
3	She runs a cinema.	She runs a laundry business.
4	two months ago	six months ago
5	$300	$100
6	$6	$2
7	a TV, a video player and some chairs	two irons, two sinks and a lot of soap
8	$15 a week	$50 a week
9	Yes, because her business is easy to run; she doesn't have to work in the daytime, she can take her children to school, the children don't have to work, Jane can afford better food and she can look after her mother.	Yes, because she doesn't have to worry about (paying) school fees, perhaps her children can go to university in the future, and she's building a house for her family.

7b Students do activity as per Coursebook.

SPEAKING

8a

Task summary: Students work for Credit Aid and they have to choose two out of four people to lend money to. First of all, each person reads about two people and takes notes of the important information. Then they compare these people with the two people their partner has read about. Then in pairs they have to choose only two people to give a loan to.

- Explain the task and task outcome. Put students into pairs; Student As read and take notes about the two people on page 112, and Student Bs read and take notes about the two people on page 118. Tell students that not all the information they will read is important, and that they should only write down what is really important.

8b Tell the pairs to discuss all four people together. They close their Coursebooks so that they are using their notes only, not reading from the information on pages 112 and 118.

- Monitor students and take notes when necessary. Focus in particular on the key language, *have to* and *don't have to*. Note: this is also a good moment to see if students are using the language of giving reasons, as well as comparative and superlative adjectives.

- When students are ready get them to compare their answers as a whole group. Ask them to explain their choices.

- Give students feedback on their language performance if necessary.

HOMEWORK OPTIONS

Students do/finish the extra practice activity 4 on page 141 in the Language Reference.

Students do the exercises on pages 62–63 of the Workbook.

10.3 SCENARIO: IN MY OPINION

IN THIS LESSON

Lesson topic and staging

The lesson looks at some of the things people do with money such as saving it or giving it away to charity. Students begin the lesson by talking about a number of quotes about money, such as *Money can buy you happiness*. Students then listen to someone conducting a survey about money. The researcher asks a couple a number of questions about what they do with money. This listening contextualises the Key Language focus on asking for and giving opinions. Students work with the meaning, form and pronunciation of the language before talking about their own views on money. This prepares them for the main focus of the lesson, the task. Students have to prepare and conduct their own survey on money. They have to make notes which they then use to write a short paragraph on the results.

Objectives

By the end of the lesson students should have:

- learned to talk about some of the ways they use money
- learned how to ask for and give opinions
- developed their awareness of and use of sentence stress to show a shift in focus
- improved their ability to form questions
- written, conducted and collated a simple survey on the topic of money
- written a short paragraph on the results of their survey

Common European Framework

Students can prepare, conduct, collate and write up the results of a simple questionnaire.

Timings

If short of time, you could drop exercises 4a and 4b.

A possible lesson break would be after exercise 4b on page 88.

Make sure you leave sufficient time at the end of the lesson to prepare for, complete and discuss the task in exercises 7, 8 and 9.

WARM-UP

This activity develops students' editing skills and revises vocabulary from Lesson 10.2.

- Write the following five sentences on the board and ask students in pairs to correct them. Tell students that there is one mistake in every sentence. The mistake can be a fact, or a problem with grammar or vocabulary, but not spelling.

1 I borrowed you £10.
2 How many interest does the bank charge?
3 Micro-credit loans are usually very big.
4 Credit Aid borrows money from poor people.
5 You can't get a loan if you earn less than one dollar a day.

- When students are ready check their answers quickly.

PREPARATION

Preteach: *charity* (an organisation that collects money and provides help for people who need it)

- Students do activity as per Coursebook.

2.31

2a Let students read the questions before playing the recording.

> **1** Probably boyfriend and girlfriend but could be married. They are doing the shopping together and know each other very well. **2** David; **3** Answers will depend on students' personality.

Track 2.31
Researcher, Katie, David

R: Excuse me, I'm working for a bank and we're doing a survey about money. Can I interview you?
K: Well, actually we're rather busy.
D: Yes, we're doing the shopping and we have to be back at the car park in ten minutes.
R: I understand, but it's only a short interview, and you can win a holiday to Thailand.
K: Really? Well, I don't see any problems.
D: But darling, we should finish the shopping.
K: Five minutes isn't a problem, is it, David? So, what's the first question?
R: Right, well, if you're sure. Erm, what's your opinion about having credit cards?
D: Well, personally, I think that they're a bad idea. It's very easy to spend more than you can afford.
R: And you, madam, what's your opinion?
K: Well, in my opinion, they're great. They give you a chance to buy expensive things when you want them. You don't have to wait for them.
R: OK madam, and do you think that saving money is important?
K: Erm, yes, I suppose it is, but to be honest, I don't save very much each month. I prefer to spend my money now.
R: And sir, do you think that saving money is important?
D: Oh yes, definitely. When you're old, you can't live without money, so I save something every month, for my pension.
R: Right. Do you think that borrowing money from friends is a good idea?

continued...

D: Oh, no, not at all. I think that it's a terrible idea because if you forget to pay them back, well, things can get very difficult, can't they?

R: Mmm, I guess so. And you, madam, do you think that it's a good idea?

K: Well, I'm not sure. It's cheaper than borrowing from banks. But you have to be careful, you shouldn't borrow a lot or often, and of course, you have to remember to pay your friend back!

R: OK. Finally, do you agree that people should give money to charity every month?

K: No, not at all. I believe that the government should look after everyone. My money is my money.

R: And you, sir? Do you agree that we should give money to charity?

D: Well, yes, I do. We should give some money, but we aren't very rich so I can't always give something, but I do try, when I can.

R: Well, thank you very much …

2b Students do activity as per Coursebook.

> **1** true (*I think that they're a bad idea. It's very easy to spend more than you can afford.*); **2** true (*They give you a chance to buy expensive things when you want them. You don't have to wait for them.*); **3** false (*… to be honest, I don't save very much each month.*); **4** false (*I save something every month, for my pension.*); **5** true (*I think that it's a terrible idea because if you forget to pay them back, well, things can get very difficult, can't they?*); **6** false (*Well, I'm not sure.*); **7** true (*No, not at all. I believe that the government should look after everyone. My money is my money.*); **8** false (*We should give some money, but we aren't very rich so I can't always give something, but I do try, when I can.*)

KEY LANGUAGE: asking for and giving opinions

2.31

3 Students do activity as per Coursebook. Pause the recording after every sentence to give students time to write their answers.

> **1** having, think, opinion; **2** think that, it is, definitely; **3** good idea, all, sure; **4** should give, believe, do

If your students are not very strong, you could put the missing words and phrases on the board in the wrong order and let them try to complete the sentences before they listen.

pronunciation

2.32

4a This exercise shows students how the main stress in a sentence can shift when the speaker wants to shift the focus from one topic, person or word to another. Write this conversation on the board and ask students why the stress moves on the two questions.

AHMED: Do you want to go to the cinema?

BEN: I'm not sure. Do *you* want to go?

• Let students read the conversation and try and mark the stress before playing the recording.

> **1** first question: important; second question: you; **2** the first question **3** the second question

> **Track 2.32**
> R: OK madam, and do you think that saving money is important?
> K: Erm, yes, I suppose it is, but to be honest, I don't save very much each month. I prefer to spend my money now.
> R: And sir, do you think that saving money is important?
> D: Oh yes, definitely. When you're old, you can't live without money, so I save something every month, for my pension.

4b Students do activity as per Coursebook.

5 Show students how to do the exercise by doing the first question in exercise 3 together. Tell them that they should only ask the question and then continue the conversation according to their opinion, as below:

STUDENT A: What's your opinion about having credit cards?

STUDENT B: Well, personally, I think they're a bad idea. What's your opinion about credit cards?

STUDENT A: In my opinion they're a good idea.

• Students continue with the exercise. Monitor their performance to see if they are shifting the main stresses correctly.

6 Students do activity as per Coursebook.

> **1b** save money; **2b** about borrowing money from friends; **3b** giving money to charity is; **4b** part-time jobs; **5b** having credit cards is

10.4 STUDY AND WRITING SKILLS

TASK: expressing thoughts and opinion

Task summary: In the task students first work in pairs to make a questionnaire on people's opinions about money. When that is ready students interview as many people as possible and note their answers. They then share the results with their partner. Students then write up their research. A successful task outcome is when each student has managed to write a simple paragraph describing the results of their survey. If they can include a table or graph (see page 39), that would be better still.

7

Preteach: *homeless people* (people with no place to live), *high salary* (a lot of money earned every month), *pocket money* (money given to children every week by their parents to spend on small things such as sweets), *retirement* (when you stop working at the end of your working life)

- Explain the task and task outcome to students. Students do activity as per Coursebook.

8a Draw students' attention to the OTHER USEFUL PHRASES and tell them to use the phrases when answering questions in the survey.

- Remind students to try to use the Key Language on page 88 and to take notes when they get people's answers so that they can share the results with their partner.

- Ask students how they got on. Ask if they were surprised by any of the answers. Give students feedback on their language performance.

8b Put students in pairs and get them to combine their results.

9 Students could write paragraphs in pairs, using the combined results, or individually.

- Refer students to page 39 if you want to revise tables and percentages.

HOMEWORK OPTIONS

If students haven't finished the paragraph, ask them to complete it for homework.

Students do the exercises on page 64 of the Workbook.

10.4 STUDY AND WRITING SKILLS

IN THIS LESSON

Lesson topic and staging

The first part of the lesson focuses on study skills involved in taking notes while listening. Students listen to a talk about British banks and the different types of student account they offer and complete a mind map with the information. The listening also contextualises some work on words and phrases of addition. Students then apply what they have learned by making a mind map based on the third part of the talk about British banks. They use these notes to write a short paragraph about two different student accounts. Students then read about other accounts, tell their partners and make a further set of mind maps to record the information.

In the second part of the lesson students learn about the structure and style of a formal letter. They also learn how to use the linking word *that* to link two clauses. The lesson finishes with students writing a formal letter to a bank to explain a problem they have had.

Objectives

By the end of the lesson students should have:

- learned (more) about British banks and the student accounts they offer
- learned how to take notes while listening by using a mind map
- expanded their knowledge and use of phrases of addition: *as well as*, *also* and *in addition*
- learned to use *that* to make longer, more complex sentences appropriate in formal letters
- analysed the style and structure of a formal letter
- written a short formal letter to a bank explaining a problem and asking the bank to resolve the problem

Common European Framework

Students can write a short formal letter outlining a simple problem and asking for the problem to be resolved.

Timings

If short of time, you could drop exercises 7 and 8 on page 90.

A possible lesson break would be after exercise 8 on page 90.

WARM-UP

This activity revises spelling and percentages, which students will need in the first half of this lesson.

- Ask students if they can remember the alphabet in English. Tell them to go through it with their partner.

- Go through the alphabet once with the class repeating it after you.

- Then go through the alphabet by pointing to different students to indicate that they should say the next letter of the alphabet.
- Write the following percentages on the board: *85.6%*, *12%*, *41.7%*, and ask students to say them for you.
- Give students the following mini dictations. Spell out the words but read out the numbers as normal. Make sure you pause between each word so students have enough time to write.

Micro Credit give loans and charge 2%.

I borrowed $5,000 at 5.6% from my bank.

STUDY SKILLS: taking notes while listening

2.33

1 Students do activity as per Coursebook. Point out that students should only complete gaps a–f.

> **a** four; **b** NatWest; **c** HSBC; **d** interest; **e** discounts; **f** 18.9%

Track 2.33
Part 1
Sue Cutler
Right, I expect you want to open a bank account while you're here, so this next part of my talk is about the banks in Britain and their student services. There are four main or high street banks in Britain. They are, first of all, NatWest, that's spelt N-A-T-W-E-S-T. Secondly, Barclays, that's B-A-R-C-L-A-Y-S. Thirdly, HSBC, H-S-B-C and finally, Lloyds TSB. That's two words. LLOYDS, double L-O-Y-D-S, then T-S-B, Lloyds TSB. All of these banks offer student bank accounts and there are some differences between these accounts.
OK, so, first of all, the NatWest student account. This account offers an interest-free overdraft. As well as this, you can get a credit card and the interest rate for that is about 18.9 percent per year. Also, the bank offers discounts on train fares in Britain.

2a Students do activity as per Coursebook.

> **1** student account; **2** interest-free overdraft; **3** credit card; **4** 18.9; **5** train fares

2b Students do activity as per Coursebook.

> As well as this, Also
> Note: both are followed by a comma.

2.34

3a Students do activity as per Coursebook.

> **g** interest-free overdraft; **h** free mobile phone insurance; **i** credit card; **j** 19.9%

Track 2.34
Part 2
The second account is with Barclays. Like the NatWest account, there's an interest-free overdraft. In addition, this bank offers a credit card with an interest rate of 19.9 percent, so it's more expensive than the NatWest card. With this account, students also get free mobile phone insurance. I imagine that's popular with many of you.

3b Students do activity as per Coursebook.

> **1** In addition; **2** also
> Note: *In addition* is followed by a comma.

4 Get students to look at the examples in exercises 2 and 3 again to answer the questions.

> They all go at the beginning of a sentence. *Also* can sit in two places; the most common position is before the main verb in the sentence, e.g. *He also has a car.*

2.35

5 Students do activity as per Coursebook.

> Students' mind maps will vary but should include the following information:
> HSBC: interest-free overdraft, credit card with interest rate of 18.9%, free driving lesson
> Lloyds TSB: interest-free overdraft, credit card with interest rate of 17.9%, no discounts or free services

Track 2.35
Part 3
Right, now the HSBC account. This account also has an interest-free overdraft. In addition, there's a credit card and the interest rate is 18.9 percent. As well as this, students get a free driving lesson.
Finally, the Lloyds TSB student account offers an interest-free overdraft. Also, students get a credit card with an interest rate of 17.9 percent. Unfortunately, this account doesn't offer any discounts or free services.
So, that's an overview of the four main banks and their student accounts. Are there any questions?

6 Students do activity as per Coursebook. Remind them to use words and phrases to introduce extra information: *and, also, as well as this, in addition*.

- Monitor students and answer any questions that arise.
- Check students' answers. There are different ways to write the texts so accept anything that is correct.

> **Possible answers:**
> The HSBC student account (also) offers an interest-free overdraft. In addition, there is a credit card and the interest rate is 18.9%. As well as this, students get a free driving lesson.
> The Lloyds TSB student account offers an interest-free overdraft. Also, students get a credit card with an interest rate of 17.9%. Unfortunately, this account doesn't offer any discounts or free services.

7 Explain that students have to read about a student account; Student A looks at page 113 and Student B at page 119. Tell students to use full sentences and to join their ideas with linkers such as *and, also, as well as this*.

- Put students in pairs. Tell them to make a mind map based on the information their partner gives them.

> Students' mind maps will vary but should include all the information from pages 113 and 119.

8 Students will probably need time to review all six accounts so give them time to do so.

- Have a brief discussion about which is the best. You could vote to see which was the overall favourite.

WRITING SKILLS: a formal letter

9

Preteach: *international money transfer* (the transfer of money between two bank accounts in different countries), *refund* (the money that is given back to you in a shop, restaurant, etc., for example because you are not satisfied with what you bought)

- Students do activity as per Coursebook.

> 1c; 2b

10 Students do activity as per Coursebook.

> 1d; 2e; 3a; 4c; 5b

11 Students do activity as per Coursebook.

You could point out the rule for opening and closing formal letters: when we know the name of the person we are writing to, e.g. Dr Hargreaves, Ms Siddique, we end the letter, *Yours sincerely*. When we don't know their name, we begin the letter, *Dear Sir/Madam* and end the letter, *Yours faithfully*.

> **1** Parts d (gap 1) and e (gap 2); **2** *3 February 2007*; **3** *I am writing, I am afraid, I am unhappy*; **4** *However, when I made ... , I am afraid that I am unhappy ... , Could you please refund ...*; **5** *I look forward to hearing from you, Yours faithfully*

12 Students do activity as per Coursebook.

> **1** I noticed **that** you charged me £25 for this service. **2** The bank assistant told me **that** the charge was only £10. **3** I am afraid **that** I am unhappy with this situation.

13 Students do activity as per Coursebook.

> **1** I thought that it was free. **2** He said that the charge was £100. **3** I realised that there was a mistake. **4** I hope that you can help me. **5** I am unhappy that this happened.

14 Students do activity as per Coursebook. Remind them to use the letter in exercise 10 to help them. They do not need to include the addresses.

If your students are strong, ask them to write two or three letters. If your students are not very strong, get them to write one letter, perhaps in pairs.

> **Model answers:**
> 3 February 2007
> Dear Sir/Madam,
> Re: Credit card application of Mr V. Singh
> I am writing to you about a problem with my recent application for a credit card.
> On 4 January, I went to the main branch of your bank in Glasgow and applied for a credit card. When I checked my credit card statement, I noticed that you charged me £20 for applying for the credit card. However, when I applied for the credit card the bank assistant said there was no charge.
> I am afraid that I am unhappy with this situation. Could you please refund this charge?
> Yours faithfully,
> Mr V. Singh
>
> Re: Overdraft application for Ms S. Parker
> I am writing to you about a problem with my recent overdraft application.
> On 4 January, I went to the main branch of your bank in Manchester and applied for an overdraft. When I checked my statement, I noticed that you charged me £30 for the overdraft application. However, when I applied for the overdraft the bank assistant said there was a £15 charge.
> I am afraid that I am unhappy with this situation. Could you please refund this charge?
> Yours faithfully,
> Ms S. Parker
>
> Re: Loan application for Mr M. Al Jabar
> I am writing to you about a problem with my recent loan application.
> On 4 January, I went to the main branch of your bank in Cardiff and applied for a loan. When I checked my statement, I noticed that you charged me £50 for the loan application. However, when I applied for the loan the bank assistant said there was no charge because it was a special offer in January.
> I am afraid that I am unhappy with this situation. Could you please refund this charge?
> Yours faithfully,
> Mr M. Al Jabar

HOMEWORK OPTIONS

If students have not finished their formal letters, ask them to do so for homework. Alternatively, you could ask students to write another letter.

Students do the exercises on page 65 of the Workbook.

Homes

11.1 MY HOME, MY CASTLE

IN THIS LESSON

Lesson topic and staging

This lesson looks at the topic of gated communities. Students read about these communities and discuss whether they are a good idea. The lesson then moves onto looking at common compound nouns such as *car park, Internet café* and *shopping centre*. The grammar focus of the lesson is *will, won't* for what we know or think about the future. Students work with the meaning, form and pronunciation of the future simple tense. The last activity of the lesson is speaking; students discuss some ideas about their own futures.

Objectives

By the end of the lesson students should have:

- learned (more) about the concept of gated communities
- revised and extended their knowledge and use of *will* and *won't* for what we know or think about the future
- learned about compound nouns such as *tennis court* and *theme park*
- discussed how life will/won't be in 2100
- talked about how their own lives will and won't change in the future

Timings

If short of time, you could drop exercises 6a and 6b on page 93. Students could do these exercises for homework.

A possible lesson break would be after exercise 6b on page 93.

WARM-UP

This is a quick vocabulary activity.

- Give students two minutes to see how many objects in the photo on page 92 they can name, for example *chair, painting,* and so on.

READING

1   Students do activity as per Coursebook. Ask a few students to tell the whole group what they talked about.

2

Preteach: *gated community* (an area where people live surrounded by high walls and fences with security guards)

- Students do activity as per Coursebook. Make sure that they don't try to read the article in too much detail yet.

i The article refers to 9/11. On 11 September 2001 America was hit by a number of terrorist attacks. It was the first time that the USA had suffered a terrorist attack of this sort and the tragic events of that day had a profound effect on the people of America and the rest of the world.

    c

3

Preteach: *facilities* (rooms, equipment or services that are available in a place)

- Students do activity as per Coursebook.

    2, 3, 4, 6

4   Students do activity as per Coursebook.

    1C; 2A, C; 3D; 4A; 5B, C

5   Students do activity as per Coursebook.

To extend this activity write the following questions on the board:

1   Are there any gated communities in your country? What types of people live there?

2   Would you like to live in a gated community? Why? Why not?

VOCABULARY: compound nouns

6a Get students to look for the compound nouns. You could tell them which paragraphs to look in (the three compounds are in paragraphs A and D).

Some students may have a problem with word stress here. Point out that the stress is normally on the first word in compound nouns, for example:

    •   •   •

security guards   play areas   business centres

    travel agencies, golf courses, police officers

6b Students do activity as per Coursebook.

    Internet café, police station, post office,
    railway station, shopping centre, sports centre,
    swimming pool, tennis court, theme park

To extend this activity and activate the vocabulary, you could ask students to tell you where the places in the exercise can be found in their town or city.

Is there a theme park near here/in X?

No, there isn't. But there's one in Y.

GRAMMAR: *will, won't*

7 Students do activity as per Coursebook.

> **1** c; **2** no; **3** can, should

To extend the activity and give some extra practice on form, draw this table on the board and ask students to copy it down. When students are ready ask them to complete the missing spaces at the bottom with examples from the text.

Affirmative (+)	Negative (–)	Question (?)
I/you/he/she/ we/you/they'll (will) + verb	I/you/he/she/ we/you/they won't (will not) + verb	Will I/you/ he/she/we/ you/they + verb?
e.g.	e.g.	e.g.

For a full explanation and further practice activities, go to pages 142–143 in the Language Reference.

8 Students do activity as per Coursebook.

> **1** will have; **2** will be; **3** won't meet; **4** won't live;
> **5** won't have to; **6** will change

9

Preteach: *relationship* (a situation in which two people are romantic or sexual partners)

- Check students' answers before they talk about the questions. Encourage students to talk as much as possible about the questions. Do an example with a student to demonstrate what you expect, getting the student to expand his/her answers as much as possible, e.g.

  TEACHER: Will there be any fish in the world in 2100?
  STUDENT: I'm not sure but a lot of people say there won't be.
  TEACHER: Why?
  STUDENT: Because the seas will be much warmer.
  TEACHER: Really!
  STUDENT: Yes. So lots of fish will die or move to colder water.

> **1** Will families be bigger or smaller than now?
> **2** Will there be any fish in the sea? **3** Will people use the Internet? **4** Will people keep all their teeth all their life? **5** Will India be the most important country? **6** Will love be important in relationships?

- Monitor students' conversations and take notes on the target language.
- Get a few students to share their answers with the whole group.
- Give students feedback on their language performance.

pronunciation

2.36

10 Explain to students that people normally use contractions when they speak unless the situation is very formal. Get students to listen and complete the sentences; focus particularly on the contracted forms.

Play the recording sentence by sentence and get students to repeat after each sentence.

> **Audioscript and answers:**
> **Track 2.36**
> **1** I'll be rich.
> **2** You'll have three children.
> **3** She'll buy a sports car.
> **4** He'll live alone.
> **5** It'll make them happy.
> **6** We'll speak excellent English.
> **7** They'll go to Australia.

SPEAKING

11

Preteach: *well known* (famous)

- Divide students into As and Bs and get them to read and respond to the questionnaire on their own.
- Write this prompt on the board: *I'll be rich in 2037.* Ask students to make it into a question using *you*.
- Write the question up, elicit an answer and then write that up. Build a model conversation this way so students know what to do.

  STUDENT A: Will you be rich in 2037?
  STUDENT B: Me! Rich!! No, I won't be rich. How about you? Will you be rich in 2037?
  STUDENT A: I don't know but …

- Ask students to start talking with their partners. Be sure to monitor and take notes on correct and incorrect uses of the key language.
- When students are finished deal with task achievement and then language performance as normal.

HOMEWORK OPTIONS

Students do/finish the extra practice activities 1, 2 and 6 on page 143 in the Language Reference.

Students do the exercises on pages 66–67 of the Workbook.

11.2 GREEN LIVING

IN THIS LESSON

Lesson topic and staging

This lesson looks at what people can do to make their homes 'greener' or more environmentally friendly. The lesson begins with a vocabulary set on 'green living', such as *save energy with low-energy light bulbs*. Students then answer a questionnaire to find out how green their house is. This leads into a listening about three people who took the same questionnaire. The listening contextualises the grammar focus: *be going to* for future plans and intentions, for example *They're going to recycle their paper*. Students then work with the meaning and form of the language. The topic changes to organising an end-of-course celebration for the class. Students make plans for the celebration, tell their classmates their plans and then vote for the best plan. Finally, they write a short description of their plans for the college principal.

Objectives

By the end of the lesson students should have:

- learned (more) about how to save energy and recycle in the house by taking a questionnaire on the topic
- learned a set of vocabulary to talk about green living
- extended their knowledge and use of *be going to* to talk about future plans and intentions
- worked as a group to organise an end-of-course celebration for their class
- written a description of their plans for the college principal

Timings

If short of time, you could drop exercise 10 and ask students to do it for homework.

A possible lesson break would be after exercise 4 on page 95 and before the grammar focus on the same page.

WARM-UP

This activity predicts the content of the lesson.

- Write the title of the lesson, *Green Living*, on the board and draw this picture as well:

- Ask students what they think the lesson will be about. Give them time to think about it and then tell you.
- Ask students to check their predictions by briefly looking at pages 94 and 95 of the Coursebook.

VOCABULARY: green living

1

Preteach: *green electricity* (electricity produced from sources which do not damage the environment; the cleanest energy sources are renewable energies like wind, solar and hydro power)

- Get students to match the sentences with the labels on the picture. If students don't know certain words, for example *saucepan* and *lid*, use the picture to teach them.

> 2F; 3B; 4A; 5D; 6E; 7H; 8C

READING

2

Preteach: *tap* (something that you turn to make water come out of a pipe)

- Students read the questionnaire and then do it in pairs.
- Students check their scores on page 121. Ask around the whole group and see who the greenest people in the class are.

LISTENING

`2.37`

3 Explain the activity and get students to look at the text and photos before you play the recording.

> 1 Martin; 2 Simon and Rachel; 3 Vicky
> Simon and Rachel are the greenest.

Track 2.37
Interviewer, Martin, Simon, Vicky
1
I: What was your score?
M: I got 36, but my flatmate, Richard, only got 25.
I: Right, and what are you going to do? What changes are you going to make?
M: Well, I'm going to have showers in the future, no more lovely hot baths for me. Richard is going to make more changes.
I: Oh yes, what's he going to do?
M: Well, he's going to recycle things, like paper and glass. At the moment he doesn't recycle anything, which is terrible. Also, he's going to turn things off, especially his CD player as he always leaves that on standby. Oh, and he's going to cover his saucepans when he's cooking – but that isn't very often!

continued…

2

I: What was your family's score?

S: Yes, well, we got 40, but we're going to make some big changes anyway.

I: Oh yes, such as?

S: Well, we're going to buy a solar panel and some low-energy light bulbs. We think that the solar panel will be a great idea for us because we'll save money. The children are young, so they can't do a lot, but they're going to recycle their paper – they do a lot of pictures and drawings. We aren't going to have showers because we haven't got a shower at the moment – only a bath.

3

I: What was your score?

V: Oh, it was very good, I got 35.

I: I see, and what are you going to do to go greener?

V: Oh, I'm too old to change a lot. I'm not going to do anything new. I recycle everything, I turn everything off. What more can I do? Solar panels are very expensive.

I: Why don't you buy green electricity?

V: Oh, I'm not sure, is that easy to do?

I: Yes, it is now. We can find a company for you and you don't need to change anything in your house.

V: That sounds a good idea. Let me think about it.

4 Students do activity as per Coursebook.

> **1** false (*I got 36, but my flatmate, Richard, only got 25.*); **2** true (*he's going to recycle things, like paper and glass … Also, he's going to turn things off, especially his CD player as he always leaves that on standby. Oh, and he's going to cover his saucepans when he's cooking …*); **3** true (*We think that the solar panel will be a great idea for us because we'll save money.*); **4** true (*we haven't got a shower at the moment – only a bath*); **5** true (*I'm too old to change a lot. I'm not going to do anything new.*); **6** false (*We can find a company for you and you don't need to change anything in your house.*)

GRAMMAR: *be going to*

`2.37`

5 Students do activity as per Coursebook.

> **1** Martin; **2** Richard; **3** Simon and Rachel's children; **4** Simon and Rachel; **5** Vicky

6a

Preteach: *intention* (something that you plan to do)

• Students do activity as per Coursebook.

> future plans and intentions

6b Students do activity as per Coursebook.

> **1** is; **2** is; **3** are; **4** not; **5** subject; **6** going to; **7** infinitive

For a full explanation and further practice activities, go to pages 142–143 in the Language Reference.

`2.38`

7 Students do activity as per Coursebook.

> **1** 'm going to find out; **2** isn't going to buy; **3** aren't going to change; **4** 're going to turn off; **5** Are, going to make; **6** 's going to cycle

> **Track 2.38**
> 1 I'm going to find out about green electricity.
> 2 She isn't going to buy a wind turbine because it's expensive.
> 3 We aren't going to change anything. We're already very green.
> 4 They're going to turn off their TVs with the on/off button.
> 5 Are you going to make any changes?
> 6 He's going to cycle to work every day.

SPEAKING

8a Get students to look back at the questionnaire.

• Get a student to tell you one of their plans. If they don't use (*not*) *going to*, prompt them to self-correct by asking them how we talk about future plans and intentions.

• Monitor students. If they don't use (*not*) *going to* prompt them to self-correct.

8b Begin this exercise with the whole group. Get them to come up with ideas and write the prompts on the board, for example *too much photocopying, glass and tin cans never recycled, students come to college by car, no energy-saving light bulbs, people waste water*, etc.

• Get students into pairs or groups to continue the exercise. Tell them to make notes so they can report ideas back to the whole group.

• When students are ready get a few ideas from them.

To extend this activity, get each pair or group to give you their top two or three most important, energy-saving ideas. Write all their ideas on the board.

• Tell students as a whole group to decide on the top eight ideas in order of importance with 1 being the most important.

• When they are ready, ask them what their top eight are.

9a Explain all three stages of the activity so that students understand the task outcome, i.e. they have to have a plan and all the plans will be voted on. The best one will be used as the basis for the letter to the college principal.

- Get students into groups to do the first part of the activity.

9b Students do activity as per Coursebook.

9c Get each group to present their plan. Tell students they can ask questions but only when each presentation is finished.

- Vote on the plans.

WRITING

10 Note: if you feel that one or more of your students' letters could eventually go to the principal, tell students this before they start to write. It would provide a real purpose to this activity and it should increase students' motivation as well.

- Help students to start the letter by asking them if it will be a formal or informal letter.

- Remind them of the formal letter on page 91. Ask them what is at the top of the letter, i.e. date and person: *Dear Sir / Madam / Dr X / Mr Y / Ms Z.*

- Ask them what should go at the bottom of the letter, i.e. *We look forward to your reply. Yours faithfully / sincerely, Class T.*

- Give them the following framework for the letter:

  Paragraph 1: say why you are writing.

  Paragraph 2: give details of time of proposed celebration and how many people are going.

  Paragraph 3: ask the principal for permission to have the celebration.

  Paragraph 4: thank the principal for his / her time and close the letter.

- Start the letter together, including the first paragraph, and then let students finish off the letter individually, in pairs or in small groups, e.g.

  Dear Dr Karanowski

  We are writing to you to ask if we could organise an end-of-course celebration for our English class.

HOMEWORK OPTIONS

Students write/complete the letter from exercise 10.

Students do/finish the extra practice activity 3 on page 143 in the Language Reference.

Students do the exercises on pages 68–69 of the Workbook.

11.3 SCENARIO: AT AN ACCOMMODATION AGENCY

IN THIS LESSON

Lesson topic and staging

The lesson looks at what is involved in renting a flat. After studying a vocabulary set on rooms, furniture and equipment, students read four adverts for flats. In the listening that follows, a student phones an accommodation agency in search of a flat. The listening contextualises the Key Language of checking understanding. Students work with the meaning, form and pronunciation of the language before tackling the main focus of the lesson, the task. Students have to prepare and conduct a role-play in which they act out the roles of a student looking for a flat and someone who works in an accommodation agency. The lesson finishes with students working in pairs and deciding which of the four flats in exercise 3 they would choose to share.

Objectives

By the end of the lesson students should have:

- learned a vocabulary set related to accommodation: location, rooms, furniture and equipment

- learned how to read adverts for flats

- learned how to check their understanding during a conversation

- developed their awareness of the use of shifting sentence stress to check meaning

- learned how to find out basic information about accommodation

Common European Framework

Students can ask for clarification in a conversation.

Students can ask basic questions to find out if accommodation is suitable for their needs.

Timings

If short of time, you could drop exercise 2.

A possible lesson break would be after exercise 5 on page 97 and before the pronunciation exercises.

Make sure you leave sufficient time at the end of the lesson to prepare for, complete and discuss the task in exercises 8 and 9.

WARM-UP

This activity revises ideas and language from Lesson 11.2.

- Ask students to imagine that they are going to share a two-bedroom flat with their class partner. Get them to think and say what they are going to do to make sure the flat is 'green'. They shouldn't use their Coursebooks or notes.

- When students are ready get several to share their ideas with the rest of the class.

PREPARATION

1 Get students to work in small groups and see how many of the words in the box they can see in the photos at the top of pages 96 and 97.

- See if students have any questions about vocabulary they don't understand.

- Check their understanding of the vocabulary by getting them to do exercise 1.

Rooms	Furniture	Equipment
bathroom	armchair	cooker
bedroom	bookcase	dishwasher
dining room	cupboard	fridge-freezer
kitchen	chair	washing
living room	desk	machine
	sofa	
	table	
	wardrobe	

To extend this activity, get students to use the new vocabulary to talk about the house or apartment where they live.

2 Students do activity as per Coursebook.

3a Students do activity as per Coursebook.

Dublin is the capital of the Republic of Ireland (not part of the UK) and one of Europe's most popular tourist cities. It is Ireland's largest port. It has also developed into the largest manufacturing and exporting city in Ireland, especially for computer hardware and software; Ireland is now the world's leading exporter of these. The city has a population of over a million and has a student population of 50,000.

1 Church St, Harbour Rd, Museum Ave; 2 Church St, Canal St, Museum Ave; 3 Canal St

3b Students do activity as per Coursebook.

- Get students to explain why they would like to live in the flats they choose.

2.39

4a Students do activity as per Coursebook.

Harbour Rd, Canal St
He doesn't decide to rent either of the flats.

Track 2.39
Estate agent, Conor
EA: Hello, Find-a-Flat-Fast. How can I help?
C: Ah, hello. I'm looking for a flat to share with a friend. Hello, can you hear me?
EA: Yes, I can. How many bedrooms do you want?
C: Two bedrooms.
EA: OK, let's see. I've got one here, it looks lovely – two bedrooms, kitchen, living room, two bathrooms … ground floor with a garden … , but there's no furniture, just a cooker and fridge-freezer in the kitchen.
C: That's OK. How much is the rent?
EA: It's 150 euros a week per person.
C: Oh, that's expensive. We're students.
EA: OK, here's another one. It's got two bedrooms, and both are large. There's a small kitchen, a dining room and a living room. There's also a large bathroom.
C: Right. What floor is the flat on?
EA: It's on the fourth floor, and I'm afraid there isn't a lift.
C: I'm sorry, could you repeat that, please?
EA: Sure. It's on the fourth floor.
C: And there isn't a lift?
EA: That's right.
C: OK, erm … what furniture is there?
EA: Well, in each bedroom there's a bed, a desk and a wardrobe. In the kitchen there's a cooker, a fridge-freezer and a washing machine. There's a table with chairs in the dining room and a sofa in the living room.
C: Just a moment. So, there's a cooker, a fridge-freezer and a washing machine. Is that right?
EA: Yes, it is.
C: What about the local area? Is it near public transport?
EA: Well, there's a bus stop about 15 minutes away.
C: I'm sorry, could you say that again?
EA: Sure. There's a bus stop about 15 minutes away.
C: A bus stop. OK. And, was that 15 or 50 minutes?
EA: Fifteen, one five.
C: What about trains?
EA: I'm afraid there isn't a local station.
C: Mmm, and how much is it?
EA: It's 90 euros a week, per person.
C: I'm sorry, did you say 19 or 90 euros?
EA: No! It isn't that cheap! It's 90, nine zero. Would you like to see the flat?
C: Well, we really need a flat near a train station, so I don't think that we will. But thanks for your help. Goodbye.
EA: Goodbye.

The photograph above exercise 4a shows O'Connell Bridge in the centre of Dublin.

4b Give students time to read through the notes before you play the recording. Tell them they don't need to write out the full words; for example, rather than writing 'kitchen' they could just put 'K'.

🔧 If your students are not very strong, break the listening up so that half your students listen for the answers to questions with even numbers and the other half listen for the answers to questions with odd numbers.

> 1 2; 2 2 bathrooms; 3 ground floor; 4 yes; 5 cooker; 6 fridge-freezer; 7 no furniture; 8 150; 9 2; 10 kitchen; 11 bathroom; 12 fourth; 13 fridge-freezer; 14 desk; 15 sofa; 16 table; 17 15; 18 90

KEY LANGUAGE: checking understanding

2.39

5   Students do activity as per Coursebook.

> 1 repeat, 2 So, right; 3 again; 4 Was; 5 did

pronunciation

2.40

6   Explain to students that often a better way to check information than just saying *I'm sorry* or *Could you repeat that?* is to use stress to draw attention to the word that you are not sure of. Write the two sentences below on the board and mark the stress to show this.

> – *It's on the fourth floor.*
>
> – *I'm sorry, was that the fourth or the fifth floor?*

- Get students to repeat the two sentences after you, then play Track 2.40 and let students do the activity as per Coursebook. You can then ask them to mark the stress on the rest of the questions from exercise 5.

> **Audioscript and answers:**
> **Track 2.40**
> 4 ... was that 15 or 50 minutes?
> 5 I'm sorry, did you say 19 or 90 euros?

7a Students do activity as per Coursebook.

> There are a number of possible answers. Accept any that are logical in the context.

2.41

7b Students do activity as per Coursebook.

> **Audioscript and answers:**
> **Track 2.41**
> 1
> – It's on the fourth floor.
> – I'm sorry, was that the fourth or the fifth floor?
> 2
> – The rent is one hundred and fifty euros.
> – Did you say one hundred and fifty or fifteen?
> 3
> – It's got a living room.
> – Was that a living room or a dining room?
> 4
> – There's a sofa in the living room.
> – Did you say there is or there isn't a sofa?
> 5
> – It hasn't got a balcony.
> – Did you say it has or hasn't got a balcony?

TASK: asking for information about accommodation

Task summary: In the task students role-play the parts of a student looking for a flat and someone who works in an accommodation agency. Students prepare for their roles and then role-play the telephone conversation. Students then swap roles and repeat the role-play with different information. A successful task outcome is when both students have managed to ask for and give the necessary information to allow for a decision to be made. If students are not sure of anything and are able to check understanding, then the outcome will be even more successful.

8   Ask students what information you need to know when you phone an accommodation agency (for example, you might want to find out about public transport).

- Get students to give you a list of things and then let them check the notes above exercise 9.

- Explain the basic task and task outcome to students.

- Divide students into As and Bs and tell them to read their roles – Bs then look at page 119.

- When students are ready see if they have any questions about their roles or the situation. Draw their attention to the OTHER USEFUL PHRASES and tell them to use it in the course of the conversation. Also remind students to try to use the Key Language on page 97.

- Students then swap roles, with As looking at page 113.

- Monitor the activity and take notes on the key language, asking for and giving information and checking meaning if necessary.

- Ask students how they got on. Did they have any problems? Did they find the right flat?

- Give students feedback on their language performance.

9 Explain the activity briefly and check that students are clear about what they have to do, i.e. decide with their partner which of the four flats they want to rent.

- As this activity represents the culmination of all the work in this lesson, monitor their conversations and take notes on correct and incorrect uses of their language.

- When students are ready ask a few pairs if they found a flat they liked. If they have, ask which one and why.

- Next discuss any notes you have made. Point out good examples of language use first before moving on to any mistakes they have made.

HOMEWORK OPTION

Students do the exercises on page 70 of the Workbook.

DICTIONARY REMINDER

Ask your students to make a note to bring their dictionaries to class for the next lesson.

11.4 STUDY AND WRITING SKILLS

IN THIS LESSON

Lesson topic and staging

The first part of the lesson focuses on examination skills. Students begin the lesson by talking about their experiences of exams. They then learn a vocabulary set related to taking exams, for example *pass/fail an examination* and *revise* for an examination. This language is used in a list of things that people should and shouldn't do when preparing for an examination. Students think about their own strategies and decide which of the 'new' ideas they could try out in the future. The lesson continues with more advice on how to relax when revising, and what to do before and after an exam. In the second part of the lesson students learn about the structure and style of an informal letter. They learn how to use the linking word *when* to join sentences as well as how to give simple directions. They apply this and the other things they have learned to write a letter inviting a friend to a party.

Objectives

By the end of the lesson students should have:

- learned vocabulary to talk about examinations

- learned (more) about preparing for and taking examinations

- learned to use *when* to make longer, more complex sentences appropriate in letters

- analysed the style and structure of an informal letter

- learned how to give simple directions

- written a short informal letter to a friend inviting them to a party

Common European Framework

Students can give simple directions.

Students can write an informal letter giving directions.

Timings

If short of time, you could drop exercise 6 page 98. Students could do this for homework.

A possible lesson break would be after exercise 6, before the Writing Skills on page 99.

WARM-UP

This activity revises vocabulary from Lesson 11.3.

- Draw the following table on the board and ask students to give you one word for each category.

Rooms	Furniture	Equipment
bathroom	sofa	fridge-freezer

- Put students in pairs and give them three minutes to write as many words as they can.

- Get students to check their answers with page 96 of the Coursebook.

STUDY SKILLS: examination skills

1 Students do activity as per Coursebook.

- Get some students to share their answers with the whole group.

2 If students have brought dictionaries, get them to work quietly on their own. Otherwise, ask them to work in small groups to find out the meaning from each other.

- Check students' answers and clarify any questions.

3a Students do activity as per Coursebook.

3b Ask students if they have any questions about the sentences.

- Ask a few pairs to tell you what they will try in the future. Encourage them to use *will*.

4 Students do activity as per Coursebook.

> **Suggested answers:** swimming, meditating, seeing friends, going to the cinema or a concert, listening to music, reading a book, etc.

5 Explain the idea of 'golden rules' to students (very important rules that should be followed).

- Ask them if they can think of 'golden rules' for exams.

- Get students to complete the rules.

> **1** Read; **2** Do; **3** spend; **4** Make; **5** watch; **6** do; **7** do; **8** Take

- After checking students' answers ask them if there were any new ideas for them. If yes, which would they try in their next exam?

6 Students do activity as per Coursebook.

WRITING SKILLS: an informal letter

7 Get students to describe the picture. Ask them why the people might be having a party – try to elicit as many different kinds of party as possible (e.g. birthday party, wedding reception, etc.).

8a Students do activity as per Coursebook. Ask students if they've ever had a housewarming party or been to one.

> She is having a housewarming party (a party to celebrate moving into a new house or flat).

8b Students do activity as per Coursebook.

> **1** true (*I'm in my new flat now, and I'm really enjoying it.*); **2** doesn't say; **3** false (*You can walk from there* [the station].); **4** doesn't say; **5** false (**That's* [the tube] *what we call the underground.*)

9 Students do activity as per Coursebook.

Formal letters	Informal letters
Full date: 3 February 2007	Short date: 9/6/07
Dear Sir/Madam	*Dear Erdem*
Opening: no greeting	Opening: *How are you?*
No contractions: *I am writing about …*	Contractions: *I'm in my new flat …*
Formal language: *I noticed that …; I am afraid that …*, etc.	Informal language: *I'm really enjoying it, Take the tube …*
Full sentences: *Could you please refund …*	Not full sentences: *[I] Hope to see you on Saturday …*
Formal closing: *Yours faithfully,*	Informal closing: *Best wishes*
Writer's full name, often with their title (*Dr, Mr, Mrs, Ms*): *Manuela Rosa*	Writer's first name: *Carla*

10 Students do activity as per Coursebook.

> **1** straight; **2** on; **3** Take; **4** Go; **5** Turn

11 Students do activity as per Coursebook.

> **Example from text:** *When you come out of the station, turn right and go up the hill.* Note the use of the comma after the *when* clause.
> 1b; 2c; 3a

12 Get students to look at the map and work out the directions in English.

- Get students to write a letter using the map. They should also use the letter on page 99 as a model. Monitor their writing and answer any questions they have.

> **Model answer:**
> … My new address is above. It's really easy to get here. Take the bus or the train to X railway station. You can walk from there. When you get off the bus, or when you come out of the station, turn left and walk to the traffic lights. Turn right at the traffic lights – then you're on my road. Go straight on for about X metres. My house is on the right.

HOMEWORK OPTIONS

If students have not finished their letters, ask them to do so for homework.

Students do the exercises on page 71 of the Workbook.

DICTIONARY REMINDER

Ask your students to make a note to bring their dictionaries to class for the next lesson.

12 Travel

12.1 CHILDREN OF THE WIND

Lesson topic and staging

This lesson looks at the topic of travel with a particular focus on 'global nomads' (young people who, because of their parents' jobs, have grown up in various countries). Students begin the lesson talking about where they would like to live, apart from their own countries. They then listen to an interview with Kirsty, a global nomad who has lived in several different countries. The listening contextualises the grammar focus of the lesson: present perfect. Students work with the meaning, form and pronunciation of the present perfect. They then read a web page about other 'global nomads' and their experiences of life. In the final activity of the lesson, students personalise the language focus by talking about their own experiences in life, such as travelling, living away from home and working or studying with someone from a different country.

Objectives

By the end of the lesson students should have:

- learned (more) about the concept of 'global nomads' by listening to and reading about such people
- revised and extended their knowledge and use of the present perfect for talking about experiences
- learned to express past experiences in their own lives

Timings

If short of time, you could drop exercise 8 on page 101. Students could do this exercise for homework.

A possible lesson break would be after exercise 5c on page 101.

This is a quick revision of strategies for effective management of examinations.

- Ask students to write down three strategies they are going to try out before, during and after the next exam they take. Also ask them to explain why and write up this prompt on the board.

  I'm going to make a revision plan because …

- Get a few students to tell the whole group their future plans.

1 Do this opening activity with the whole group.

- Get a couple of students to tell the class about their experiences.

2.42

2a Students do activity as per Coursebook.

> She is happy.

Track 2.42
Peter, Kirsty
P: G'day.
K: Hi there!
P: My name is Peter Knight. I'm doing research into people who grow up in different countries and I'm talking to people here at the university today. Is it OK if I ask you a few questions?
K: Sure, go ahead.
P: Well, first, tell me, have you ever lived abroad?
K: Yes, I have.
P: Oh, that's lucky for me! What's your name?
K: Kirsty Andrews.
P: OK, Kirsty. Which countries have you lived in?
K: Erm … England, Oman and Japan. That's it, I think.
P: Why have you lived in so many places?
K: Because of my Dad's job.
P: I see. And … erm … what's your favourite country?
K: Australia! No, seriously, I really like Japan. It's amazing! It's so different.
P: Can you speak Japanese?
K: A little bit, yeah [yes].
P: Have you ever worked in any of these countries?
K: No, I haven't.
P: OK. Next question. Has your experience changed you in any way?
K: OK. Let me see … well … I know a lot more about the differences between cultures … and I don't think that my way is the best way or the only way.
P: What about friends? I mean, do you see your old friends from the different countries?
K: Yeah, that's a problem. My best friend is in Japan. She's visited me once or twice here and we send emails all the time but I still miss her a lot.
P: I can understand that. Right … final question … are there any other countries you'd like to live in?
K: Well, I've never lived in a poor country. I think it could be an important experience. Maybe an African country, or something like that. And I haven't lived in South America. I'd like to spend some time there. Maybe I'll do these things after graduation.
P: Right … I'll let you get on with your lunch. Thanks a lot for your time, Kirsty.

2b Students do activity as per Coursebook. Give students time to look at the form and try to complete any gaps they can before playing the recording.

> 1 England; 2 Japan; 3 Japan; 4 amazing, different;
> 5 Japanese; 6 cultures; 7 friends; 8 poor; 9 South

GRAMMAR: present perfect

[!] Some students may have problems with this tense because it doesn't exist or is used differently in their language. They may produce mistakes like the following:

I've been to Senegal in Africa last year.

Learning a new concept in another language is a process. That means that students will often get it right and then make a mistake. This process of getting it 'right and wrong' can take some time. A good strategy is to continue to remind or prompt the students so they can self-correct. For example:

STUDENT: I've been to Russia last summer.
TEACHER: Present perfect? / I've been last summer?
STUDENT: Oh, no. I went to Russia last summer.
TEACHER: Right. That's the correct grammar. And what did you think of Russia?

This process of acquiring language requires both students and teachers to be patient.

3 Students do activity as per Coursebook.

> The speaker does not say when.

4 Students do activity as per Coursebook.

> 1 've; 2 haven't; 3 worked; 4 Have; 5 Has
> **Note:** *ever* means at any time in the past up to now.

For a full explanation and further practice activities, go to pages 144–145 in the Language Reference.

GRAMMAR TIP

Read through the box with students; irregular past participles are covered in exercise 9.

5a Students do activity as per Coursebook.

> 1 've visited; 2 've changed; 3 's talked;
> 4 's watched; 5 've moved

2.43

5b Students do activity as per Coursebook.

> **Track 2.43**
> 1 We've visited a lot of interesting places.
> 2 I've changed a lot in the last ten years.
> 3 She's talked to people from a lot of countries.
> 4 He's watched films in different languages.
> 5 They've moved house several times.

5c Write this question on the board and ask students what possible answers there are:

Have you visited another country?

- Students should be able to come up with *Yes, No, Yes, I have, No, I haven't.*

- Drill the short answer forms. One way is to give prompts to students, i.e.
  TEACHER: Has he been to France? (Positive.)
  STUDENTS: Yes, he has.
  TEACHER: Has he been to France? (Negative.)
  STUDENTS: No, he hasn't.

- Tell students to work individually to turn the sentences in exercise 5a into questions, and check their answers.

- Get students to work in pairs to ask and answer the questions.

- When students are ready get them to tell the whole class one thing their partner said, using third person, for example:

  Daniela has been to a lot of interesting countries: France, Mali and Poland.

READING

Preteach: *to feel at home* (to feel comfortable in a place), *to be good at something* (someone who is good at something can do it well), *independent* (responsible for yourself, making your own decisions and not needing help from other people), *proud* (pleased because you think that something you have achieved or are connected with is very good), *lonely* (unhappy because you are alone), *close to someone* (if two people are close, they like or love each other very much)

6 Students do activity as per Coursebook. As this is a gist question encourage the students to read the text quickly. Give them a time limit of 40 seconds to match the reasons with the person who is writing.

> 3

7 Students do activity as per Coursebook.

> 1 Maria; 2 Andy; 3 Nina; 4 Nina/Maria; 5 Students ideas will vary.

8 Students do activity as per Coursebook. Have a classroom discussion by asking students if they want to be 'global nomads'. Why (not)?

Suggested answers:

Advantages	Disadvantages
A good life with large homes and nice holidays. Well-educated, international citizens. Experience a lot. Good at learning new skills and meeting people. See the world. Speak different languages. Independent and strong. Comfortable with people from all over the world.	Can feel different from others. Can't stay in one place for long. May not feel at home anywhere/feel like a stranger everywhere. Can feel lonely at times.

GRAMMAR TIP

Look at the box with students. Ask them if they know any other examples of irregular past participles.

9a Students do activity as per Coursebook.

> to grow → grown; to do → done; to feel → felt;
> to become → become

9b Students do activity as per Coursebook. Get them to look at page 159 and find the past participles.

- You should check the whole class's pronunciation by getting them to repeat the verbs after you.

> drive → driven; eat → eaten; fly → flown;
> live → lived; read → read; travel → travelled;
> visit → visited; work → worked; study → studied

For a full explanation and further practice activities, go to page 144 in the Language Reference.

SPEAKING

10 Give students some time to think about the questions they will ask. They can check the past participles but don't let them write out the questions in full.

- Students work in pairs and ask and answer questions. Monitor the activity.
- Get them to tell you some of the things they discussed.
- Look at their language performance if you feel it is important.

HOMEWORK OPTIONS

Students do/finish the extra practice activities 1 and 2 on page 145 in the Language Reference.

Students do the exercises on pages 72–73 of the Workbook.

12.2 JOURNEYS OF A LIFETIME

IN THIS LESSON

Lesson topic and staging

This lesson looks at the travels and writing of the well-known comedian and actor, Michael Palin. Students begin the lesson by reading about four travel books by Palin. They then read short extracts from the four books before examining collocation (the tendency for words to occur regularly with other words) between adjectives and nouns, for example a *crowded train* or *still water*. Students then read an interview with Palin in which he talks about his experiences as a traveller and writer. The reading provides the context for the grammar focus: present perfect and past simple. Students study how these two tenses work together in conversation, the present perfect being used to open conversations about experiences in life, and the past simple to find out when these experiences happened. After working with the meaning and form of the language, the lesson finishes with a speaking activity. Students talk about a variety of experiences they have had.

Objectives

By the end of the lesson students should have:

- read about the well-known British travel writer Michael Palin
- learned about how certain adjectives collocate with certain nouns
- learned how the present perfect contrasts with the past simple when talking about experiences in life
- learned to talk about past experiences they have had

Timings

If short of time, you could drop exercise 3 and ask students to do it for homework.

A possible lesson break would be after exercise 5 on page 103.

WARM-UP

This activity revises common regular and irregular past participles.

- Divide students into As and Bs. Both groups have to write down 10 verbs, for example *go, walk, be, become*, etc. Tell students that they have to know how to say and spell the past participles but they shouldn't write them down.
- As then ask Bs for the past participle form of the verbs. Elicit and write the question on the board: *What is the past participle of ___ ?*
- When As have finished, Bs ask their ten questions.

VOCABULARY: adjective + noun

1 Get students to look at the four photos of different places and the man in the middle. Ask them if they know where these places are and what the connection is between them and the man.

- Students do activity as per Coursebook.

> 1C; 2A; 3D; 4B

ⓘ Photo A shows the village of Ghandruk, with the Annapurna and Machhapuchhre peaks in the background.

Photo B shows the Heart Reef on the Great Barrier Reef near Queensland, Australia.

Photo C shows two Adelie penguins on an iceberg in the Antarctic.

Photo D shows the Sahara Desert.

2 Students do activity as per Coursebook. There may be some words students don't know but do not preteach any of them yet, because students work with the vocabulary in the next activity. Make sure students match the extracts with the book titles and descriptions in exercise 1, not with the photos.

- After you check the answers, ask students which books they want to read and why.

> A 1; B 4; C 2; D 3

3a Students do activity as per Coursebook.

> 1 still; 2 lonely; 3 crowded; 4 empty; 5 pale; 6 bare

3b Explain to students that there are many adjective + noun combinations in English, for example *a difficult question*. Ask students if they can think of any other examples.

> 1 crowded; 2 pale; 3 empty; 4 lonely; 5 bare; 6 still

💡 Tell students that it is important to note these adjective + noun combinations. They can create a special section headed *Adjective + noun combinations* in their notebooks. For example: *a hard exam* or *a serious problem*.

READING

4 Make sure students read the questions before they read the article.

> a 5; b 2; c 1; d 6; e 4; f 3

5 Students do activity as per Coursebook.

1 true (*I made a TV series – Around the World in 80 Days – and wrote a book about that trip, and so I started this great career.*); **2** true (*I've written six travel books – one for each TV series.*); **3** false (*Peru … the most wonderful, magical place I've ever been to in all my travels.*); **4** false (*I've eaten insects and a snake. I ate that when I was in China, in 1985.*); **5** false (*Ah, my favourite place is in Peru.*); **6** true (*The most important thing that I have learned is that people are warm, kind and fun all over the world …*)

✎ To extend this activity, you could ask students to write two questions they would like to ask Palin about his experiences. Of course, they will never get the answers but you can always get them to imagine Palin's answers and tell their classmates what they think he would say!

GRAMMAR: present perfect and past simple

⚠ Students commonly make mistakes with these two tenses. It may help students to visualise the difference by writing two model sentences and drawing two timelines on the board.

In the first sentence the action happened in the past but we do not know when or it is not important: the focus is on the experience. The arrows show that the action happened some time in the past, and that it is relevant to the present.

I've been to Spain.

In the second sentence the action happened in the past AND we know when it happened.

I went in 2003.

6 Students do activity as per Coursebook.

> 1a, d; 2 past simple; 3 present perfect

GRAMMAR TIP

Read through the box and make sure that students understand the meaning of *I've gone*. Point out that we use *gone* only when somebody or something hasn't returned.

For a full explanation and further practice activities, go to pages 144–145 in the Language Reference.

7a Students do activity as per Coursebook.

> **2** haven't been; **3** went; **4** visited; **5** 've worked; **6** 've visited; **7** worked; **8** had; **9** was; **10** studied

7b

- Students need to use the model in exercise 7a to do this. Get students to make notes about their travel experiences. Tell students that this doesn't have to be trips abroad. If they haven't been abroad, they should write about their trips within their country.

- Get students to use the text in 7a as a model to write their travel histories. Monitor the activity and help students when needed.

- Get a few students to read out their experiences to the whole class. Ask other students to note places they have been to or places they want to visit.

- When students have finished ask other students to comment, for example:

  Luke's been to India. I've been there too.

  Luke's been to Moscow. I want to go there.

🔧 If (some) students haven't travelled much in their own country, you can get them to write about a person they know who has travelled. Alternatively, tell them this is the opportunity to live out their dreams of travelling. Tell them to write an imaginary history and include all the places they have always wanted to visit!

SPEAKING

8a

Preteach: *campsite* (a piece of land where you can stay in a tent), *to climb a mountain* (to move towards the top of a mountain)

- Explain the activity to students and divide them into As and Bs.

- Give them time to read the tables and prepare their questions in their heads.

- Model a typical exchange by acting out the dialogue in exercise 8a.

- Let students ask and answer the questions and monitor the activity.

8b Get different students to tell the whole class one thing about their partner. Remind them to use the third person.

- Give feedback on the task and the language performance.

HOMEWORK OPTIONS

If students haven't finished their short travel histories, they can do it for homework.

Students do/finish the extra practice activities 3, 4, 6 and 7 on page 145 in the Language Reference.

Students do the exercises on pages 74–75 of the Workbook.

12.3 SCENARIO: AROUND THE WORLD

IN THIS LESSON

Lesson topic and staging

The lesson is based around a board game. The game continues the topic of travel and recycles language from the whole course. Students start the lesson talking about a number of famous places around the world, from the Great Wall of China to Machu Picchu, the incredible Inca city in Peru. In the listening that follows, a woman talks about visiting the Empire State Building in New York. Students then move on to the main focus of the lesson, the task. The task is based on a board game in which students travel around the world in pairs visiting six famous places they want to see. When they land on a tourist attraction they have to talk about a topic for 30 seconds. When a student has visited all six of the attractions that they wanted to see they have to head back to the starting point. The first student to reach Heathrow Airport, the starting point of the game, wins.

Objectives

By the end of the lesson students should have:

- learned (more) about a number of famous tourist attractions around the world like the Djenne Mosque, Easter Island and Uluru

- revised language from the whole course

- improved their fluency when speaking in English

- relaxed and had fun playing a board game in English

Timings

Make sure you leave sufficient time at the end of the lesson to prepare for, complete and discuss the task in exercises 4a and 4b.

WARM-UP

This activity revises the present perfect and the past simple from Lesson 12.2.

- Write the following prompts on the board:

  1 Have/ever/fail an exam? What …? When …? Why …?

  2 Have/ever/eat an insect? When …? What…?

  3 Have/ever stay up all night? When …? Why …?

  4 Have/ever meet anyone famous? Who …? When …?

- Ask students to read them and then ask them: *What is the past participle of* fail, eat, stay *and* meet?

- Ask them to form the four questions from the prompts in number 1, i.e. *Have you ever failed an exam? What exam did you fail? When did you fail it? Why did you fail it?*

- Tell students to pick two questions that interest them, to write out the questions and to talk to their partner about the experience.
- Invite students to share any answers they want to with the whole group.

PREPARATION

1 Put students in pairs to talk about the places.

- Move students into larger groups to teach each other about places they don't know about.
- Open the discussion to the whole group. Ask students if there are any places they don't know about.

i Heathrow Airport is the main airport in London.

Table Mountain is the famous mountain in Cape Town, South Africa.

The Coliseum is a giant amphitheatre in the centre of the city of Rome. It was the largest ever built in the Roman Empire and was completed in AD 80 under emperor Titus.

The Taj Mahal, or 'Crown Palace', is a beautiful white marble Islamic tomb built by the emperor Shah Jahan for his second wife, Mumtaz Mahal, in 1631.

The Great Wall of China was built some 2,000 years ago and is 6,700 kilometres long. It stretches from east to west and was built to protect China from the nomadic Hsiung Nu tribes north of China.

Angkor Wat is an ancient temple in Cambodia, Southeast Asia. This magnificent temple was built in the 12th century to honour the Hindu god, Vishnu. The temple symbolises Hindu cosmology.

Mount Fuji or Fujisan is Japan's highest mountain at 3,776 meters. It is actually a dormant volcano and can be climbed between July and August every year.

Uluru is a huge rock formation in the middle of Australia. It is the only pilgrimage site visited by Aborigines and is a sacred place for these indigenous people of Australia. It is also visited by thousands of tourists. Most non-Aborigines call it Ayers Rock.

Easter Island is an isolated island in the South Pacific Ocean. It is famous for its *moai*, or giant stone statues, which were built by the Rapa Nui. These people mysteriously disappeared, probably because of a man-made ecological disaster. Nobody knows exactly why the stone statues were built.

The Grand Canyon is a deep narrow valley with steep sides in Colorado, USA. It was made by the Colorado River, which runs through the canyon. It is enormous: 446 kilometres long and between 1,524 and 1,829 metres deep.

Machu Picchu is an Inca city built high in the mountains in Peru. This incredible city is about 500 years old and was hand-built with stone.

The Empire State Building is one of New York's most famous tourist attractions. The building was finished in 1931 and has 102 stories. Since the tragedy of 9/11 it is the tallest building in New York at just over 443 metres tall.

The Amazon Forest is the biggest rain forest in the world: an amazing seven million square kilometres. It is in South America. Tragically, the forest is in danger – some scientists say it could disappear in just 50 years!

The Djenne Mosque is a mosque in Mali, West Africa. It was originally built in the 13th century but has been rebuilt twice since then. It is the largest mud-brick building in the world. Every year after the rainy season the people who live there help to repair the mud that covers the brick walls.

`2.44`

2a Students do activity as per Coursebook.

The Empire State Building in New York.

Track 2.44
Interviewer, Woman
I: What's the tallest building you've ever seen?
W: The tallest building? Well … let me see … erm … I haven't seen many really tall buildings, but last year I went to New York and I visited the Empire State Building, and I really liked it. Erm … I first saw the building from the plane. That was fantastic; it made me think of the film King Kong. Then I visited the building the next day. It's very tall and it's also beautiful, I think. It's different from most tall buildings because erm … it's made of bricks and has a lot of windows. Other tall buildings are all glass, so it's very different, and that's why I think that it looks beautiful. Anyway, I went to the top of the building in the lift, and the view from the top is wonderful. You can see all of Manhattan in every direction – the yellow taxis look so small, like tiny insects! Well, what else? Oh yes, I also went up the building at night. That was great – you can see all the lights of New York City below your feet. That was a very special moment for me. So, that's the tallest building I've seen.

2b Students do activity as per Coursebook. Remind them to take notes and not to write full sentences.

Suggested answers:
1 last year; 2 from the plane; 3 the next day, also went up the building at night; 4 fantastic, very tall, beautiful, different from most tall buildings because it's made of bricks and has a lot of windows, view from the top is wonderful, you can see all of Manhattan, you can see all the lights of New York City

2c Students do activity as per Coursebook.

> **Students should tick:** then, so, let me see, also, what else?, I think

🔧 If students find this exercise difficult, get them to look at the audioscript on page 156 and underline the OTHER USEFUL PHRASES in context (see above).

3 Get students to do the task and try to use as many of the OTHER USEFUL PHRASES as they can.

TASK: giving short talks

Task summary: This task is different from the other tasks in the Coursebook. It consists in playing a board game. Every time students land on one of the tourist attractions (2–16) in exercise 1 they have to talk for 30 seconds about a topic. The aims of the game are to improve students' fluency when speaking, to revise language areas from the Coursebook and to have fun. A successful task outcome is when students manage to achieve all three of the aims.

4a Students do activity as per Coursebook. Stress that the six must come from at least three different continents.

4b Hand out the dice and counters. If you don't have any counters, get students to use coins.

- Get students to read the rules and then carefully check they understand them.

- Tell students to read the *Topics for your talks* section and see if they have any questions.

- Do an example or two with the class to model the activity. Remind students about the OTHER USEFUL PHRASES and let them start the game.

- Monitor the activity and help students if they have any problems. Also take notes on examples of correct an incorrect language use.

- Ask students how they got on. What did they find out about their partners? How helpful was the OTHER USEFUL PHRASES when they were talking? Did they have any problems?

- Give students feedback on their language performance if necessary.

HOMEWORK OPTION

Students do the exercises on page 76 of the Workbook.

12.4 STUDY AND WRITING SKILLS

IN THIS LESSON

Lesson topic and staging

The course is about to finish and this is the last lesson in this Coursebook. Appropriately, the first part of the lesson focuses on learning English outside the classroom. Students look at a number of different ways to continue learning English, especially using the Internet to practise reading, listening and writing. This part of the lesson finishes on a good piece of advice about memory and learning. In the second part of the lesson students learn how to write a postcard. They examine the subject matter, style and structure of two postcards. Next students look at the common use of extreme adjectives in postcards such as *disgusting* rather than *not very good* and *awful* rather than *unpleasant*. Students then apply this use of adjectives and the other things they have learned to write a postcard to a friend or member of their family.

Objectives

By the end of the lesson students should have:

- learned (more) about how to continue learning English outside the classroom

- learned about how we can remember more about what we study

- analysed the subject matter, style and structure of postcards

- written a postcard to a friend or family member describing their holiday

Common European Framework

Students can write a simple description of their holiday.

Timings

If short of time, you could drop exercises 7 and 8.

A possible lesson break would be after exercise 6 on page 106.

WARM-UP

This activity prepares students for the topic of the lesson, learning outside the classroom.

- Write these questions on the board and ask students to talk about them.

  1 What do you do to learn English outside the classroom?

  2 Can you think of other ways to practise English that you don't do? For example, listen to an English-speaking radio channel.

- Get a few students to talk to the whole group about their ideas.

STUDY SKILLS: learning outside the classroom

1 Students do activity as per Coursebook.

2

Preteach: *Internet message board* (a place on the Internet where people can talk about topics of interest to them such as technology, food, sports, different kinds of music, computer games and so on)

- Students do activity as per Coursebook. Get the whole group to exchange ideas.

3 Students do activity as per Coursebook.

- Check students answers and see if any of them have done these things.

  A 1; **B** 3; **C** 2

> 2.45

4a

Preteach: *chat room* (a place on the Internet where people can talk to each other by typing in messages in real time)

- Students do activity as per Coursebook.

  message boards, video clips, language-learning websites

Track 2.45

OK, now I'm going to talk about technology and learning. First of all, the Internet. There are several ways you can use it to improve your English, because you can read, listen and write.

Writing practice is excellent for your learning; it's almost as important as speaking. On the Internet there are two places where you can write – message boards and live chat rooms. Live chat rooms are great for improving your fluency, because you have to write quickly. It's like a conversation. A message board is good for both fluency and accuracy because you can think and prepare before you write. Both are excellent for communication practice. Now, the Internet is a good place to practise your listening. You should visit a good news site, such as the BBC, and watch the short video clips. Before you watch, you can read about the story, and then you can watch the clip as many times as you want. Often these are short and you can watch clips about news and sports, even music. In order to improve your listening, you have to be an active listener: make notes, try to write down the main points, try to write down new vocabulary.

Finally, on the Internet there are many sites for English language learning. Have you visited the website for this book? There are extra practice exercises and reading materials. The BBC World Service also has an excellent site for learning English, with special message boards for learners.

The best thing about the Internet is that it gives you the chance to do things with the language, and that's very important. All right? Good, now I'm going to talk about …

4b Students do activity as per Coursebook.

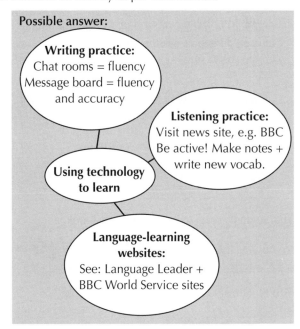

Possible answer:

Writing practice: Chat rooms = fluency / Message board = fluency and accuracy

Listening practice: Visit news site, e.g. BBC / Be active! Make notes + write new vocab.

Using technology to learn

Language-learning websites: See: Language Leader + BBC World Service sites

5 Students do activity as per Coursebook.

> 2.46

6

Preteach: *quote* (words that come from a book, poem, etc.)

- Get students to read the quote and then to try and complete it with the words in the box.

- Play the recording so that students can check their ideas. Give them time to think about the text and compare answers with a partner before checking the whole group's answers.

  1 see; **2** say; **3** read; **4** hear; **5** see; **6** say; **7** do

---

Track 2.46

In conclusion, the important thing is to do lots of different things: 'We remember 20 percent of what we read, 30 percent of what we hear, 40 percent of what we see, 50 percent of what we say, 60 percent of what we do and 90 percent of what we read, hear, see, say and do.' So, follow my advice and enjoy practising your English outside the classroom.

- Ask students what they could learn from the quote from Flanagan.

WRITING SKILLS: a postcard

7 Get students to discuss the questions in pairs.

- When they are ready ask a couple of students to tell the whole group what their partner said.

8 Students do activity as per Coursebook. Write their answers on the board.

- Ask students to elaborate on their choices by asking questions like *What do people write about famous buildings in postcards?* If students say something unusual like *jobs*, ask them to explain their choice as all the words and phrases could be possible given the right context.

  Suggested answers: famous buildings, food, hotels, activities, interesting places, the weather

9 Students do activity as per coursebook.

  famous buildings, activities, interesting places, the weather

10a Students do activity as per Coursebook.

  1 really; **2** amazing; **3** dresses; **4** temple; **5** OK; **6** Lots

10b Students do activity as per Coursebook.

  1d; 2f; 3e; 4a; 5b; 6c

11 Students do activity as per Coursebook. Ask students what BS8 2HP is called in English (the postcode).

  Sarah Gilbert
  49 Clifton Road
  Bristol
  BS8 2HP
  UK

12 Students do activity as per Coursebook.

  She is enjoying her trip. Words and phrases that show this are:
  Everyone is really friendly and the palace is amazing!
  I've bought lots of beautiful dresses!
  Everyone said it's beautiful and they're right.
  I've seen some incredible sunsets …
  He's really nice.
  … a lovely boat trip …

13 Students do activity as per Coursebook. When you go through the answers, point out to students the strength of Mariam's language in the adjectives she uses. Demonstrate the strength of adjectives like *disgusting* and *terrible* by getting students to order the following adjectives and adjectival phrases along a line such as the one below: *OK, disgusting, very good, not very good, fantastic.* The correct order is *fantastic, very good, OK, not very good, disgusting.*

  ☺ _____ ☺ _____ ☹

  Mariam is having the worst holiday.

14 Explain the writing task to students and get them to decide who they are going to write to. That will help them decide on the appropriate style.

- Look at the two models and get students to underline stock phrases for opening and closing a postcard. You could put them on the board in a table.

Openings	Closings
Hi Sarah	I hope you're well. Take care. Love, Hannah
Dear Mum and Dad	Hope everything is OK at home. See you soon. Lots of love, Hannah

- Tell students to decide on the topics and the order in which they are going to write about them.
- Get them to make notes on the topics.
- When they are ready ask students to write the postcards. Monitor their writing and answer any questions they have.

HOMEWORK OPTIONS

If students have not finished their letters, ask them to do so for homework. Alternatively, you could ask students to write another letter.

Students do the exercises on page 77 of the Workbook.

Review

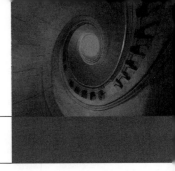

UNITS 10–12

GRAMMAR

1

> **1** have helped; **2** should; **3** are people going to;
> **4** visited; **5** has been; **6** should; **7** have; **8** won't;
> **9** have found; **10** should; **11** are going to run;
> **12** will

2

> **1** false (*New technology and small, modern cars
> have helped our roads and environment but
> scientists say we should be even greener.*); **2** false
> (*… you have to plug your electric car into the
> electricity every evening …*); **3** true (*It's currently
> the most popular green choice.*); **4** true (*Do you
> recycle your vegetable oil and animal products?
> You should do this because one day these
> 'biofuels'…*)

3 Students could discuss this in pairs or you could have
a class discussion.

4

> 1c; 2e; 3a; 4f; 5d; 6b

5 First get students to decide on the three places that
their partner is going to ask them questions about;
they should tell their partners what these places are.

- Give students a few minutes to prepare their
  questions. Remind them that they need to make new
  questions using phrases a–f – they shouldn't just
  repeat the questions in exercise 4.

VOCABULARY

6

> 1a; 2c; 3b; 4a; 5c; 6b; 7a; 8b; 9a; 10c

7 Ask the whole group to give you one advantage of
creditnow.com – for example, you can get a loan
quickly on line.

- Let students make a list of other advantages in pairs.
- When students are ready ask them to list the
  advantages.

Suggested answers:
Quick loans; buy things you want today and don't
pay any interest for one year; take a loan online
today and you don't have to pay anything back
for six months; receive a credit card; get discounts
with the credit card; get interest-free credit for six
months with the credit card

8 Students do activity as per Coursebook.

KEY LANGUAGE

`2.47`

9 This section revises the Key Language section from
Lesson 11.3 (checking understanding, page 97).

> **1** bike; **2** two; **3** £50; **4** CD; **5** opened/used; **6** £30

Track 2.47
2 Men
1
M1: Hello.
M2: Hello. I'm interested in the bike for sale.
M1: OK. Great. Well, it's about two years old.
M2: Sorry, did you say two?
M1: Yes. And it's 50 pounds.
M2: Sorry, was that 15 or 50?
M1: Fifty. It's a mountain bike.
M2: That sounds good.
M1: What else do you want to know about it?
M2: Erm, I don't know really.
M1: Well, would you like to see it then?
M2: Yes, I could come this afternoon …
2
Man, Woman
M: Hello.
W: Hello. I'm interested in the CD player for sale in the
  paper.
M: OK. Well, it's new. It's still in the box.
W: Sorry, what did you say?
M: It's in the box. I've never opened it.
W: Oh. And how much is it?
M: I paid 50 pounds for it. So it's 30 pounds. OK?
W: Sorry, can you repeat that?
M: It's 30 pounds.
W: OK. Could I come and see it?
M: Sure.
W: Where do you live exactly?

10a

> 1b; 2f; 3e; 4a; 5g; 6c; 7d

10b

> First conversation: **1**b, **5**g, **3**e, **2**f
> Second conversation: **6**c, **7**d, **4**a

11

> **1** Can you repeat that, please?
> **2** Sorry, was that 15 or 50?
> **3** What else do you want to know about it?
> **4** Could I come and see it?

12 Students do activity as per Coursebook

LANGUAGE CHECK

13

> **1** to; **2** did; **3** not; **4** personally; **5** to; **6** be; **7** right;
> **8** have (second); **9** has; **10** never

LOOK BACK

14

> give advice: 10.1, exercises 9 and 10; give your
> opinion about money: 10.3, exercise 1; talk about
> the year 2100: 11.1, exercise 9; plan a party: 11.2,
> exercise 9; give directions to your house: 11.4,
> exercise 12; read about people who have grown
> up abroad: 12.1, exercise 6; talk about places
> you've visited: 12.2, exercise 8a; write a postcard:
> 12.4, exercise 14

Extra practice key

Unit 1

1 2 's; 3 're; 4 are; 5 is; 6 's; 7 are
2 2 ✓; 3 ✓; 4 ✗ No, they **aren't**. 5 ✓; 6 ✗ No, **I'm not**. I'm French.
3 1c; 2a; 3f; 4e; 5b; 6d
4 2 There **are** not any cars in Venice.
  3 Is there a film at the cinema today? – No, **there** isn't.
  4 In Chicago, **are** there any good theatres?
  5 In Kyoto, there are a lot **of** old buildings.
5 2 I'm; 3 is; 4 are; 5 isn't; 6 a; 7 Are
6 1d; 2e; 3c; 4a; 5b
7 The library is opposite the university/between the park and the market/next to the park/next to the market.
9 Tokyo
10 2 hot; 3 quiet; 4 big; 5 expensive; 6 new; 7 cold; 8 cheap
11

Buildings	Stations	Shopping
(museum)	bus	market
cinema	railway	bookshop
temple		shopping centre

Unit 2

1 2 live; 3 flies; 4 study; 5 buys; 6 goes; 7 has; 8 meet
2 2 doesn't; 3 isn't; 4 don't; 5 don't; 6 don't; 7 don't; 8 don't
4 1 don't; 2 What; 3 Are; 4 Does, doesn't; 5 What; 6 Is; 7 Where; 8 Do, don't
5 2e; 3d; 4a; 5c
6 2 pilot; 3 lawyer; 4 web designer; 5 lecturer; 6 fashion buyer
7 1 live in a hall of residence; 2 do a course; 3 go to university; 4 give classes; 5 score of 100
8 2 salary; 3 duties; 4 filing; 5 qualifications

Unit 3

1 2 When/How; 3 Why; 4 Where; 5 What; 6 Which; 7 When; 8 Who
3 1 always; 2 often; 3 never; 4 occasionally; 5 once a week; 6 sometimes
4 2 ✓; 3 ✗ I play tennis every week. 4 ✓; 5 ✓; 6 ✗ He is always at school. 7 ✗ How often are you in London? 8 ✓
5 2 sounds; 3 don't want; 4 don't, go; 5 having; 6 meet
6

Sea words	Desert words
(shark)	rock
dolphin	plant
ocean	cactus
whale	sand
seagull	

7 2 drum dance; 3 workshop; 4 notebook; 5 DVD player; 6 whiteboard; 7 coursebook; 8 blackboard
8 They are all one word, except *drum dance* and *DVD player*.
9 2 (b)oils; 3 (s)wim; 4 (u)nderstand; 5 (m)ean; 6 (c)ook; 7 (j)ump

Unit 4

1 2a; 3e; 4b; 5c
2 2 a; 3 an; 4 a; 5 a; 6 the
3 2 The festival … 3 … enjoy thrillers. 4 … take the children … 5 … an accountant. 6 The director … 7 … in the garden. 8 … in the cinema …
4 2 Can/does; 3 doesn't; 4 makes; 5 to; 6 do
6 2b; 3e; 4g; 5c; 6d; 7a; 8f
7 2 animations; 3 westerns; 4 historical; 5 Thrillers
8 1 do aerobics; 2 go swimming; 3 play football; 4 do yoga; 5 go running; 6 play basketball; 7 play tennis
9

Accommodation	Entertainment
campsite	kids' club
chalet	painting class
double room	satellite TV
family room	
sea view	

Unit 5

1 2 more beautiful; 3 cheaper; 4 older; 5 better; 6 faster; 7 hotter; 8 easier
2 2 fastest; 3 most comfortable; 4 worst; 5 best; 6 most important; 7 shortest; 8 most romantic
4 1 nice(e)r; 2 eas(y)ier; 3 expensive(r); 4 bigg(g)est; 5 worse(r); 6 be(s)tter; 7 bus(y)iest; 8 lat(t)est
5 2c; 3e; 4d; 5f; 6a
7 2b; 3e; 4a; 5c; 6d
8 1 topic sentence; 2 final copy; 3 paragraph; 4 sentence(s); 5 mind map

Unit 6

1

Countable nouns	Uncountable nouns
city	(food)
cinema	coffee
pilot	money
film	rain
vitamin	rice

2 1 Bread is good for you. 2 We work in an office. 3 Green tea is a super drink. 4 Nurses work in hospitals. 5 Olive oil is good on salad.
3 2 any; 3 any; 4 any; 5 some; 6 any; 7 some; 8 some; 9 any; 10 some
4 2 Many; 3 much; 4 a lot of; 5 many; 6 a lot of
6 2 has got; 3 has got; 4 haven't got; 5 have got
7 2c; 3f; 4b; 5d; 6a
8

Fruit	Meat	Fish	Vegetables	Drinks
(banana)	roast beef	caviar	broccoli	coffee
orange	burger	salmon	carrot	green tea
strawberry(ies)	chicken	sardine	garlic	milk
	chilli con carne	sushi	red pepper	
	lamb (kebab)		potato(es)	
			tomato(es)	

10 2 medicine; 3 diet; 4 illness; 5 memory

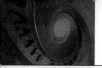

Unit 7

1 2 're buying; 3 are going; 4 's meeting; 5 're doing;
6 isn't working; 7 're sitting; 8 's not raining

2 2 I'm organising; 3 are visiting; 4 helps; 5 she's doing;
6 are staying; 7 I'm trying; 8 eat

3 2 What are you doing? 3 Who are you phoning?
4 Where are they going? 5 How are you feeling?

4 2b; 3a; 4f; 5c; 6e

5 1b; 2a; 3g; 4c; 5e; 6f; 7d

6 1 pay; 2 spend; 3 try; 4 checks; 5 buy; 6 spend

7 1 supermarket; 2 customer; 3 online shopping;
4 product; 5 furniture; 6 hypermarket; 7 price;
8 stationery

8 1 petrol; 2 highway; 3 car; 4 motel; 5 centre; 6 mall;
7 store

Unit 8

1 2 Was; 3 wasn't; 4 was; 5 was; 6 were; 7 Were;
8 weren't; 9 were; 10 was; 11 Was; 12 Were; 13 were;
14 was

2 2 Was the teacher here? 3 Where were you yesterday
evening? 4 Was it a good film? 5 Who were you with?

4 2 can't; 3 could; 4 could; 5 can, couldn't; 6 couldn't;
7 can

5 2 what; 3 can; 4 help; 5 when; 6 give; 7 where

6 b 2; c 4; d 1; e 7; f 3; g 6

7 2 window; 3 painting; 4 door; 5 gate; 6 garden

8 2 on; 3 on; 4 about; 5 in; 6 onto

9 2 wooden; 3 circular; 4 wide; 5 rectangle; 6 weigh

Unit 9

1 2 went; 3 returned; 4 built; 5 held; 6 worked;
7 drove; 8 stood; 9 helped; 10 studied; 11 travelled;
12 invented

2 1 returned/travelled; 2 helped; 3 studied;
4 enjoyed; 5 drove/travelled; 6 studied/worked;
7 built/invented; 12 built

3 2 They did not see him. Did you? 3 Did you drive
here in your car? 4 What time did you leave? 5 Where
did you live before you lived in Morocco? 6 Did they
say 'yes'? – Yes, they did. 7 My brother was not born
in hospital. 8 Some of our friends did not come to the
party last night.

4 2 He sat … 3 The Romans wore … 4 They didn't like
… 5 Did you enjoy … 6 She wasn't interested …

7 b 3; c 4; d 1

8

Parts of the body	Machines
(bones)	scanner
skin	microscope
teeth	

9 1g; 2c; 3a; 4j; 5h; 6i; 7b; 8f; 9d; 10e

Unit 10

1 2 You should move to a more beautiful city. 3 You
should change your account. 4 He should be more
careful. 5 You should ask for the money (back). 6 You
should shop on the Internet.

2 **Suggested answers:** 2 They shouldn't go out all the
time and never study. They should spend more time
at home and study more. 3 He shouldn't smoke
50 cigarettes a day. He should try to stop. 4 You
shouldn't watch so much television. You should
read more. 5 She shouldn't spend all her money on
clothes. She should wear her old clothes more.

3 2 Should we walk? 3 Should he do the exam this
term? 4 Should I get a credit card?

4 2 have to; 3 don't have to; 4 has to; 5 doesn't have to;
6 Do, have to; 7 don't have to; 8 Do, have to; 9 does,
have to

5 2d; 3f; 4b; 5g; 6h; 7a; 8e

6 2g; 3b; 4i; 5c; 6f; 7d; 8a; 9e

Unit 11

1 2 'll; 3 will; 4 won't; 5 won't; 6 'll; 7 will; 8 won't; 9 'll

3 2 Are you going to watch TV? 3 He isn't going
to do anything new. 4 Is John going to visit his
grandmother? 5 We aren't going to change our plans.
6 Are Bertrand and Tijana going to build a house?
7 They're going to find out about flight times. 8 What
are we going to recycle?

4 2 it; 3 say; 4 repeat; 5 Was

5 b A laptop. c About 18 months. d Eighteen. One-
eight months. e I'd like £200. f Two hundred pounds.
g Yes, it was.

6 1 centre; 2 park; 3 station

7 1 (wardrobe), bed; 2 lid, saucepan, cooker, cupboard,
dishwasher, fridge-freezer, table, washing machine;
3 armchair, bookcase, sofa; 4 bath, shower

8 1 revise; 2 revision; 3 pass; 4 fail; 5 practice;
6 Relaxation

Unit 12

1 2 Have, looked; 3 Has, (ever) driven; 4 've eaten;
5 Have, watched; 6 Have, talked; 7 've been;
8 's gone

2 2 see → seen; 3 went → gone; 4 have → had;
5 growed → grown; 6 maked → made

3 1 made; 2 have been; 3 ate; 4 she left; 5 she's ever
been; 6 didn't play; 7 haven't met; 8 have never been

4 2a; 3e; 4c; 5d

5 2 perhaps; 3 so; 4 also

6 2 empty; 3 fascinating; 4 kind; 5 well-educated;
6 unpleasant

7 2 pale colour; 3 bare feet; 4 empty bottle; 5 lonely life

Teaching notes for photocopiable activities

1A Mega cities (use after Lesson 1.2) **

Aim: to practise grammar (*to be, there is, there are*) and vocabulary (adjectives to describe a city and places in a city)

Grouping: groups of four

Procedure:

- Write *mega city* on the board and explain that mega cities are cities with ten million people or more. Ask students if they know any mega cities (the ten largest mega cities in the world, in order of size, are Tokyo, Mexico City, Seoul, New York, São Paulo, Mumbai, Delhi, Shanghai, Los Angeles, Osaka).

- You may want to preteach all or some of the following: *climate* (weather), *skyscraper*, *river*, *centre* (of a place), *pyramid*.

- Explain the activity: students work in groups of four. Each student has a text about a different mega city and a table. Students read about their city and then complete their part of the table.

- Once students have completed their table, take the texts away. Students then work in their groups asking and answering questions to complete the rest of the table. You may want to elicit the questions needed and write them on the board, i.e.:

  Are there any museums/skyscrapers (there)? Is there a river (there)? Is the climate good?

- When students have finished, ask them which city they would like to visit and why.

1B Old town, new town (use after Lesson 1.3) **

Aim: to practise saying where places are; to revise the names of places

Grouping: pairs

Procedure:

- Ask students to look at the symbols on page 10 of the Coursebook and see how many place names they remember.

- Put students into pairs and explain the activity. Student A has a map of a street in a town, but the map is very old and now has some mistakes. Student B has the correct map: there are six differences. Student A has to correct his/her map by asking Student B questions. He/She must only ask questions – they shouldn't show each other their maps. For example:

  Is there a market? – Yes, there is. It's opposite …

- The activity is finished when Student As have corrected all six mistakes in their map.

- Hand out the maps and elicit the question about the market: *Is there a market?*

- Remind students of the three possible responses: *Yes, there is. No, there isn't. I'm not sure.*

- You could ask students if they think the changes to the town are good or bad.

2A What's my job? (use after Lesson 2.2) **-***

Aim: to practise grammar (present simple questions and short answers) and vocabulary (jobs and places of work)

Grouping: groups of three to six

Procedure:

- Brainstorm as many different jobs with the students as possible.

- Hand out a copy of the worksheet to each group and explain the first part of the activity: students match the sentence halves to form questions that can be used to ask about jobs.

- Go over the answers and explain the second part of the activity: students take it in turns to choose one of the jobs illustrated on the worksheet (they shouldn't tell the others which they've chosen). The other students in the group have to ask *Yes/No* questions to try to work out which job the first student has chosen. They can use the questions on the worksheet, or any of their own.

- Demonstrate the activity by telling students to ask you questions to find a job you are thinking about, for example *teacher*. Reply to their questions with short answers, i.e. *Yes, I do. No, I don't. Yes, I am. No, I'm not.*

- Get students to do the activity. Monitor and help when necessary.

2B Off to university (use after Lesson 2.3) **

Aim: to practise grammar (present simple questions and answers) and vocabulary

Grouping: pairs

Procedure:

- Explain the activity: students first work in two groups. Student As are foreign students who want to find out information about a university, Student Bs work at the university's Students' Information Office.

- Get students into groups of As only and Bs only and hand out the material to the students. Student As work together to complete questions they want to ask. Student Bs read their information sheet and fill in the headings.

- When students are ready, put them into pairs of As and Bs. Write the first two lines of the conversation on the board and tell students to start.

  INFORMATION OFFICER: Hello. Can I help you?

  FOREIGN STUDENT: Yes, please. I'm a foreign student and I want information about the university …

- Monitor the activity and take notes if necessary.

3A Questions! Questions! (use after Lesson 3.2) **-***

Aim: to practise grammar (question words and formation), vocabulary and information from Units 1–3

Grouping: groups of two to four

Materials: one dice for every group of students and one counter per student; students can use a coin instead of a counter

Procedure:

- Revise/Elicit the question words from page 23 of the Coursebook.
- Give out copies of the board game to each group and tell them to complete the questions with any one of the question words.
- Check students' answers.
- Hand out the dice and counters.
- Explain the activity: students take it in turns to roll a dice, move their counters and answer the question. If they can't answer the question they have to move back one square. If they land on a 'Move' square, they have to follow the instruction. The first player to land on or cross the 'Finish' square is the winner.

> **Suggested answers** (where appropriate):
> **2** in a court; **3** to search for food; **4** Mumbai; **7** Chile; **10** sharks (other answers are possible); **13** Ireland; **15** Ankara; **16** ten million or more; **17** about 30 percent; **19** Africa; **20** about 60 percent; **24** China; **26** different jobs in an office, such as answering the phone, writing and sending emails and letters, filing, photocopying; **28** He's an American businessman. His company, Microsoft, makes Windows, the popular computer program. **29** a tuna; **30** Warsaw

3B Festival fun (use after Lesson 3.3) **

Aim: to practise grammar (question formation), vocabulary (words related to festivals) and Key Language (making suggestions)

Grouping: groups of four

Procedure:

- Write the names of the following four festivals on the board: *The Notting Hill Carnival, La Tomatina, The Pan-African Film and Television Festival, Quebec City Winter Carnival*. Ask students if they know anything about them.
- You may want to preteach all or some of the following: *steelpan band* (a group of people that play music on drums made of metal), *costumes* (the special clothes people wear at festivals), *fireworks* (things that you light so that they explode into bright lights in the sky), *float* (a lorry that is decorated and takes people and music bands through a carnival), *dogsled race* (people race each other pulled by dogs).
- Explain the activity: students work in groups of four. Each student has a text about a festival and a table. Students read about their festival and then complete their part of the table.
- Once students have completed their table, take the texts away. Students then work in their groups asking and answering questions to complete the rest of the table. You may want to elicit the questions needed and write them on the board, i.e.:

Where is it? How many days is it? When is it? How many visitors does it have? What activities are there?

- Once students have completed their tables, give out the set of preference cards (cut out from the bottom of the photocopiable page) – each student in the group should have a different card. Tell students to read their cards, and then discuss which festival to go to. There is no correct answer, and students will not be able to match all their preferences from their card. You may want to revise the language for making suggestions on page 27 of the Coursebook before they do this.

4A A dream hotel (use after Lesson 4.3) **-***

Aim: to practise grammar (articles), Key Language (asking for information) and vocabulary (sports, activities, accommodation and hotel facilities)

Grouping: from pairs to multiples of four to six students

Procedure:

- Tell students they are going to build the hotel. Preteach *facilities* (rooms, equipment or services that are available in a place).
- Ask them what things they need to think about, for example where the hotel is (in the mountains, on an island, by the sea, in a desert, in Europe, in Asia, etc.).
- Explain the activity. Show the students the handout. At each of the nine steps they have to talk about and agree on their answer to the question before they move on to the next question.
- Give students the handouts and elicit one or two answers for each question.
- When they have discussed the questions they should create a poster for their hotel which contains some reference to all nine points.
- When students are ready they present their poster to the whole class. Encourage students to ask the presenters further questions. You could refer them to the Key Language on page 36 of the Coursebook.
- Finally, you could get the class to vote on the best project. If you do this, make sure that this idea is clear to students before they begin to do the activity.

4B Bingo (use after Lesson 4.4) *-**

Aim: to practise numbers

Grouping: whole class to pairs

Procedure:

- Write the following numbers on the board and quickly check students can say them:

5.5	*50*	*55.5*	*500*	*550*
5,000	*5,500*	*5,555*	*50,000*	
55,000	*5 million*	*½*		

- Tell students that you are going to play 'Bingo'. If students do not know the game, explain the rules. Each student has a bingo card with nine spaces on it. They have to write in nine different numbers out of the 16 that you will write on the board.

Teaching notes for photocopiable activities

- Write the following 16 numbers on the board and let students complete their bingo cards:

12 million	*7.7*	*½*	*25,000*
12.4	*7 million*	*9,000*	*345*
8,456	*4 million*	*60*	*16*
333	*657*	*1,200*	*8 million*

- Tell them you will read out all the numbers and they will have to cross out the numbers on their cards. When a student has three numbers horizontally, vertically or diagonally they shout 'Bingo!'. Explain *horizontally*, *vertically* and *diagonally* with a diagram on the board.

- Read out the numbers slowly and clearly in this order:

8 million	*9,000*	*12.4*	*12 million*
345	*½*	*333*	*7.7*
4 million	*25,000*	*7 million*	*657*
60	*16*	*8,456*	*1,200*

- When someone shouts 'Bingo!' stop the game and check their numbers are correct. The winner is the one who crosses out all the numbers on his/her card.

5A Good, better, the best – a quiz (use after Lesson 5.3) **

Aim: to practise grammar (comparative and superlative adjectives) and information from Units 1–5

Grouping: pairs or groups of four to six

Procedure:

- Give each group a copy of the worksheet. Students look at the sentences and decide if they think they are correct or not. They tick (✓) or cross (✗) accordingly.

- Students then bet on their answer (minimum £1 and maximum £10) depending on how sure they are, and write down the amount in the 'Bet' column.

- Allow them about ten minutes for this, and then tell them to stop and check their answers. If students have bet on a correct sentence they write the amount that they bet in the 'Win' column. If they have bet on an incorrect sentence, they write the amount in the 'Lose' column.

- Get students to add up the amounts in the 'Win' and the 'Lose' columns, then subtract the 'Lose' column from the 'Win' column. The group with the most money is the winner.

> 1 true; 2 false; 3 true; 4 true; 5 false; 6 true; 7 false; 8 false; 9 false; 10 false; 11 false; 12 true; 13 false; 14 false; 15 false; 16 false; 17 false; 18 true; 19 true; 20 true; 21 true; 22 false

5B What's the best car? (use after Lesson 5.4) **–***

Aim: to practise grammar (comparative and superlative adjectives) and vocabulary (cars and adjectives to describe cars, e.g. fast, safe, etc.)

Grouping: small groups/pairs

Procedure:

- Show students the pictures of the two types of car and elicit their names: a *4x4* and an *estate car*.

- Get students to work in small groups, see how many differences they can find between the 4x4 and the estate car and note down their answers. For example, *An estate car is usually cheaper than a 4x4.*

- Check students' answers and explain the next activity as you hand out the first photocopy (the sections headed 'Student A' and 'Student B'): students work in pairs, As and Bs, and have to ask and answer questions to complete the missing information about the two cars.

- Model the first question and answer with two students. You may want to elicit the questions needed and write them on the board, i.e.:

  How much does it cost? What is its top speed? How many seats does it have? What size is it? How many stars does it have for safety? How many stars does it have for comfort?

- In the final stage, students have to look at information about two people, Tanya and Simon, who both want to buy a car. They then have to try to decide which car is suitable for which person. Hand out the information to each group, and explain the activity. Different answers are possible, so make students justify their answers.

- Preteach: *vet* (an animal doctor), *decorator* (someone whose job is to decorate rooms and buildings).

- Encourage students to use comparatives in their discussion. You might also like to give them some useful expressions, e.g.:

  I think … The 4x4 is … but the estate car is … What do you think about the … I think the 4x4 is better for … because …

> **Suggested answers:**
> **Tanya**
> The best choice for her is probably the 4x4 because it has enough space for her partner and their two big dogs. It has lots of space for golf clubs and skis too. In her job as a vet, Tanya will often need to use a 4x4 to travel around the countryside and across fields and even small streams to get to sick animals. The 4x4 will also be useful on their adventure holidays. Furthermore, Tanya can probably afford a 4x4 on the money she earns as a vet.
> **Simon**
> The best choice for Simon is probably the estate. It has enough seats for the family and enough space to store their things for weekends and for holidays. It might be too small for a camping holiday but they only go once a year. The estate is also big enough to do a weekly shop and for Simon to put in all his paint, brushes, etc. for decorating. Although the 4x4 is an attractive option it is much more expensive than the estate: almost double!

6A Food, drink or dish (use after Lesson 6.3) **

Aim: to practise grammar (*some, any, many, much, a lot* and question formation) and vocabulary (food, drink and dishes)

Grouping: pairs or larger groups

Procedure:

- Quickly brainstorm the vocabulary of food, drink and dishes. You could draw a mind map on the board (suggested bubble headings: *fruit, meat and fish, drinks, dishes, vegetables, others*) to go over this.

- Preteach: *flour* (white or brown, used for making bread, cakes, etc.), *beans*.

- Hand a copy of the worksheet to each pair or group. Explain the activity: students are going to play a guessing game. They first have to match the questions to the answers on the worksheet, and then they have to guess which food, drink or dish is being referred to (it is different for each question/answer pair).

- Once you have checked the answers, get students to take it in turns to think of a food, drink or dish of their own. The other students then have to ask questions like those on the worksheet to try to work out the food.

> **Suggested answers:**
> 1e carrot ; 2c fruit (other answers are possible);
> 3a pepper; 4b orange (and other fruit);
> 5i pasta, noodles, bread; 6f sushi; 7d milk;
> 8g tomato/cheese; 9h chilli con carne

6B What am I bid? (use after Lesson 6.2) **

Aim: to practise grammar (countable and uncountable nouns; *some, any, much, many, a lot of*)

Grouping: pairs and whole class

Procedure:

- Preteach: *auction* (an event at which things are sold to the person who offers the most money), *to bid for something* (to offer to pay a particular price for something in an auction).

- Ask students what people normally buy at an auction, for example old furniture, paintings, etc.

- Tell students that they are going to work in pairs and bid for things in an auction. However, in this auction they don't bid for furniture but for sentences that are grammatically correct. Tell them each pair has £500 and a list of 12 sentences.

- Put students in pairs and hand each pair a copy of the auction worksheet. Tell them to read the sentences and decide which are correct and which are incorrect. They should only bid for the sentences they think are correct and they can bid as much money as they want on each sentence, as long as they don't spend more than their £500 in the whole game.

- Give students about six or seven minutes to read through and talk about the sentences with their partners.

- When students are ready tell them that the auction will begin. They can only put their hands up and say the price they want to pay for the sentence. Play the 'auctioneer' and encourage them to bid for each sentence by encouraging them to buy. For example:

This is a beautiful sentence, ladies and gentleman. It is made of perfect English and is a typical sentence from the 21st century. OK, what am I bid for it? Yes, the woman in the blue top over there? £30? Am I bid more? £50 by the gentleman in the corner? £50. Any other bids?

- Continue the auction until all 12 sentences have been looked at – some may not be bought!

- When the auction is finished go back over all the sentences and check the grammar. Get students to correct any that are wrong.

- Finally, find the most successful bidders – the pair who bought the highest number of correct sentences.

> **Corrected sentences:**
> 2 Vegetables are my favourite type of food.
> 3 Do you write many/a lot of emails every day?
> 5 Milk is my favourite drink.
> 8 Children don't often drink much water.
> 9 A doctor works in a hospital.
> 11 Can I have some cheese and some bread, please?

7A Find the differences (use after Lesson 7.3) *-**

Aim: to practise grammar (present continuous or actions happening now) and vocabulary (shops, shopping and things we buy)

Grouping: pairs

Procedure:

- Tell students they are going to work in pairs. Each pair has two pictures which contain ten differences. Students shouldn't look at their partner's picture. They have to find the differences by describing and asking questions. For example:

In my picture, there's a man. He's buying a DVD.

How many children are walking in the street in your picture?

Hand out the pictures for Students A and B. Give students five to ten minutes to find the ten differences.

- Go over the answers and discuss correct and incorrect uses of the tense if necessary.

Teaching notes for photocopiable activities

1 A woman walking out of *Coco Fashion* with two/six bags.
2 A young man buying a book/DVD in *Music World*.
3 A man putting shopping/golf clubs in his car.
4 A woman walking along the street with no hat/a hat.
5 A young man sitting outside Whale Café reading a book/newspaper and drinking coffee.
6 A man crossing the road, holding hands with a small child/two small children.
7 A man/woman looking at something in the window of Whale Café.
8 A woman walking out of/into Whale Café.
9 An old man/woman walking a dog.
10 A man paying the waiter outside Whale Café with money (a note)/a credit card.

7B Say 'Yes!', say 'No!' (use after Lesson 7.4) **_***

Aim: to practise Key Language (giving advantages and disadvantages) and vocabulary (shops and shopping)

Grouping: groups of four

Procedure:

- Get students to brainstorm types of shop. Preteach: *butcher's* (a shop where you buy meat), *baker's* (a shop where you buy bread), *greengrocer's* (a shop where you buy fruit and vegetables), *pub* (a place where people meet to have a drink), *town council* (a group of people who are in charge of and decide things for a town).

- Explain the activity: there are plans to build a big supermarket in the small town of Greenbanks. Students have to study information about the town and decide whether to build the supermarket or not.

- Divide the students into pairs, As and Bs. Tell the As that they live in the town and are *against* the supermarket. Tell Bs that they work for the town council and are *for* the supermarket.

- Hand out the 'Factfile'. Ask As to read it and underline or circle everything they think is a disadvantage of building the supermarket. Get Bs to read through and underline or circle all the advantages.

- When the students are ready put them in groups of four – there should be one pair of As and one pair of Bs in each group. Refer them to the Key Language on page 62 in the Coursebook.

- Ask students to discuss the advantages and disadvantages in their groups. After discussing the issue they have to vote 'Yes' or 'No' on the proposal.

- When students are ready ask the whole group how they would personally vote in a situation like this. Count the 'Yes' and 'No' votes to find out the result.

8A When you were a child (use after Lesson 8.2) **

Aim: to practise grammar (*could* to talk about ability and possibility in the past)

Grouping: Students work individually, walking around the classroom talking to as many people as possible. The activity can also be done in pairs or small groups.

Procedure:

- Tell students they are going to complete a questionnaire. There are questions about what people could or couldn't do when they were younger, and there are also two gaps for students to write their own questions.

- Get students to read the questionnaire and complete the two blank spaces (9 and 10) with their own ideas. To complete the questionnaire students have to ask each question to others in the class until someone answers 'Yes'. They then write the person's name next to the question.

- Write these answers on the board:

  Yes, I could. No, I couldn't. I can't remember.

- Demonstrate the activity by walking around the classroom and asking the question *Could you walk when you were one?* until someone says 'Yes'.

- Hand out the questionnaires and remind students to write down the names of the people who say 'Yes'.

- When students have finished get them to tell you who could do the things in the questionnaire.

8B Could you … ? (use after Lesson 8.3) **

Aim: to practise Key Language (polite requests and responses)

Grouping: groups of three or four

Procedure:

- Explain the activity. This is a card game in which students have to collect pairs of cards with pictures showing actions. There are two types of cards: polite request cards (marked by … *please?* at the bottom of the card) and response cards (marked by *Yes*). Students collect as many pairs as possible.

- In the game students have to make requests and respond to requests. Elicit and write the two request forms from page 70 of the Coursebook on the board, i.e.:

  Could you … (open the door, please)?

  Could you tell me … (where the bank is, please)?

- Revise the OTHER USEFUL PHRASES from page 71 of the Coursebook. Elicit some possible responses to the requests above and write them on the board, e.g.:

  Sure, no problem.

  Yes, of course. Go down this road and turn right.

- Tell students to move into groups of three or four. Hand out the cut-up request and response cards and tell one of the students in each group to deal out all the cards to everyone in the group. Each student should have an equal number of request cards and of response cards.

- Students don't show their cards to each other.

- Students look at the cards they've been given and see if they have any pairs of cards that go together. They put these to one side.

- The dealer of the cards then starts the game. He or she chooses a request card, and makes a sentence based on the picture – he or she can make a request to anyone in the group. If the other person has a matching response card, he or she should answer the request positively and give the first player the response card. If the person doesn't have a response card, he or she has to turn down the request. The game then moves to the next player on the right.

- The first person to get a response card for all their request cards says 'Stop' and the game ends. Everyone counts their cards and the person with the most pairs of cards is the winner. Note: it is possible that there are two or even three winners.

9A Match! (use after Lesson 9.1) ***

Aim: to practise the pronunciation of the past simple tense and the form of some irregular verbs

Grouping: pairs or groups of three or four

Procedure:

- Write the following four headings on the board:

  /t/   /d/   /ɪd/   Irregular verbs

- Ask students which column the following verbs should go in: make, wait, play, talk.

- Explain the activity: students have a pile of 20 mini-cards with verbs on them, and a card with the four headings. A student picks up a verb card and they have to decide which group, /t/, /d/, /ɪd/, or Irregular verbs, the verb goes in. They should put the verb cards under the correct headings to make columns.

- Check students' answers and write them on the board. Alternatively, let students go to the board to write in their answers.

- Finally, you could ask students in their groups to write the past simple form of the regular and irregular verbs. This is a good way of checking their spelling.

/t/	/d/	/ɪd/	Irregular verbs
work	travel	need	go
cook	stay	invite	have
finish	live	want	be
help	study	grade	do
shop	move	start	get

9B TV or car? (use after Lesson 9.3) **-***

Aim: to practise Key Language (giving advantages, disadvantages and reasons)

Grouping: pairs and small groups of four to six

Procedure:

- Explain the activity: students will have a discussion about two important inventions of the 20th century – the car and the TV. Student As will argue for the car, and Bs for the TV.

- First put Student As together in pairs or small groups, and the same with the Bs. Give them five or ten minutes to think of advantages for their invention and disadvantages for the other invention, and to fill in their sheet. Monitor and help as necessary.

- When students have prepared their arguments, move them into pairs or small groups of As and Bs together. You might like to revise the Key Language from page 78 of the Coursebook. Students then have a discussion in their groups; Student As say why they think Student Bs' invention isn't good and then why their invention is better/more important. Student Bs then do the same.

- At the end of the discussion students vote on which invention they think is more important.

10A Money (use after Lesson 10.2) ***

Aim: to practise vocabulary (money, phrases connected with money)

Grouping: individuals, pairs or small groups

Procedure:

- Ask students if any of them do crosswords. Tell them that they are going to do a crossword on the topic of money.

- Explain how clues are organised 'across' and 'down'. Hand out the crossword and let students do it. You could tell them to look at pages 84 and 86 of the Coursebook if they have problems.

- Check students' answers when most of them are finished.

Across: 3 loan; **5** wallet; **6** cheque; **8** borrow; **9** earn; **10** credit card
Down: 1 coin; **2** note; **4** cashpoint; **7** purse

Teaching notes for photocopiable activities

10B Help me, please! (use after Lesson 10.3) **

Aim: to practise grammar (*should, shouldn't*) and Useful Language (*I think that …, In my opinion, …*)

Grouping: groups of three or more

Procedure:

- Write all the necesssary structures, i.e. *should/shouldn't* as well as the OTHER USEFUL PHRASES on page 89 of the Coursebook, on the board.

- Tell students they are going to play a card game. Each group has a pile of 15 cards placed face down. The cards all show a problem, for example a person stuck in traffic. The first student picks up a card and tells the other students the problem. Each student in the group has to give advice to the person using the phrases on the board. The student with the card listens, decides who has given the best advice and gives the card to that student. The next player picks up the next card in the pile. At the end of the game the student with the most cards is the winner.

- Demonstrate the activity. Preteach: *to be stuck in a traffic jam* (to be in a long line of cars that is moving very slowly). Pick up a card and tell students that you are stuck in traffic. Ask them to give you advice using the structures on the board. For example:

  You should telephone your office.

  You shouldn't panic.

  I think that you should relax.

- Get students into small groups and hand out the cards. Let students play the game and monitor by answering their questions when necessary. Remind them to try and use the OTHER USEFUL PHRASES from page 89 of the Coursebook.

- When most students are ready stop the game and get them to work out who the winners are.

11A A safe future? (use after Lesson 11.2) **

Aim: to practise grammar (*will, won't*) and vocabulary (green living)

Grouping: pairs or groups of four

Procedure:

- Tell students they are going to talk about the future. They have to read a number of statements and decide what they think about them.

- Hand out the worksheet and demonstrate the activity by discussing the first statement with the class: *The world will not be hotter.*

- Students then work in the groups, discussing the other statements and making a note on the worksheet about what they thought. You might like to look again at the OTHER USEFUL PHRASES on page 89 of the Coursebook, and encourage students to use it in their discussions.

- Once students have finished, go over some of their opinions as a class.

11B Design your flat (use after Lesson 11.3) **-***

Aim: to practise grammar (*be going to*), OTHER USEFUL PHRASES (making and responding to suggestions) from Lesson 3.3 and vocabulary (rooms, furniture and equipment)

Grouping: pairs or groups of three or four

Procedure:

- Quickly revise the ways students have learnt to make suggestions. Write the following structures on the board:

  Why don't we …

  Let's …

  What about …

  I'd like …

- Ask students what form the main verb would take after each structure, using the phrase *rent a flat*. You could also ask students which of the three would end with a question mark and which with a full stop when written as part of a complete sentence.

- Elicit some positive and negative responses – some from the OTHER USEFUL PHRASES box on page 27 of the Coursebook can be used here, e.g.:

  That sounds good. I don't want to do that.

- Explain the activity: students are going to design a studio flat to live in. They can put in new walls and windows, and also furnish the flat.

- Hand out the floor plans and give students 10–15 minutes to complete their plan.

- Join the groups together to form larger groups. Remind them of how we use *be going to* when we talk about plans and intentions. Get students to present their flats to the other groups using the structure; they could then vote on the best idea.

12A Have you ever … ? (use after Lesson 12.2) **-***

Aim: to practise grammar (present perfect and past simple) and vocabulary (from throughout the Coursebook)

Grouping: groups of three or four

Procedure:

- Explain the activity: students are going to work in groups and talk about experiences. Each group is given a set of cards with a phrase on each; the first student picks up a card from the top of the pile and uses the phrase given to form a question in the present perfect, e.g. *Have you ever failed an exam?*

- The student asks the question to the others in his/her group. If somebody answers *Yes, I have*, the first student asks *When?* The student who answered *yes* should then describe the experience – remind students that at this point they should use the past simple. Students take it in turns to pick up a card and ask a question until the cards run out.

- Hand out the cards and let students do the activity.

12B A holiday postcard (use after Lesson 12.4) **

Aim: to revise a number of tenses (present perfect, past simple and *going to*), to develop students' editing skills

Grouping: individuals, pairs or small groups

Procedure:

- Hand out the postcards and tell students to read them and decide if they would like to visit this place.
- Ask students if they know anything more about Grenada.
- Tell them there are ten mistakes in the text. There are mistakes in grammar, spelling and capitalization. Ask them to read the postcards again and underline and correct the mistakes.
- When most students are ready check their answers.

Corrected text:

Dear Greg and Anna

How are you? I'm in **Grenada** in the Caribbean. I **arrived** here last week and I'm having a great time. It's a beautiful island – there are beaches with BLACK sand! The **people** are very **friendly** and the food **is** fantastic.

I've seen a lot of the island. I **went** to a forest and on Saturday I **went** to St. George's, the capital of Grenada. There were **many / a lot of** tourists there but that was OK.

Tomorrow I**'m going** to Carriacou – that's the island next to Grenada.

See you soon. Lots of love,

Christine

Tokyo

Tokyo is the capital of Japan and it's on the island of Honshu. It's a mega city with over 34 million people. The city is modern and is famous for skyscrapers. There are old temples, museums, parks and a lot of shops. There isn't a river and there aren't any beaches. The climate is good; it isn't hot or cold.

	Tokyo	Mexico City	Shanghai	Cairo
Skyscrapers				
Temples/ Churches				
Museums				
Parks				
River/Beach				
Pyramids				
Climate				

Mexico City

Mexico City is the capital of Mexico. It's a mega city with over 25 million people. The city is old and big. It's famous for museums. There are parks and churches and a lot of shops too. There isn't a river and there aren't any beaches; the city is in the centre of Mexico. The climate is good; it isn't hot or cold.

	Tokyo	Mexico City	Shanghai	Cairo
Skyscrapers				
Temples/ Churches				
Museums				
Parks				
River/Beach				
Pyramids				
Climate				

Shanghai

Shanghai is in the east of China and it's on the Huangpu river. It's a mega city with over 20 million people. There are two parts of the city. Pudong is the modern part of the city and it's famous for skyscrapers. Puxi is the old part of Shanghai. There are a lot of museums in Puxi. The winter is very cold and the summer hot. There aren't any beaches in Shanghai.

	Tokyo	Mexico City	Shanghai	Cairo
Skyscrapers				
Temples/ Churches				
Museums				
Parks				
River/Beach				
Pyramids				
Climate				

Cairo

Cairo is in the north of Egypt and is the capital. It's a mega city with over 16 million people. The city is on the river Nile. It is a very old and busy city. It is famous for the pyramids and temples. There are museums, parks and a lot of shops. There aren't any beaches in Cairo. The climate is warm all year.

	Tokyo	Mexico City	Shanghai	Cairo
Skyscrapers				
Temples/ Churches				
Museums				
Parks				
River/Beach				
Pyramids				
Climate				

Student A

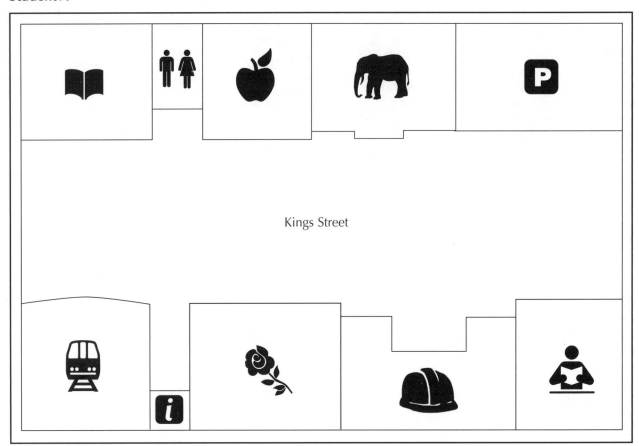

Student B

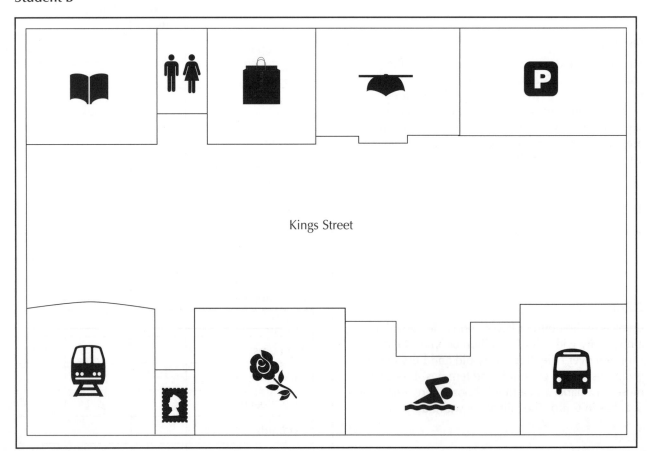

Photocopiables ©Pearson Education Limited 2008

1 Do you work … ....

2 Do you need … ....

3 Do you use … ....

4 Do you sell … ....

5 Do you travel … ....

a) … with people/numbers/students?

b) … by car in this job?

c) … special qualifications?

d) … in an office/in a shop?

e) … the Internet?

f) … special clothes or tools?

g) … things in this job?

h) … to other countries?

i) … or buy things?

j) … a computer in this job?

PEARSON
Longman

Student A

Complete the questions with the words below.

| foreign visa residence work classes exams qualifications |

Questions to ask

1 Does the university take .... students?

2 What .... do I need to go to the university?

3 Does the university help with my .... application?

4 Does the university have English language ....?
   When are they?

5 Are there .... for the language classes?

6 Do foreign students ....?

7 Do foreign students live in halls of ....?

✂ -

Student B

Complete the information sheet with the headings below.

| Visa applications   Work permits   Language qualifications
Help with language   Accommodation |

Information for foreign students

....

Students need a minimum score of IELTS 6.0 or TOEFL 550.

....

The university helps all foreign students.

Note: no visa necessary for students from European Union countries – Austria, Belgium, Cyprus, Czech Republic, Denmark, Estonia, Finland, France, Germany, Greece, Hungary, Ireland, Italy, Latvia, Lithuania, Luxembourg, Malta, Poland, Portugal, Slovakia, Slovenia, Spain, Sweden, The Netherlands, United Kingdom.

....

English language course for foreign students:

Tuesday 6 to 8 and Thursday 6 to 8

English language students have two exams, in December and June.

....

Many students from the European Union work when they are at university. It is not possible for students to work if they are not from the European Union.

....

Foreign students are always given a place in one of the university halls of residence. However, it is also possible for foreign students to live in private flats.

Start

1 .... your favourite song?

2 .... does a lawyer work?

3 .... do animals come out at night in a desert?

4 .... city in India is famous for films?

5 .... do you pronounce *dictionary*?

6 .... your teacher's first name?

Move to question 10.

7 .... is the Atacama desert?

8 .... does your English class start?

9 .... is the President of the USA?

10 .... fish are dangerous?

11 .... often do you play sport?

12 .... qualifications do you have?

Move back to question 4.

13 .... does the group U2 come from?

14 .... do you want to learn English?

15 .... is the capital of Turkey?

16 .... many people live in a mega city?

17 .... percentage of the world's deserts are sand?

18 .... is your favourite restaurant?

Move to question 21.

19 .... is the Sahara desert?

20 .... percentage of your body is water?

21 .... much water do you normally drink every day?

22 .... do you normally see your friends?

23 .... is your favourite TV programme?

24 .... country is Shanghai in?

Move back to question 15.

25 .... do you love?

26 .... does an office assistant do?

27 .... does your English lesson finish?

28 .... is Bill Gates?

29 .... of these three animals is a fish – a whale, a penguin or a tuna?

30 .... is the capital of Poland?

Finish!

PEARSON
Longman

©Pearson Education Limited 2008 Photocopiables

FESTIVAL FUN

The Notting Hill Carnival, London

This two-day festival takes place on the last weekend in August every year. The carnival starts on Saturday; there is a competition between steel bands. Sunday is Children's Day and the main parade is on Monday. There are a lot of floats with steelpan bands or sound systems. A lot of people wear costumes and everybody dances! About one million people go to the carnival every year.

La Tomatina

This seven-day festival takes place at the end of August near Valencia in Spain. There is music, parades, dancing and fireworks. On Wednesday there is the 'Tomatina' or tomato fight: 30,000 people throw tomatoes at each other for one or two hours!

The Pan-African Film and Television Festival of Ouagadougou (FESPACO)

FESPACO is a film festival that takes place in Ouagadougou, the capital of Burkina Faso in West Africa. This seven-day festival takes place every two years. There are a lot of activities: presentations, seminars, a fashion show, music and an African film library. About 40,000 people go to the festival and they see about 200 African films.

Quebec City Winter Carnival

This 17-day festival in February takes place in Quebec City, Canada. There are a lot of activities: winter sports, the carnival parade, dogsled races … Visit the Ice Palace and see the fantastic Ice Sculpture festival too. About one million people go to the festival every year.

Festival	Where	Days/When	Visitors	Activities
Notting Hill Carnival				
La Tomatina				
FESPACO				
Quebec City Winter				

Festival	Where	Days/When	Visitors	Activities
Notting Hill Carnival				
La Tomatina				
FESPACO				
Quebec City Winter				

You prefer:

to go in summer

lots of people

film or music

You prefer:

to go for more than a week

to go in winter

sports

not too many people

You prefer:

to go for a short time

lots of people

films or music

You prefer:

to go somewhere far away

lots of people

sports or music

 Photocopiables ©Pearson Education Limited 2008

PEARSON Longman

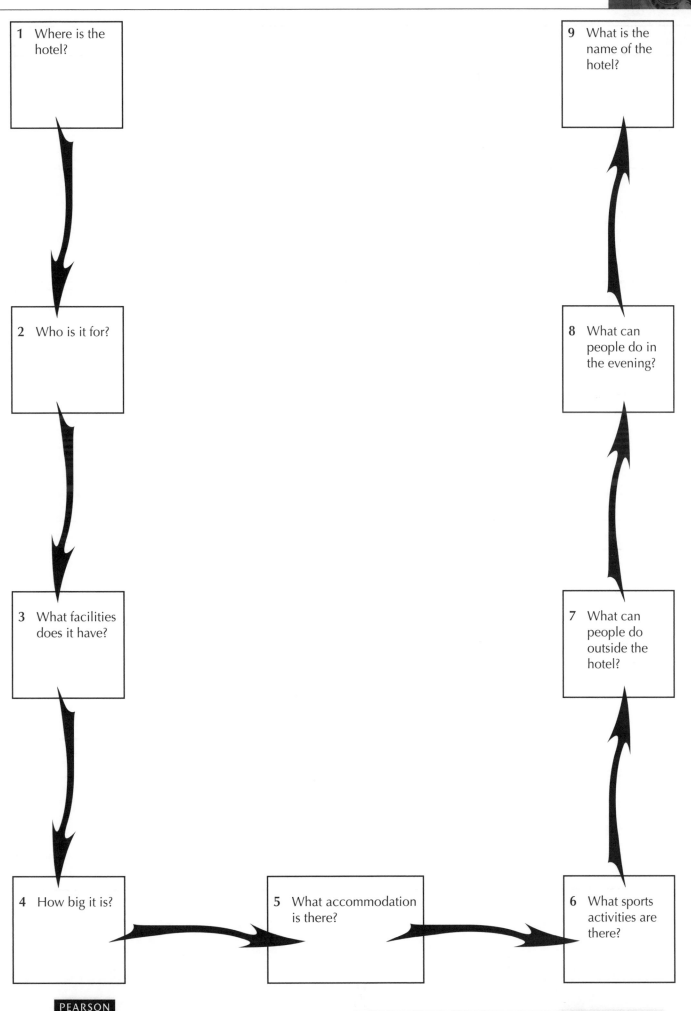

1 Where is the hotel?

2 Who is it for?

3 What facilities does it have?

4 How big it is?

5 What accommodation is there?

6 What sports activities are there?

7 What can people do outside the hotel?

8 What can people do in the evening?

9 What is the name of the hotel?

PEARSON
Longman

BINGO

Name		

Name		

Name		

Name		

 Photocopiables ©Pearson Education Limited 2008

PEARSON
Longman

GOOD, BETTER, THE BEST – A QUIZ

5A

	✓ / ✗	Bet	Win	Lose
1 São Paulo in Brazil is hotter than Kraków in Poland in summer.				
2 Sydney, Australia is smaller than Cambridge, England.				
3 A mile is longer than a kilometre.				
4 A lawyer normally makes more money than an office assistant.				
5 A letter is normally faster than an email.				
6 *Photocopy* has more syllables than *lecturer*.				
7 A Turkish person normally uses more water in a day than an American.				
8 A penguin can live better in a desert than a snake.				
9 A single ticket is normally more expensive than a return ticket.				
10 Cycling is the most popular sport for women in England.				
11 The highest mountain in the world is Mount Fuji.				
12 A blue whale weighs more than an elephant.				
13 A sentence is longer than a paragraph.				
14 Twelve hours is longer than 740 minutes.				
15 The fastest train in the world is the French TGV.				
16 Berlin is the largest city in Europe.				
17 The biggest city in the USA is Chicago.				
18 The London Underground is the oldest metro system in the world.				
19 It is normally more expensive to fly business than economy class.				
20 Mumbai, India produces more films than Paris, France.				
21 It is cheaper to get a book from a library than a bookshop.				
22 Food is more important for survival than water.				

--✂

	✓ / ✗	Bet	Win	Lose
1 São Paulo in Brazil is hotter than Kraków in Poland in summer.				
2 Sydney, Australia is smaller than Cambridge, England.				
3 A mile is longer than a kilometre.				
4 A lawyer normally makes more money than an office assistant.				
5 A letter is normally faster than an email.				
6 *Photocopy* has more syllables than *lecturer*.				
7 A Turkish person normally uses more water in a day than an American.				
8 A penguin can live better in a desert than a snake.				
9 A single ticket is normally more expensive than a return ticket.				
10 Cycling is the most popular sport for women in England.				
11 The highest mountain in the world is Mount Fuji.				
12 A blue whale weighs more than an elephant.				
13 A sentence is longer than a paragraph.				
14 Twelve hours is longer than 740 minutes.				
15 The fastest train in the world is the French TGV.				
16 Berlin is the largest city in Europe.				
17 The biggest city in the USA is Chicago.				
18 The London Underground is the oldest metro system in the world.				
19 It is normally more expensive to fly business than economy class.				
20 Mumbai, India produces more films than Paris, France.				
21 It is cheaper to get a book from a library than a bookshop.				
22 Food is more important for survival than water.				

Student A

	4x4	Estate car
Price	£35,000	....
Top speed	....	210kph
Seats	6 seats	....
Size	....	4.77m/1.82m
Safety	****	....
Comfort	....	****

✂ -

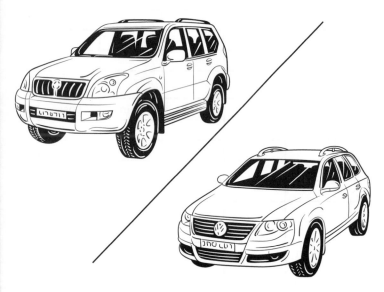

Student B

	4x4	Estate car
Price	....	£18,000
Top speed	170kph	....
Seats	....	5 seats
Size	4.80m/1.90m	....
Safety	....	*****
Comfort	*****	....

✂ -

Profile 1: Tanya is married to Halil. They don't have children but they do have two large dogs!

They both love sport, especially golf, skiing and adventure holidays.

Tanya is a vet and needs a car for work because she travels to farms around the area where she lives.

Profile 2: Simon is married to Jane. They have two children aged ten and 12.

They do a lot together as a family: holidays and weekends away. They go camping once a year and Simon and Jane both enjoy playing tennis and fishing, which they do with their two children.

They live in a small village and use a car for shopping in town at the weekend. Simon needs a car for his job; he is a decorator.

 Photocopiables ©Pearson Education Limited 2008

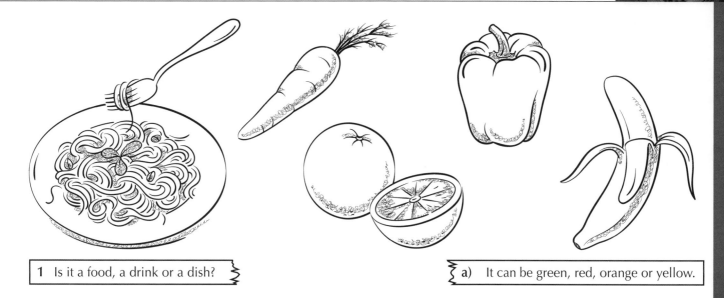

1 Is it a food, a drink or a dish?	**a)** It can be green, red, orange or yellow.
2 Is it a fruit, a vegetable, meat or fish?	**b)** No, it doesn't. It has a lot of vitamin C.
3 Is it green, orange, red or yellow?	**c)** It's a fruit.
4 Does it have any vitamin B?	**d)** You can have it any time. A lot of children have it for breakfast.
5 Is it made with flour and water?	**e)** It's a food … an orange vegetable.
6 Which country is it from?	**f)** From Japan. It's very popular there.
7 Do you normally have it for breakfast, lunch or dinner?	**g)** Yes, it's in most types of pizza.
8 Do you use it to make pizza?	**h)** Yes, it does. It also has tomatoes, beans, garlic and chilli.
9 Does it have meat in it?	**i)** Yes, it is.

PEARSON
Longman

6B

WHAT AM I BID?

Sentences	Correct (✓) or incorrect (✗)	Bid
1 There's a lot of traffic in London.	☐	....
2 Vegetables is my favourite type of food.	☐	....
3 Do you write much emails every day?	☐	....
4 Are there any cold drinks?	☐	....
5 A milk is my favourite drink.	☐	....
6 Do you want some coffee?	☐	....
7 I don't have much money at the moment.	☐	....
8 Children don't often drink many water.	☐	....
9 Doctor works in a hospital.	☐	....
10 Some restaurants in Paris are expensive.	☐	....
11 Can I have some cheese and a bread, please?	☐	....
12 Does she eat much fruit?	☐	....

Sentences	Correct (✓) or incorrect (✗)	Bid
1 There's a lot of traffic in London.	☐	....
2 Vegetables is my favourite type of food.	☐	....
3 Do you write much emails every day?	☐	....
4 Are there any cold drinks?	☐	....
5 A milk is my favourite drink.	☐	....
6 Do you want some coffee?	☐	....
7 I don't have much money at the moment.	☐	....
8 Children don't often drink many water.	☐	....
9 Doctor works in a hospital.	☐	....
10 Some restaurants in Paris are expensive.	☐	....
11 Can I have some cheese and a bread, please?	☐	....
12 Does she eat much fruit?	☐	....

Sentences	Correct (✓) or incorrect (✗)	Bid
1 There's a lot of traffic in London.	☐	....
2 Vegetables is my favourite type of food.	☐	....
3 Do you write much emails every day?	☐	....
4 Are there any cold drinks?	☐	....
5 A milk is my favourite drink.	☐	....
6 Do you want some coffee?	☐	....
7 I don't have much money at the moment.	☐	....
8 Children don't often drink many water.	☐	....
9 Doctor works in a hospital.	☐	....
10 Some restaurants in Paris are expensive.	☐	....
11 Can I have some cheese and a bread, please?	☐	....
12 Does she eat much fruit?	☐	....

Sentences	Correct (✓) or incorrect (✗)	Bid
1 There's a lot of traffic in London.	☐	....
2 Vegetables is my favourite type of food.	☐	....
3 Do you write much emails every day?	☐	....
4 Are there any cold drinks?	☐	....
5 A milk is my favourite drink.	☐	....
6 Do you want some coffee?	☐	....
7 I don't have much money at the moment.	☐	....
8 Children don't often drink many water.	☐	....
9 Doctor works in a hospital.	☐	....
10 Some restaurants in Paris are expensive.	☐	....
11 Can I have some cheese and a bread, please?	☐	....
12 Does she eat much fruit?	☐	....

PEARSON Longman

PEARSON
Longman

Factfile for Greenbanks

Location: town on the river Tern

Population: 5,000 people

Facilities:

    a small library ☑   two schools ☑   a clothes shop ☑

    two churches ☑   a cinema ☒   petrol station ☒

Shops:

2 greengrocer's, 3 butcher's, 2 baker's, 2 small stores, 2 pubs, a factory

Additional information:

    The local factory is closing; 30 people work there.

    There are some local farms. They sell meat, fruit, vegetables and flour to the local shops.

    The supermarket will also sell CDs, DVDs and cheap clothes.

    The company that wants to build the supermarket also plans to build a petrol station next to the supermarket.

- -

Factfile for Greenbanks

Location: town on the river Tern

Population: 5,000 people

Facilities:

    a small library ☑   two schools ☑   a clothes shop ☑

    two churches ☑   a cinema ☒   petrol station ☒

Shops:

2 greengrocer's, 3 butcher's, 2 baker's, 2 small stores, 2 pubs, a factory

Additional information:

    The local factory is closing; 30 people work there.

    There are some local farms. They sell meat, fruit, vegetables and flour to the local shops.

    The supermarket will also sell CDs, DVDs and cheap clothes.

    The company that wants to build the supermarket also plans to build a petrol station next to the supermarket.

- -

Factfile for Greenbanks

Location: town on the river Tern

Population: 5,000 people

Facilities:

    a small library ☑   two schools ☑   a clothes shop ☑

    two churches ☑   a cinema ☒   petrol station ☒

Shops:

2 greengrocer's, 3 butcher's, 2 baker's, 2 small stores, 2 pubs, a factory

Additional information:

    The local factory is closing; 30 people work there.

    There are some local farms. They sell meat, fruit, vegetables and flour to the local shops.

    The supermarket will also sell CDs, DVDs and cheap clothes.

    The company that wants to build the supermarket also plans to build a petrol station next to the supermarket.

Photocopiables ©Pearson Education Limited 2008

Who could...	Name	Who could...	Name
1 walk when they were one?		6 sleep at a friend's when they were ten?	
2 talk when they were two?		7 go out until 10pm when they were 14?	
3 read when they were four?		8 drive when they were 16?	
4 ride a bicycle when they were five?		9	
5 go to school on their own when they were eight?		10	

Who could...	Name	Who could...	Name
1 walk when they were one?		6 sleep at a friend's when they were ten?	
2 talk when they were two?		7 go out until 10pm when they were 14?	
3 read when they were four?		8 drive when they were 16?	
4 ride a bicycle when they were five?		9	
5 go to school on their own when they were eight?		10	

Who could...	Name	Who could...	Name
1 walk when they were one?		6 sleep at a friend's when they were ten?	
2 talk when they were two?		7 go out until 10pm when they were 14?	
3 read when they were four?		8 drive when they were 16?	
4 ride a bicycle when they were five?		9	
5 go to school on their own when they were eight?		10	

Who could...	Name	Who could...	Name
1 walk when they were one?		6 sleep at a friend's when they were ten?	
2 talk when they were two?		7 go out until 10pm when they were 14?	
3 read when they were four?		8 drive when they were 16?	
4 ride a bicycle when they were five?		9	
5 go to school on their own when they were eight?		10	

PEARSON
Longman

©Pearson Education Limited 2008   Photocopiables

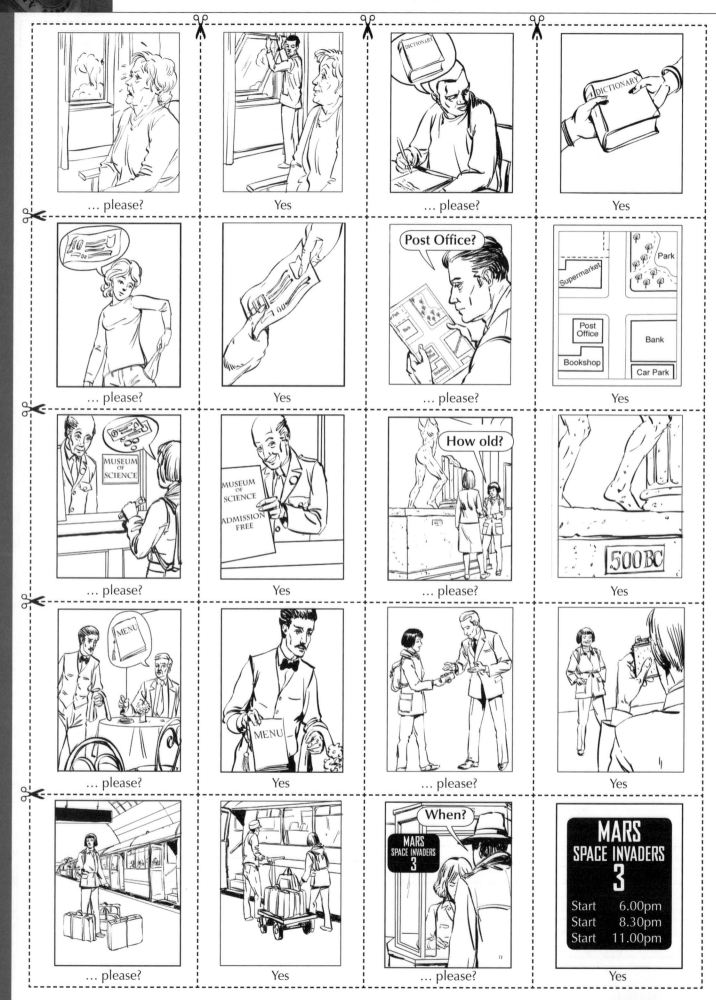

PEARSON
Longman

MATCH!

work	go	need	travel
stay	cook	have	invite
want	grade	finish	be
do	live	study	help
shop	start	get	move

/t/	/d/	/ɪd/	Irregular verbs

work	go	need	travel
stay	cook	have	invite
want	grade	finish	be
do	live	study	help
shop	start	get	move

/t/	/d/	/ɪd/	Irregular verbs

work	go	need	travel
stay	cook	have	invite
want	grade	finish	be
do	live	study	help
shop	start	get	move

/t/	/d/	/ɪd/	Irregular verbs

PEARSON Longman

©Pearson Education Limited 2008 Photocopiables 161

Student A

Advantages of the car

1 ....

2 ....

3 ....

4 ....

Disadvantages of television

1 ....

2 ....

3 ....

4 ....

✂ -

Student B

Advantages of television

1 ....

2 ....

3 ....

4 ....

Disadvantages of the car

1 ....

2 ....

3 ....

4 ....

 Photocopiables ©Pearson Education Limited 2008

PEARSON Longman

Across

3 You ask a bank or a person for this when you need more money than you have.

5 A small flat case for carrying paper money.

6 You use this piece of paper to pay for things, using the money in your bank account. You write the amount of money, the date and the name of the person you are paying on the paper.

8 Take money from a person or a bank and give it back to them later.

9 When you get money from a job, you _____ it.

10 A small plastic card that you use to buy things and pay for them later.

Down

1 A piece of money made of metal.

2 A piece of paper money.

4 You can use this machine to get money from your bank account without going into the bank.

7 Women use these small containers to carry money.

Across

3 You ask a bank or a person for this when you need more money than you have.

5 A small flat case for carrying paper money.

6 You use this piece of paper to pay for things, using the money in your bank account. You write the amount of money, the date and the name of the person you are paying on the paper.

8 Take money from a person or a bank and give it back to them later.

9 When you get money from a job, you _____ it.

10 A small plastic card that you use to buy things and pay for them later.

Down

1 A piece of money made of metal.

2 A piece of paper money.

4 You can use this machine to get money from your bank account without going into the bank.

7 Women use these small containers to carry money.

Across

3 You ask a bank or a person for this when you need more money than you have.

5 A small flat case for carrying paper money.

6 You use this piece of paper to pay for things, using the money in your bank account. You write the amount of money, the date and the name of the person you are paying on the paper.

8 Take money from a person or a bank and give it back to them later.

9 When you get money from a job, you _____ it.

10 A small plastic card that you use to buy things and pay for them later.

Down

1 A piece of money made of metal.

2 A piece of paper money.

4 You can use this machine to get money from your bank account without going into the bank.

7 Women use these small containers to carry money.

PEARSON
Longman

©Pearson Education Limited 2008 Photocopiables

HELP ME, PLEASE!

PEARSON
Longman

A SAFE FUTURE?

Statement	We agree	We aren't sure	We disagree
1 The world will not be hotter.			
2 China will be the most powerful country in the world.			
3 Cars won't use petrol.			
4 Most energy will come from the sun.			
5 People will only use plastic, not glass.			
6 There won't be any problems with water.			

Statement	We agree	We aren't sure	We disagree
1 The world will not be hotter.			
2 China will be the most powerful country in the world.			
3 Cars won't use petrol.			
4 Most energy will come from the sun.			
5 People will only use plastic, not glass.			
6 There won't be any problems with water.			

Statement	We agree	We aren't sure	We disagree
1 The world will not be hotter.			
2 China will be the most powerful country in the world.			
3 Cars won't use petrol.			
4 Most energy will come from the sun.			
5 People will only use plastic, not glass.			
6 There won't be any problems with water.			

Statement	We agree	We aren't sure	We disagree
1 The world will not be hotter.			
2 China will be the most powerful country in the world.			
3 Cars won't use petrol.			
4 Most energy will come from the sun.			
5 People will only use plastic, not glass.			
6 There won't be any problems with water.			

Statement	We agree	We aren't sure	We disagree
1 The world will not be hotter.			
2 China will be the most powerful country in the world.			
3 Cars won't use petrol.			
4 Most energy will come from the sun.			
5 People will only use plastic, not glass.			
6 There won't be any problems with water.			

DESIGN YOUR FLAT

Floor plan	Useful vocabulary

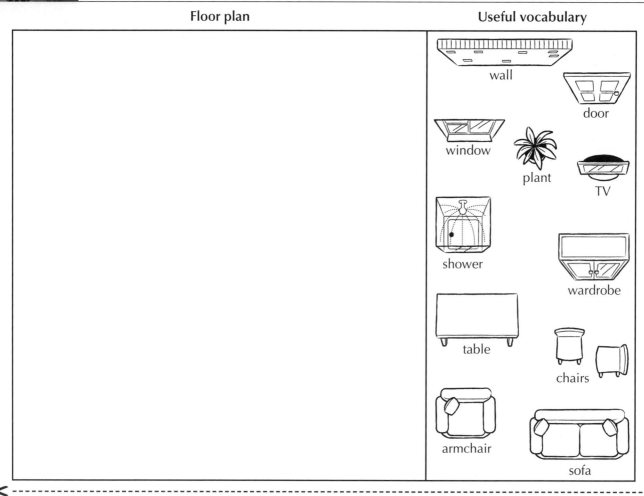

Floor plan	Useful vocabulary

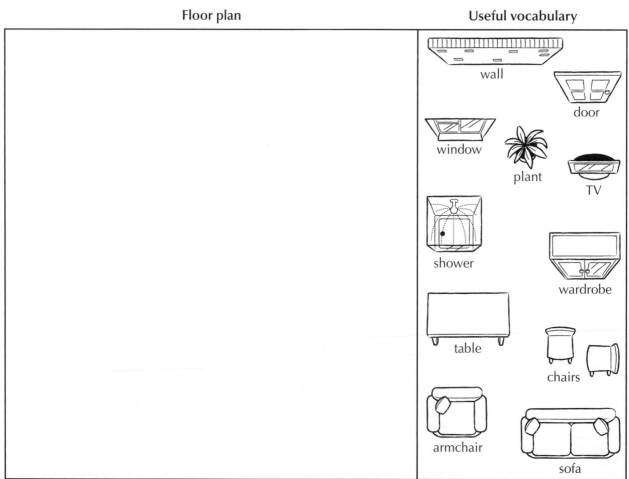

 Photocopiables ©Pearson Education Limited 2008

fail an exam	lose lots of money	go scuba diving	fail an exam	lose lots of money	go scuba diving
go to another country	borrow money from a bank	see somebody famous	go to another country	borrow money from a bank	see somebody famous
eat an unusual type of food	play in a band	recycle something	eat an unusual type of food	play in a band	recycle something
lend money to a friend	sleep on a train	ride a horse	lend money to a friend	sleep on a train	ride a horse
go wind-surfing	buy something on the Internet	do yoga	go wind-surfing	buy something on the Internet	do yoga
fly somewhere business class	lose a purse/wallet	ride a motorbike	fly somewhere business class	lose a purse/wallet	ride a motorbike
fail an exam	lose lots of money	go scuba diving	fail an exam	lose lots of money	go scuba diving
go to another country	borrow money from a bank	see somebody famous	go to another country	borrow money from a bank	see somebody famous
eat an unusual type of food	play in a band	recycle something	eat an unusual type of food	play in a band	recycle something
lend money to a friend	sleep on a train	ride a horse	lend money to a friend	sleep on a train	ride a horse
go wind-surfing	buy something on the Internet	do yoga	go wind-surfing	buy something on the Internet	do yoga
fly somewhere business class	lose a purse/wallet	ride a motorbike	fly somewhere business class	lose a purse/wallet	ride a motorbike

September 17th

Dear Greg and Anna

How are you? I'm in grenada in the Caribbean. I've arrived here last week and I'm having a great time. It's a beautiful island – there are beaches with BLACK sand! The peoples are very frondly and the food are fantastic.

I've seen a lot of the island: I've been to a forest and on Saturday I've gone to St George's, the capital of Grenada. There were much tourists there but that was OK.

Tomorrow I went to Carriacou – that's the island next to Grenada.

See you soon. Lots of love,

christine

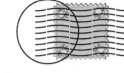

Address

G. Jones and A. Smith

10, Victoria Street

Bournemouth

BH1 1PL

UK

September 17th

Dear Greg and Anna

How are you? I'm in grenada in the Caribbean. I've arrived here last week and I'm having a great time. It's a beautiful island – there are beaches with BLACK sand! The peoples are very frondly and the food are fantastic.

I've seen a lot of the island: I've been to a forest and on Saturday I've gone to St George's, the capital of Grenada. There were much tourists there but that was OK.

Tomorrow I went to Carriacou – that's the island next to Grenada.

See you soon. Lots of love,

christine

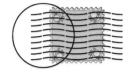

Address

G. Jones and A. Smith

10, Victoria Street

Bournemouth

BH1 1PL

UK

PEARSON
Longman